LIFELINES

SHARAN B. MERRIAM
M. CAROLYN CLARK

LIFELINES

Patterns of Work, Love, and Learning in Adulthood

SHARAN B. MERRIAM
M. CAROLYN CLARK

 Jossey-Bass Publishers

San Francisco • Oxford • 1991

LIFELINES
Patterns of Work, Love, and Learning in Adulthood
by Sharan B. Merriam and M. Carolyn Clark

Copyright © 1991 by: Jossey-Bass Inc., Publishers
350 Sansome Street
San Francisco, California 94104
&
Jossey-Bass Limited
Headington Hill Hall
Oxford OX3 0BW

Library of Congress Cataloging-in-Publication Data

Merriam, Sharan B.
    Lifelines : patterns of work, love, and learning in adulthood / Sharan
B. Merriam, M. Carolyn Clark.
        p.   cm. — (The Jossey-Bass social and behavioral science
series) (The Jossey-Bass higher and adult education series)
    Includes bibliographical references and index.
    ISBN 1-55542-364-7
    1. Adulthood.   2. Adult learning.   3. Work.   4. Love.   I. Title.
II. Series.   III. Series: The Jossey-Bass higher and adult education
series.
HQ799.95.M47   1991
305.24 — dc20   91-10280
                                                                   CIP

Manufactured in the United States of America

The paper in this book meets the guidelines for
permanence and durability of the Committee on
Production Guidelines for Book Longevity of
the Council on Library Resources.

JACKET DESIGN BY CASSANDRA CHU

FIRST EDITION

Code 9171

A joint publication in
The Jossey-Bass
Social and Behavioral Science Series
and
The Jossey-Bass
Higher and Adult Education Series

Contents

Preface

Freud reportedly said that maturity is the capacity "to work and to love." Simple yet profound, this definition captures most aspects of human activity. Working and loving structure our lives and give our existence meaning. People define their identities in terms of work and love. Ask people to "identify" themselves and they will respond in terms of work (a teacher, a construction worker, a salesperson), or love (a parent, a spouse, a friend). Society has developed institutions in both areas. A person usually works for a company or a bureaucratic structure of some sort, and love usually finds expression within the social institutions of marriage and family.

Work has most often been studied by those in sociology, organizational behavior, and management, while psychologists and marriage and family therapists have investigated love. There is some research on the integration of work and love in terms of how adults manage family and career, how much time is devoted to each segment, how people achieve a satisfactory balance of the two, and so on. Most recently, women in particular have been studied with regard to coping with a family (love) and a career (work). However, only a few studies have examined the interaction between work life and relational life. Many questions remain unanswered. For example, do things need to be going well in both arenas for a person to feel productive? Do activity and energy in one area stimulate activity in the other? Or is the energy devoted to one at the expense of the other?

Another question involves the way this interaction between work and love is related to learning in adult life. Life transitions (either work or family related) often motivate adults to engage in formal learning. But extensive learning also occurs informally, through engagement with particular life events or more indirectly through the accumulation of life experiences. How do these learning activities — both formal and informal — correlate with work and love experiences? And what learnings are deemed most significant? More important, what role does learning have in the development of our capacity to work and to love?

In this book, we are concerned with the intersection of work, love, and learning. We have interwoven several strands of thought: the psychosocial and developmental literature on work and love, our own research into the patterns of work and love using a journal-like instrument and in-depth interviews, and an analysis of how formal and informal learning are interrelated with various patterns of work and love.

While there are a number of books that relate to our topic, none focuses specifically on the interrelationship of work, love, and learning in adult life. Baruch, Barnett, and Rivers's *Lifeprints: New Patterns of Love and Work for Today's Women* (1983) comes closest in examining love and work, but it does so only in relation to women and does not consider interaction patterns or the place of learning in those patterns. In *Themes of Work and Love in Adulthood* (1980), Smelser and Erikson address our subject from a variety of perspectives. Their work, along with Rohrlich's *Work and Love: The Crucial Balance* (1980), offers a theoretical base for our research and analysis of the interaction of the two arenas. Numerous other publications in the field of life-span and adult development have also influenced our study. Investigators such as Erikson (1963), Vaillant (1977), and Levinson and others (1978) include work and love in their theories of development, but they do not structure their theories around these domains, nor do they consider the role of learning. Those books that do address learning from a developmental perspective, such as Daloz's *Effective Teaching and Mentoring* (1986), Belenky, Clinchy, Goldberger, and Tarule's *Women's Ways of Knowing: The*

Development of Self, Voice, and Mind (1986), and Mezirow and Associates' *Fostering Critical Reflection in Adulthood: A Guide to Transformative and Emancipatory Learning* (1990), focus on the nature and process of learning in adulthood, but they do not directly integrate learning, working, and loving.

Lifelines: Patterns of Work, Love, and Learning in Adulthood thus brings together several strands of knowledge in an original way. In addition to this new focus, our book integrates our own research on work, love, and learning. Specifically, we report the results of our study that delineated three distinct patterns of work-and-love interaction, and the place of significant learning experiences within those patterns of interaction.

Although there have been numerous studies of work and love in adulthood, our particular focus on the interaction of the two domains, along with the development of a procedure for visualizing the interaction, resulted in the discovery of three distinct patterns of interaction. We consider this discovery to be a major contribution to a better understanding of adult growth and development. We anticipate that these three patterns will be further refined in subsequent research, leading to an even more in-depth understanding of adult life. Furthermore, the three patterns of interaction and what we discovered about the role of learning within each pattern can be put to immediate use by counselors, educators, and others in the helping professions.

Audience

This book is intended partly for counselors, educators, human resource managers, and social service personnel who work with adults. We anticipate that practitioners can easily convert our framework for understanding adult life into interventions and workshops with adult clienteles. In addition, we expect that our "Work, Love, and Learning in Adulthood" questionnaire can be used as a diagnostic tool by a wide variety of practitioners in the helping professions.

General readers who want to better understand the dynamics of their life experiences will find this book of special interest. In fact, one of our goals is to foster self-understanding on the part of readers. Our inclusion of the "Work, Love, and Learning in Adulthood" questionnaire is a means toward that end. A reader using the questionnaire will be able to determine his or her own pattern of work, love, and learning, becoming personally engaged with the material in the book. Excerpts from our interviews will also help bring these concepts to life, encouraging readers to reflect on the similarities and differences between their experiences and our findings.

Overview of the Contents

Lifelines: Patterns of Work, Love, and Learning in Adulthood has eleven chapters arranged so that we present the findings from our study only after we have introduced the theoretical underpinnings of each idea.

In the first chapter, we trace the origins and development of the concepts of work and love. We discuss various interpretations of work and love, pointing out that what constitutes acceptable behavior in these areas depends on the sociocultural and historical context. Finally, we review what is known about how people learn to work and to love as they move from infancy to childhood to adolescence.

Chapter Two begins where Chapter One leaves off, with the manifestations of work and love in adulthood. The centrality of work and love in adults' lives is played out in two arenas: externally in the workplace and in the home, and internally within the psychological development of the individual. This chapter reviews studies from both perspectives.

Chapter Three explores how work- and love-related life events motivate adults to engage in learning. Most of the social roles characteristic of adult life are work or love related and also serve to distinguish adult learning from the learning that takes place in childhood. In this chapter, we also review how adults learn from everyday life experiences.

Proceeding from the theoretical base presented in the first three chapters, Chapter Four describes how our study originated: among other things, it discusses precedents for using graphs as a means of uncovering insights about developmental processes. We explain how we designed the "Work, Love, and Learning in Adulthood" questionnaire, how we collected the data, and how we analyzed them. We also provide summary information on the people who participated in our study, including the nineteen who were interviewed in depth.

Chapters Five, Six, and Seven present the three broad patterns of interaction between work and love that we discovered in our study. The *parallel pattern* discussed in Chapter Five reveals that these two areas of life are intertwined; change in one area is reflected by change in the other. There is an overall sense of constancy in this pattern; change is minimal. The *steady/fluctuating pattern* presented in Chapter Six shows one area remaining steady (rated consistently the same), while the other fluctuates. In this pattern the steady domain—whether it be work or love—appears to function as a stabilizer or source of security, and people tend to locate their personal identity in this area. Chapter Seven presents the third pattern, which we have labeled *divergent*. Work and love appear to exist independent of and often in opposition to one another. Change is frequent and is often self-initiated. Each of these chapters contains graphs depicting the pattern type, and each pattern is illustrated with excerpts from the interviews—excerpts that bring to life the parallel, steady/fluctuating, or divergent mode of interaction.

Chapter Eight delineates the insights about work and love that we gained from comparing the three patterns. For example, we saw that each pattern has a different stabilizing factor that created a sense of organization and harmony. The final section of this chapter considers stability and change as they are manifested in the three patterns.

Chapters Nine and Ten report the findings from our study with regard to learning and its relationship to work and love patterns. By interfacing the learning events on each person's work-and-love graph we were able to see when the most significant learning occurred. We were surprised to find that it usually occurred when things were going well in both the work and love domains. Chapter Ten focuses on how learning is related to the development of the capacity to work and to love. We review some of the key work in this area and then present our analysis of what makes learning significant for adults. To do this, we used data from our interviews and from the questionnaire.

In the final chapter of *Lifelines: Patterns of Work, Love, and Learning in Adulthood,* we discuss what we consider to be four major contributions of our study to the literature of adult development and learning. These are (1) the discovery of three distinct patterns of interaction, (2) the uncovering of a stabilizing factor in each pattern, (3) the lack of gender differences in any of our findings, and (4) the role that learning plays in the development of the capacity to work and to love. We also suggest how these findings might be put to use by individual readers, and by practitioners in the helping professions and in adult education.

Acknowledgments

We wish to take this opportunity to thank those whose help made this book possible. First and foremost, we thank our colleagues in adult education who distributed the "Work, Love, and Learning in Adulthood" questionnaires, the participants who took the time to fill them out, and the nineteen men and women who consented to being interviewed about their work and love patterns. Their reflections allowed us to understand the unique characteristics of each of the three patterns. We are particularly grateful to the W. K. Kellogg Foundation for its financial support to us both and for its support of the faculty development workshops where the idea for this study first emerged. Also among the participants of this study were more than twenty recipients of the Kellogg Career Enhancement Award for Georgia educators, and we would like to thank Catherine Zeph, a Kellogg Fellow and staff person in the Georgia Cooperative Extension Service, for her help in organizing this aspect of our study.

Others have been of invaluable assistance to us in various stages of the project. Gracia Alkema's encouragement early on when she was at Jossey-Bass, followed by Rebecca McGovern's enthusiastic support, helped bring this project to fruition. Colleagues Lee Burkett, Joan Dominick, Lea McGregor, and Arthur Wilson helped us to validate our findings by individually (independently of each other) deriving the same three patterns of work and love interaction from analyses of the graphs. A special thanks is due Susan Carse-McClocklin and Elizabeth Tisdell, who spent nine months of their graduate assistantships coding and analyzing data on all components of the study. Their comments, insights, and suggestions greatly strengthened our analysis. Thanks also to Judy Huang and Thomas Valentine, who helped with setting up and running the data analysis, and to Leslie Lamb for her assistance at the computer in assembling the final manuscript and especially for her consummate skill in figuring out how to "draw" dozens of work and love graphs on the computer. Crucial to strengthening the final version were the insightful, helpful, and wonderfully thorough evaluations of the first draft of this manuscript by Laurent Daloz, Kathleen Hulbert, and Carol Kasworm. Finally, we wish to thank our other colleagues at the University of Georgia, our friends, and our family members for their loving support while we worked on this project.

Athens, Georgia   Sharan B. Merriam
June 1991   M. Carolyn Clark

The Authors

Sharan B. Merriam is professor of adult education at the University of Georgia. She received her B.A. degree (1965) from Drew University in English, her M.Ed. degree (1971) from Ohio University in English education, and her Ed.D. degree (1978) from Rutgers University in adult education. Before coming to the University of Georgia, she served on the faculties of Northern Illinois University and Virginia Polytechnic Institute and State University.

Merriam's research and writing activities have focused on adult development and learning, and on qualitative research methods. Currently she is coeditor of *Adult Education Quarterly*, the major journal of research and theory in adult education. She is also coeditor with Phyllis M. Cunningham of the 1990 *Handbook of Adult and Continuing Education*. This encyclopedic work is commissioned once every ten years by the American Association for Adult and Continuing Education (AAACE) to provide an updated overview of the field of adult education.

Merriam has served on steering committees for the annual North American Adult Education Research Conference and the Commission of Professors of Adult Education. She has written or coauthored a number of books, including *Philosophical Foundations of Adult Education* (with J. Elias, 1980); *Coping with Male Mid-Life: A Systematic Analysis Using Literature as a Data Source* (1980); *Adult Education: Foundations of Practice* (with G. Darkenwald, 1982), winner of the 1986 Cyril O. Houle World Award for Literature in Adult Education; *Themes of Adulthood Through Literature* (1983); *A Guide to Research for Educators and Trainers of Adults* (with E. L. Simpson, 1984); *Adult Development: Implications for Adult Education* (1985); *Case Study Research in Education: A Qualitative Approach* (1988); and *Learning in Adulthood: A Comprehensive Guide* (with Rosemary M. Caffarella, 1991).

M. Carolyn Clark is assistant professor of adult and extension education at Texas A&M University. She received her B.A. degree (1966) from the University of Maryland in English literature, her M.A. degree (1984) from Creighton University in Christian spirituality, and her Ed.D. degree from the University of Georgia in adult education.

Clark's research focus is on adult development and learning, with particular emphasis on perspective transformation and the development of wisdom. She has published several articles on these topics in *Adult Education Quarterly, Educational Gerontology,* and *The International Journal of Lifelong Education.* She is also a contributor to the forthcoming *Theological Interpretations of Adult Education,* edited by Peter Jarvis. She has made several presentations at the annual conferences of both the American Association of Adult and Continuing Education and the Adult Education Research Conference.

Clark has extensive experience in ministry, having served in various capacities as a pastoral minister and counselor in the St. Louis area. There her responsibilities included directing programs in adult spiritual formation, developing church outreach programs, and conducting leadership workshops. She was also an addictions counselor and worked in that capacity in outpatient and residential programs for several years.

LIFELINES

CHAPTER ONE

The Essence of Adulthood

Human beings have always tried to make sense of their experience. The desire to know the meaning of life and to understand why people behave as they do has kept philosophers and clerics busy for centuries. In modern times, writers and researchers have focused on many of the same questions through the study of human behavior and the social institutions people create to channel that behavior. One organizing framework for thinking about and investigating how people make sense of their lives was suggested by Freud. When he was asked what it means to be a mature, healthy adult, he is reputed to have said that it is to have the capacity to work and to love.

Clearly, if broadly defined, our work-related and our love-related concerns structure our lives, offer opportunities for growth and development, and render meaning to our lives. If work is thought of as task-oriented behavior focusing on achievement, and love is thought of as people-oriented behavior emphasizing feelings and relationships, then it is difficult to imagine what aspect of our lives could not be included within one domain or the other. But how do we develop skills in these two crucial areas? We suggest that learning is the linchpin in this process. Life experiences, whether they are work or love related, offer us opportunities for learning. "We have learned," Daloz writes, "from our families, our work, our friends. We have learned from problems resolved and tasks achieved but also from mistakes confronted and illusions unmasked. Intentionally or

1

not, we have learned from the dilemmas our lives hand us daily"
(1986, p. 1). Life experience shapes us by influencing how we
think about and give value to ourselves and our world. What
most people learn from the interaction with life experiences leads
to a greater capacity to work and/or to love—hence to "maturity." And because experience is something we never run out
of, this type of learning never stops. New learnings, even major
ones, are always possible.

We can illustrate the key role that learning plays in the
maturation process with two examples of life experience learning we encountered in our study of work, love, and learning
in adult life. One reflects a love-related experience; the other
is work related.

Ann matured from her experience of parenting. She and
her husband had wanted children, and over the years they found
the experience of raising their son and daughter both challenging and deeply satisfying. For Ann herself, though, there was
an unexpected and intensely significant personal learning that
resulted from parenting. Her own childhood had been troubled
by ongoing psychological abuse by both her parents, who themselves had been abused as children. Her positive experience with
her own children taught her that unconditional love for another
human being was possible, and in learning that she also found
that she could understand and forgive her parents for their failure
to love her adequately.

Frank spoke about an experience that was instrumental
in changing his career. A former Air Force pilot, he had gone
to work in the aerospace industry designing flight simulators
when he retired from active duty. The military had been more
than a career for him; it was a way of thinking as well as a way
of being in the world, and it provided a frame of reference that
he never questioned. In 1970, however, he witnessed the May
Day demonstrations in Washington, D.C., and he saw armed
military troops lining the bridges going into the city. That experience of seeing troops deployed for possible action against
U.S. citizens made him begin to question the value of his work
within the military: "If I do a real good job here, what am I
doing but training people to drop bombs and kill people?" He

spoke of that experience as changing how he saw the world and his role in it, and not long after that he left the aerospace industry.

Work and love not only structure our lives, but also define us as adults. In addition, learning is the mechanism by which our capacities to work and to love are developed. Our study explored the intersection of these three constructs of work, love, and learning. In this chapter, we lay part of the foundation for the study by reviewing the concepts themselves and by exploring the way the capacities for work and love develop in childhood and adolescence. The two subsequent chapters explore work and love as they manifest themselves in adult life, and consider the important role that learning plays in this process.

What Did Freud Mean?

Although it often is assumed that Freud said that maturity or mental health involve the capacity to work (*arbeiten*) and to love (*lieben*), he actually used the terms *Leistung* and *Genuss*, which literally translate as achievement and enjoyment (Fine, 1983, p. 252). Freud also wrote that the "parents of human civilization" were work and love (Rohrlich, 1980, p. 33). But he did not say much about the interrelationship of work and love or achievement and enjoyment. Rather, Freud's fairly narrow interpretations of work and love are bound by his notion of the domination of the unconscious.

For Freud, all behavior could be interpreted as "products of the driving force of the sexual instinct and of the counterforces that kept it in check" (Gaylin, 1988, p. 44). The drive for sexual gratification became known as the "pleasure principle," which for a long time in psychoanalytic theory was thought to be the only motivating force for all human behavior. Both work and love, then, were driven by "the search for the same goal: more lasting, realistic, and socially responsible pleasure. Artistic creation and scientific discovery are the highest and most intensely enjoyable kinds of work because in them, sublimated energies of sexuality and aggression play a major role. . . . Optimal love includes the working through of ambivalence, fantasy, disgust, and narcissism. Optimal love also includes the adult union of sexuality and affection in marriage and caring for the young" (Hale, 1980, p. 30).

Love for Freud was thus primarily related to sexual gratification. Tenderness and affection were feelings that tied people together during passionless moments, or were the result of sexual desires blocked, for example, because of the incest taboo between parents and children or among siblings. Freud felt that women, more than men, were best suited for the love arena, just as the "work of civilization" was "the business of men" (Freud, quoted in Hale, 1980, p. 38). Freud's notion of work, which he saw as stemming from libidinous instincts, also contributed to a person's identity and to establishing meaning in life: "No other technique for the conduct of life attaches the individual so firmly to reality as laying emphasis on work; for his work at least gives him a secure place in a portion of reality in the human community. The possibility it offers of displacing a large amount of libidinal components, whether narcissistic, aggressive, or even erotic, on to professional work and on the human relations connected with it, lends it a value by no means second to what it enjoys as something indispensable to the preservation and justification of existence in society" (Freud, 1961, p. 27).

Freud's ideas of love and work, guided by the "pleasure principle" and a commitment to preserving civilization, were unable to satisfactorily accommodate unselfish, altruistic, self-sacrificing instincts. Freud's focus on what Murstein (1988) calls acquisitive love (benefiting the lover), versus benevolent love (benefiting the beloved), resulted in his "never discover[ing] the nature of love because he was trapped in a limited concept of pleasure" (Gaylin, 1988, p. 53). Erikson, however, felt that Freud did have a broader conceptualization in mind: "When Freud said 'love' he meant *genital* love, and genital *love;* when he said love *and* work, he meant a general work-productiveness which would not preoccupy the individual to the extent that he might lose his right or capacity to be a genital and loving being" (1963, p. 265).

Expanding the Concepts of Work and Love

Since Freud, new approaches to understanding working and loving have appeared. Frankl, who developed a form of psychotherapy called *logotherapy* in Vienna following his concentration camp experiences in World War II, felt that personal happiness or pleasure did not motivate human beings. Rather, it was the "will to meaning" — that is, people worked and loved to find meaning in life. Happiness was a by-product of the search, not the end product. For Frankl, meaningful work and meaningful love were capable of transcending self-interest (Lukas, 1983).

Erikson, whose psychosocial stages of development draw heavily from Freud's psychosexual theories, has done the most to expand the concepts of working and loving. He argued that the capacity to work and to love develops throughout the life span, with eight different stages of development all leading up to the mature culmination of working and loving in midlife. This midlife stage Erikson called *generativity,* defined as "the concern in establishing and guiding the next generation; it implies *productivity* and *creativity"* (1963, p. 267). Erikson defined generativity as going beyond libidinal love and work productiveness; for him it involved caring. In an interview, he said, "I use 'care' in a sense which includes 'to care to do' something, to 'care for' somebody, to 'take care of' that which needs protection and attention, and 'to take care not to' do something destructive (Evans, 1967, p. 53).

Working and loving have been construed by others as mastery and pleasure, instrumental and expressive behavior, agency and communion, and being and doing. Perhaps closest to Freud's work-and-love dictum is the notion of mastery and pleasure. In a study of women's well-being, for example, Baruch, Barnett, and Rivers defined working as mastery, that which "is strongly related to the doing side of life, the 'instrumental' side," and pleasure as "closely tied to the feeling side of life — the quality of one's relationships with others" (1983, p. 18).

The terms *instrumental* and *expressive* come from Parsons, who proposed a theory of social systems. For him, the instrumental orientation involves "action . . . oriented to the achievement of a goal which is an anticipated future state of affairs, the attainment of which is felt to promise gratification." In contrast, the expressive orientation is not directed toward the attainment of a future goal, but involves "the organization of the 'flow' of gratifications (and the warding off of threatened deprivations)" (Parsons, 1964, pp. 48–49). In a study of dual-career couples' happiness, Nicola and Hawkes focused on instrumental and expressive behaviors and defined them as follows: "Instrumental behaviors are those associated with getting a job done. They are behaviors concerned with work, accomplishment, mastery, and achievement. Expressive behavior has to do with emotions and the expression of those feelings and relating to other people. Instrumental behavior is task oriented. Expressive behavior is people oriented" (1985, p. 50). Smelser makes the point that instrumental and expressive or work and love behaviors are more easily distinguishable at the social level than in individual behavior:

> At the personality level we clearly observe people at work and people in love. . . . Yet I would argue that the distinction, to be useful at this level, should be regarded as identifying aspects of human action but not discrete orientations, because in fact the two orientations are often so inextricably meshed that it becomes difficult to distinguish between them. For example, one can love one's work, and one can — indeed, is well-advised to — work at love. What we call "work" invariably has some kind of expressive dimension and what we call "love" is never without an instrumental component. . . . At the social-structural level, each of the two orientations may be compartmentalized in various ways. This is most clearly seen in the pervasive tendency to institutionalize the "instrumental" or "work" orientation into discrete occupational roles, governed by an array of norms in relative isolation from other arenas of life. And . . . institutionalized norms of love, marriage, kinship, and friendship clearly define the

times, places, and situations in which impulses are
and are not to be gratified, and feelings are and are
not to be experienced [1980b, pp. 105-106].

Smelser has identified a central tension in the literature
on work and love: the extent to which they are opposing forces.
Rohrlich (1980) points out that they can be construed either as
conflicting or as highly interdependent phenomena. They are
conflicting in the sense that work provides structure and order,
boundaries and goals, whereas the essence of love is freedom
from these restraints. From this standpoint, "the challenge," according to Rohrlich, is "to develop, balance, and harmonize
working and loving" (p. 232). But we can also view work and
love as closely interrelated. Both can serve as vehicles for personal identity. Ask a person who he or she is and responses will
be in terms of work (a teacher, a police officer) or love (a parent, a friend). Both depend on social interaction. Human society has "constructed some of its major institutions to specialize
in work and love. In particular, the spectacular development
of the modern occupational-bureaucratic complex has provided
the locus of most of the work activities of society, and the modern
family has become the preferred institutional arena for the cultivation and expression of love" (Smelser, 1980a, pp. 4-5). Indeed, such "evident similarities" lead Smelser to suspect that
working and loving might be "different names for a very similar process of human adaptation" (1980a, p. 5).

Somewhat more philosophical and/or religious conceptions of work and love are found in the literature as agency and
communion and being and doing. Bakan's (1966) discussion of
agency and communion sounds very much like Rohrlich's (1980)
discussion of how we can view work and love as conflicting
forces. Bakan observes that "agency manifests itself in the formation of separations; communion in the lack of separations. . . .
Agency manifests itself in the urge to master; communion in
noncontractual cooperation" (p. 14). He sees agency associated
more with men, and communion more with women. Kegan,
building on Bakan's notion of agency and communion, sees development as a spiraling helix in which there is tension between

preserving the self and merging with others. He, too, suggests there may be gender differences in the movement between these polarities: "Men," he says, "tend to be more oriented toward differentiation," and women "tend to be more oriented toward inclusion" (1982, p. 208). Erlich and Blatt, however, do not separate the two, seeing "seeds of both dimensions" (being and doing) in the "same event, act, or situation" (1985, p. 72).

Finally, in yet another way of construing the dualities of working and loving, Lancereau (1986) writes that they can be interpreted as (1) domains of experience characterized by occupation and marriage and the roles of worker and spouse, (2) modes of organizing experience (working and loving), or (3) developmental tasks of identity and intimacy. Her study of young married women using these three approaches to work and love is reviewed in the next chapter.

In summary, from Freud's identification of working and loving or achievement and enjoyment as the two pillars of a healthy, mature adult life, and his rather narrow definition of these two forces, we have seen an expansion of the concepts to include Erikson's notion of generativity (arising from the successful resolution of identity and intimacy tasks), mastery and pleasure, instrumental and expressive modes of organizing life, agency and communion, and being and doing. Thus we have a far more nuanced and complex way of thinking about these fundamental aspects of adult life. And an additional factor shapes our understanding of these concepts: How we view work and love may also be a function of our historical and social context.

Work and Love as Culturally Defined

While working and loving might be fundamental forces in everyone's lives, views about what constitutes acceptable *behavior* in work and love depend on the sociocultural and historical context. In one interesting study, Smelser (1980b) examines the historical development of work and love in Great Britain and America in the nineteenth century. In England, the aristocracy valued *not* working, either professionally or at home (servants did that). The British middle class stressed rationality, work, and discipline and "split the world of work from the world of sentiment, giving the former to men and the latter to women" (Smelser, 1980b, p. 111). It was not until the late nineteenth century that middle-class women began to work outside the home, and then only in acceptable occupations like teaching or secretarial work. In contrast, the British working class (before the Industrial Revolution) consisted of working families functioning as an economic unit. Thus the instrumental and expressive domains of life were fused. With wage labor, more and more working-class women and children entered the workforce. Members of the extended family took on domestic responsibilities, with the resulting "instrumentalization" of the working-class family.

In America, class structure was less distinct and working-class women were less involved in wage-earning activities and more concerned with maintaining the family. But like their English counterparts, Americans have split the instrumental and expressive domains of life: "The cultural dynamics of the modern West have tended to put work and related instrumental activities into one joyless category and love and related affects into a separate category, and then to represent them as mutually exclusive. This cultural opposition has dominated the structure of Western thought for several centuries and has limited the number of moral and psychological solutions for the dilemmas of human existence" (Smelser, 1980b, p. 108).

Fine echoes Smelser's analysis in his discussion of how Weber's Protestant Ethic has dominated the West's view of work. This ethic involves working hard, making more and more money, and justifying it on religious grounds. Fine makes a case for replacing the Protestant Ethic with what he calls the Analytic Ideal, which amounts to Freud's view of work and love: "According to this ideal, [a human being] achieves the greatest happiness when he [or she] loves, is sexual, enjoys pleasure, feels, yet allows his [or her] feelings to be governed by reason, has a role in a family, has a social role, has a sense of identity, can work, communicate, be creative, and is free from psychiatric disturbance" (1983, p. 252).

Historically, then, society has treated work and love as

separate arenas, with social class influencing the specific roles they play in people's lives. Rohrlich traces the evolution of attitudes from the early Christian belief that "work was punishment for original sin" through the Calvinistic notion that "work was the will of God" to the current Western perspective that "work does not serve God so much as it serves the psychological development and enrichment of the individual" (1980, p. 31). Recent work on the development of work and love, however, stresses the mutual interdependence of the two domains (usually operationalized as work and family), and their social-class or cultural context. Thus Mortimer, Lorence, and Kumka (1986) look at how the social class values of a person's family of origin are transmitted to children and help to determine their occupational attainment. And in a reexamination of a cross-cultural study of gender differences in socialization (boys learn to be more independent and achievement oriented while girls learn to be nurturing and affiliative), Hendrix and Johnson conclude that "socialization varies more among societies than between the sexes" (1985, p. 593).

Work and love have also been subject to sociocultural constructions of gender. Women have been seen as attending to love and family-related matters while men are devoted to work. This of course has changed dramatically as women have entered the workforce and men have become more conscious of the family/attachment/affective dimension of their lives. Spade has proposed a "sex-integrated" approach to studying interconnections between work and family. This model is based on two assumptions: "that occupational conditions shape the values, orientations, and behavior of both men and women; and that the values, orientations, and behaviors that are shaped by job conditions influence men's and women's behavior in their roles as parents and husbands and wives" (1989, p. 190). While this model is designed to capture current shifts in gender identifications of work and love, what constitutes appropriate behavior in work and love arenas is still greatly influenced by gender.

Learning to Work and to Love

Most investigations of how people learn to work and to love are from the perspective of developmental psychology. This is because learning to work and to love is a process that happens over time. Some writers trace the development back to infancy, where attachment and separation are major issues. Gilligan writes that "attachment and separation anchor the cycle of human life, describing the biology of human reproduction and the psychology of human development. The concepts of attachment and separation that depict the nature and sequence of infant development appear in adolescence as identity and intimacy and then in adulthood as love and work" (1982, p. 151).

Erikson's (1963, 1968, 1980) eight-stage theory of the life cycle is the best-known framework for understanding how the capacity to work and to love develops. According to this theory, each stage of life, beginning with infancy, is confronted with a particular developmental task. These tasks are presented in terms of oppositions such as trust versus mistrust, intimacy versus isolation, and so on. The goal is always to achieve a favorable ratio of the positive over the negative.

In the infancy stage of trust versus mistrust, the ego strength to be developed is trust, a necessary prerequisite to mature loving. It is also about the struggle between attachment and separation: "The infant's first social achievement . . . is his [or her] willingness to let the mother out of sight without undue anxiety or rage, because she has become an inner certainty as well as an outer predictability" (Erikson, 1963, p. 245). In the second stage the young child seeks autonomy, and in the third stage seeks to express initiative. This is the age of play, in which the child is "eager and able to make things cooperatively, to combine with other children for the purpose of constructing and planning" (p. 258). This is also the stage when a child differentiates male from female. The fourth stage, industry versus inferiority, centers on learning to be productive: "To bring a productive situation to completion is an aim which gradually supersedes the whims and wishes of play" (p. 259). The child learns attention, perseverance, and how to handle the tools and technology of the culture. Knowledge and skills needed for adult work are firmly developed in this stage.

The locus of the development of mature working and loving can be found in the adolescent stage of identity versus role confusion, and in the young adulthood stage of intimacy versus isolation. Identity versus role confusion is the psychosocial stage between childhood and adulthood. The task at this stage is to acquire the sense of self that well-adjusted adults need. Identity formation in adolescence is an evolving process in which youths are faced "with tangible adult tasks ahead of them" (p. 261). This partly involves choosing a meaningful and economically feasible occupation. "Love" is also developing, but adolescents, even though physically mature, are "as yet unable either to love in that binding manner which only two persons with reasonably formed identities can offer each other, or to care consistently enough to sustain parenthood" (Erikson, 1968, p. 242).

Mature working and loving also depend on the successful resolution of the young adulthood task of intimacy versus isolation. Here, "the young adult, emerging from the search for and the insistence on identity, is eager and willing to fuse his [or her] identity with that of others." The young adult "is ready for intimacy, that is, the capacity to commit himself [or herself] to concrete affiliations and partnerships and to develop the ethical strength to abide by such commitments" (Erikson, 1963, p. 263). In the young adulthood stage of intimacy versus isolation, a person develops "the capacity to commit . . . to concrete affiliations and partnerships and to develop the ethical strength to abide by such commitments, even though they may call for significant sacrifices and compromises" (p. 263).

Erikson's theory offers a framework for tracing antecedents to work and love in adulthood. It has, however, been criticized as being a "male" model that fails to capture the development of these capacities in women. One argument centers on the sequencing of stages — that for women, the development of intimacy seems to come before or at least is concurrent with the development of identity (Hodgson and Fischer, 1981; Dimidjian, 1982; Morgan, 1982; Josselson, 1987). The second argument posits that male and female identity formation follow different trajectories altogether. According to Gilligan (1982), Erikson's model emphasizes separation, independence, and productiveness as bases for identity. Females, however, develop their sense of identity "by a standard of responsibility and care" (p. 160). She goes on to say that "in their portrayal of relationships, women replace the bias of men toward separation with a representation of the interdependence of self and other, both in love and in work. By changing the lens of developmental observation from individual achievement to relationships of care, women depict ongoing attachment as the path that leads to maturity" (p. 170).

Gilligan builds on Chodorow's (1978) theory that because girls share the same gender with their mothers, they "come to define and experience themselves as continuous with others; their experience of self contains more flexible or permeable ego boundaries. Boys come to define themselves as more separate and distinct, with a greater sense of rigid ego boundaries and differentiation. The basic feminine sense of self is connected to the world; the basic masculine sense of self is separate" (p. 169). At least one study seems to support Chodorow's position. Aries and Olver (1985) found male infants developed greater separation from their mothers than females do.

Studies that have looked at the development of work and love competencies in adolescents and young adults have had mixed results with regard to the order of development and gender differences. Lidz (1976) makes a case for a reciprocal relationship between identity and intimacy, arguing that the developmental paths of these processes are concurrent and interrelated. Loewenstein's reflections on her own development echo Lidz's position: "My identity as an educator was neither forged in adolescence nor consolidated through marriage. For me — and I think this is true for many women — the sequential stages of identity, intimacy, and generativity, regardless of the order in which they are proposed . . . do not describe the order of my life. Self-definition came first through motherhood and later, more autonomously, through work and competence. I had to proceed simultaneously on all fronts to master the complexities of many roles" (1980, p. 11). On the other hand, Marcia's (1980) extensive investigations into adolescent identity formation suggest that the achievement of a stable ego identity in adolescence is a prerequisite to intimacy in young adulthood. Raskin found support for intimacy preceding identity in the young women of her sample but not for older subjects. "The question," she concludes, "remains unanswered" (1986, p. 179).

In another study, identity and intimacy development among eighty-eight college students were explored (Kacerguis and Adams, 1980). The authors found that more advanced stages of identity development were associated with higher levels of intimacy formation and that occupational identity predicted intimacy for both men and women: "Both women and men who experience a self-imposed period of occupational exploration prior to commitment are significantly more likely to develop more mature and deep interpersonal commitments than their peers who are in role confusion or who have made commitments without exploration" (p. 125).

Rather than looking at gender differences, Looney and Lewis (1983) tried to determine what made for good or superior levels of psychological adjustment in adolescence. They evaluated twenty-two adolescents — eleven whites from middle- and upper-middle-class families and eleven African Americans from lower-income, working-class families — in terms of their capacities for work, play, and love. African Americans had more part-time jobs, and their heterosexual interests began earlier; whites tended to think of work in terms of tasks around the house and began thinking about the opposite sex about the time car dating was possible. Overall, however, they were alike in the development of their capacity to work and to love, a factor the researchers attributed to healthy family situations.

Thus, it would seem from this sampling of studies on the development of work and love that there is no consensus as to either sequence or gender differences. Some feel the antecedents of work and love — identity and intimacy — develop in the order Erikson presents. Others feel that they develop simultaneously. The question of gender differences in the development of identity and intimacy also remains unanswered.

Summary

According to Freud and others, a healthy, mature adult has developed the capacity to work and to love. Work and love, if defined broadly enough, encompass nearly all the experiences of our daily lives, both painful and joyful. Much psychological and sociological research has focused on how these two domains develop and how they relate to each other.

In this chapter we have reviewed different conceptualizations of the meaning of work and love. Freud's notions of working and loving were limited by his psychosexual orientation. Others have construed the terms more broadly, relating them to identity and intimacy, or instrumental and expressive orientations, or defining them as mastery and pleasure, agency and communion, being and doing. Some see working and loving as opposing forces, while others see them as similar processes, perhaps even two dimensions of the same thing. At any particular point in time, the concepts of work and love also reflect historical and sociocultural assumptions.

Finally, we have traced the development of work and love primarily through Erikson's theory of ego development. We have covered questions about the sequence of development and gender specificity, and have pointed out that there are no definite answers yet to either of these questions. But regardless of how work and love develop, they still play a central role in people's lives. The next chapter explores the way they interact in adulthood.

CHAPTER TWO

How Work and Love Interact

What do we think about as we go about our daily lives? Not surprisingly, work- and love-related concerns dominate our thoughts, structure our lives, and absorb most of our time and energy. In one study, for example, men and women were asked what they had just been thinking about as they approached tables set up in two New York City locations. Thoughts were classified into nine content areas: work, material concerns, politics, food, future plans, immediate environment, friends and relatives, love, and the self. Work and love were two of the top three concerns at both locations. Interestingly, "only one area exhibited a significant difference" between men and women: "Work was thought about more significantly by females" (Shaw, Francois, Filler, and Sciarillo, 1981, p. 294). Most of what we know about working and loving in adult life is derived from research on one domain or the other, but work has most often been studied by those in sociology, organizational behavior, and management, while love has been investigated by psychologists and marriage and family therapists. Only recently have the two arenas been examined in relation to each other.

This chapter presents what we know from previous research about the *interaction* of the two domains. But the research we review is limited in a fundamental way, because work and love are defined in highly conventional and rather narrow terms. Work is located within what we might call the industrial context, where it is clearly separated from the home both conceptually

16

and functionally. While this approach reflects the way work is most commonly experienced in our bureaucratic, industrial society, it does not reflect all experience. Missing are such experiences as work done in a family context, such as a family farm or a home-based business, or the creative work of writers and artists. The work done by homemakers is also obscured; in the bureaucratic definition, this does not count as work at all. The definition of love is equally traditional and narrow, reflecting the social structures of marriage and family. Not represented are forms of relationship that exist outside these structures, including experiences such as significant friendships, gay marriages, and membership in religious communities.

It is clear that these conventional definitions of work and love result in a limited picture of the interaction of work and love in our society, but they are the constructs underlying most of the research that has been done in this area. We present that research in this chapter even though we are aware of its limitations, since it gives us a starting point for discussing how the domains interact.

When considered together, work and love in adulthood have been studied by psychologists as intimacy and identity in young adulthood, and as generativity in midlife. The research on intimacy and identity in adulthood is sparse since most of what has been done has focused on the development of these arenas with adolescents or college students. There is "little empirical knowledge of the ways in which contemporary men and women in early adulthood negotiate issues of love and friendship" (Raskin, 1986, p. 170), despite several social trends that might certainly have an impact on how men and women "form and dissolve intimate relationships" (p. 169). Neither has the notion of generativity as mature working and loving been studied in and of itself (see Hardin, 1985, for one exception). Rather, the interaction of work and love at this stage of life is most often embedded in studies of middle age (see Vaillant, 1977; Rubin, 1979; Perosa and Perosa, 1984–85; Hinand, 1984).

More commonly, work and love have been examined in terms of their institutionalized forms of career and marriage, or work and family. A traditional sex-role bias imbues much of this literature. That is, investigators take it for granted that men work, and research on men and work focuses on working conditions, career development patterns, and work satisfaction. "The impact of men's jobs on their families is generally ignored with the exception of research on the effects of atypical work schedules and demanding careers on family life, or studies of the influence of fathers' social class on sons' occupational choices and social mobility. These analyses deemphasize the part men play in interpersonal relationships within the family" (Spade, 1989, p. 185). However, when working women are studied, the focus shifts from work factors to the "problem" work creates for the family, for the marriage, for children, and so on: "The focus of the majority of these studies is to understand the perceived disruption resulting from women moving out of their homes and into the labor force" (Spade, 1989, p. 186). Interestingly, this concern with the effects of women's *employment* on family and interpersonal relationships is reversed for men; studies with men focus on the deleterious effects of their being *unemployed.*

The work-and-family literature does offer some insight into the interaction of work and love from a social perspective. For example, research has shown that work determines the "economic resources, social status and identity, interpersonal relationships, and connection to the wider community" of the worker and the family unit (Mortimer, Lorence, and Kumka, 1986, p. 1). A person's family of origin socializes its members into certain attitudes, values, and work roles. Likewise, the original family setting "influences the occupational attainments of its members. Family economic needs provide a major motivation for both men and women to seek employment and to be successful in the occupational career." In addition, "there is evidence that families generally impede women's careers, but support the careers of men" (Mortimer and Sorensen, 1984, p. 142).

Whether construed from a sociological or a psychological perspective, work and love are the two most central forces in the life of an individual. This chapter examines what we know about the interaction of work and love, with the caveat that they are rather narrowly defined, reflecting industrial notions of work and traditional manifestations of love as located in marriage and family. The first section reviews research that has focused on women. The second section considers studies conducted with male samples. The final part of this chapter reveals what researchers who have studied *both* men and women have found out about the interaction of work and love.

Work and Love in Women's Lives

The increasing number of women entering the workforce has spawned interest in the women who seem to do it all — work full time, take care of a husband's needs, keep up a home, raise children, and still see to their own needs. Articles on the "superwoman" complex, on balancing job and family, on managing stress associated with running a career and family, and so on permeate the media. While this focus has its value in raising both women's and men's consciousness about the burden of trying to do it all, as well as about the need for social policy, it does little to advance our understanding of the interaction of work and love in women's lives. The literature on work and love that focuses on sex-role socialization and on psychological maturity is more pertinent to our study.

Sex-Role Socialization. Work and love manifest themselves in the social institutions of occupation and family. The underdevelopment of women's work potential begins in childhood where girls are socialized to the roles of wife and mother (and perhaps teacher and nurse) rather than worker. Borman and Frankel (1984) note that in the training ground of children's games, for example, girls are usually excluded from those that involve the negotiating of power, rules, and roles — just as they are excluded from the adult version of these games in organizational settings. Mortimer and Sorensen (1984) contend that women unconsciously overdevelop traditionally feminine qualities and behaviors — nurturer, supporter, wife, mother, caregiver. Jobs most often associated with femininity, such as nursing, teaching, and clerical work, are actually referred to as "women's jobs" or "female occupations." Working women dominate these jobs, reinforcing the stereotype of women as nurturers and creating a false linkage between work and love. In 1987, for example, women represented 80 percent of all administrative support (including clerical) workers, but only 9 percent of all precision production, craft, and repair workers. Women were 69 percent of all retail and personal services sales workers, but only 38 percent of all executives, managers, and administrators" (U.S. Department of Labor, 1988).

This sex-role segregation of the workforce — in which women as a class are kept subordinate to men — results in significantly lower occupational attainment for women. This situation is dramatically underscored by the fact that "women still earn only 65 cents for every dollar that men earn. This modest increase from 59 cents [of a decade or so ago] has been attributed to women's growth in the professions and, to a lesser degree, their entry into male-dominated crafts and other occupations. However, the majority of women continue to be concentrated in the lower-paying female-dominated clerical and service occupations" (Ford Foundation, 1989, p. 11). That working women still shoulder the major responsibility for home and family has led to role overload and strain, which has in turn often led to reduced work involvement.

The sex-role socialization of women into lower-paying and lower-status jobs can be related to at least three "cultural axioms" — axioms that serve to support the dominant position of men — according to a 1985 report of the National Academy of Sciences. The three axioms are "those related to women's 'natural' role in the home; those related to the male-female relationship, with women subordinate; and those related to stereotyped notions of innate differences between the sexes. . . . Women's supposed manual dexterity and passivity are offered to explain their employment as clerical workers, while construction firms cite women's alleged weakness and intolerance of harsh working conditions as reasons for denying them jobs" (cited in Ford Foundation, 1989, p. 17).

This sex-role socialization phenomenon is reflected in research exploring the relationship between the work and family life of women. In reviewing the research on the effect of family life on work, Nieva and Gutek (1981) found that women's presumed greater interest in family life led to lower-prestige jobs, that work roles were more often than not extensions of family roles, and that the jobs women had were those that allowed them to accommodate family demands. When they approached this from the other direction — the effect of work on family life, rather than of family life on work — the authors found an increased sense of competence and well-being, increased power in the marriage, a mixed effect on marital satisfaction (some studies showed a positive, others a deleterious effect), and an increase in workload overall.

The notion that work has a generally positive effect on a woman's sense of self and a mixed effect on the marriage was borne out in the interviews. Nadine, a fifty-seven-year-old homemaker, for example, speaks of the role of work in her life: "Work satisfactions earlier were mostly in the area of teaching school, and there is a great deal of satisfaction in that I really enjoyed that because you can see the progress that kids make and you can hear from them later. . . . I guess at Burlington I was more independent; I was in charge. So I had more pressure, in a way, because if it failed or succeeded, it was going to depend on me. . . . But because it succeeded, I felt a great deal of satisfaction. At the same time, Larry was very busy, and he had always depended on me to help him with his work. We had a stressful time because I wasn't on call for him. I was doing my own thing and I was really pleased with what I was doing. So there was conflict." Nieva and Gutek also note that "problems of integrating work and family life are more severe for women than men because women have traditionally been assumed to be available during the day. . . . This situation leads to more role overload on working mothers and wives than on working husbands and fathers" (p. 47).

From the perspective of social structure and childhood socialization, Gerson wanted to understand how women born into the same historical period develop different work and family patterns. She discovered that

> women's adult choices are neither the predetermined result of early childhood socialization nor mere reflections of static, purely coercive social

structures, although each of these factors plays a
role.

Women's decisions for or against motherhood
and for or against committed work ties develop out
of a negotiated process whereby they confront and
respond to constraints and opportunities, often unanticipated, encountered over the course of their
lives. The process is dynamic, not stable and fixed.
It depends on how women define and perceive their
situations as well as on the objective circumstances
that structure these perceptions [1985, p. 213].

Studies that specifically address the interaction of work
and family have linked the interaction to the variables of women's
health and well-being. Sorensen and Mortimer (1988), for example, ask what implications the dual roles of work and family
have for women's health. Competing conclusions could be drawn,
they discovered, from the wide array of studies on the topic.
Sorensen and Mortimer propose four models under which the
research can be categorized: (1) the stress model, which posits
that work (actually the role overload and conflict as a result of
work) threatens a woman's health; (2) the health-benefits model,
which suggests that the social and personal advantages of work
lead to better health; (3) the role expansion model, which "posits
that multiple roles and responsibilities, despite their attendant
conflicts and pressures, are health-enhancing" (p. 174); and (4)
the person-environment fit model, which argues that health is
based on the "fit" of the person with the job. The authors call
for more research that addresses "particular *combinations* of work
and family roles that are encountered as women go through the
life cycle. Just as work experiences have varying effects on job
satisfaction, depending on age, so too may the constellations
of work and family responsibilities, pressures, and opportunities have differing implications for the health of women in different phases of their lives" (p. 181).

Thus, while sex-role socialization has certainly shaped the
nature of work that women do, which subsequently can affect
family life, research suggests that the effect of this interaction

is less than clear-cut. The models of physical and emotional health proposed by Sorensen and Mortimer (1988) reflect divergent findings. Studies to be reviewed next focus on the interaction of love and work and their relationship to psychological maturity and well-being.

Psychological Maturity. The accelerated research interest in women's work and love patterns can be attributed to two factors: the growing interest in adult development overall, and Gilligan's (1982) research on women in particular. Gilligan found that "attachment and separation anchor the cycle of human life" (p. 151); however, men's identity is defined by separation and an ethic of justice and rights, while in women's development, "identity is defined in a context of relationship and judged by a standard of responsibility and care" (p. 160). Gilligan sees maturity for both women and men as the discovery of the complementarity of the two voices and an achievement of balance in life between the two.

The notion that "balance" between love and work is somehow related to maturity or psychological well-being is certainly inherent in Freud's dictum about working and loving. Other research seems to support this idea. In a study of 163 women in a university nurse-practitioner training program, for example, White found that higher levels of ego development went "hand in hand with an awareness of emotional interdependence and granting of appropriate autonomy to others as well as to the self. If this seems a complex blend of caring and autonomy, the data suggest that it is precisely this complexity that the individual at higher ego levels is successfully mastering" (1985, p. 572). Lancereau's in-depth study of the work and love experiences of young married women found the relationship between the two to be neither static nor sequential, but oscillating: There was "no true homeostasis, only a tentative balance" (1987, p. 195).

Lancereau also found considerable overlap of work and love, rather than a separation of the two. One woman commented that "sometimes my relationship seems like work," while another observed that "my work involves some of the qualities

of a relationship" (p. 174). Josselson's study of women's identity suggests the same kind of "overlap." She found that "women
do not leave their relating selves behind when they go to work"
(1987, p. 183); neither does "women's embeddedness in relatedness . . . detract from their capacities to work" (p. 185). Women also work at relationships—"to care is active; it is an expression of effort" (p. 184). Josselson concludes that "a woman
does not make a clear separation between relating and work"
(p. 184). Mickelson echoes this position in her analysis of why
women continue to achieve academically in view of the limited
rewards society affords for what they accomplish: "Women's experience is characterized by systems of interdependencies, relationships, and networks. Women are not as likely as men to
see family responsibilities as distinct from and competing with
professional responsibilities. For women, the two are part of one
reality and must be accommodated simultaneously. . . . Women
approach their lives by weaving diverse elements into a single
tapestry of public and private roles. A world view such as this
inevitably will affect the way women evaluate the meaning and
significance of education in their lives. This perspective suggests that returns from education are refracted not only through
the lens of income, status, and career ladders but through familial
and community roles" (1989, pp. 59–60).

Balancing or making connections between work and love
seems to be related to psychological well-being. The central question Baruch, Barnett, and Rivers (1983) addressed was how work
and love affected women's sense of well-being. Their sample consisted of women representing six different constellations of work
and family status. For example, some respondents were single
and employed, others were married with children and not employed, still others were divorced with children and employed,
and so on. The investigators found that both work and love,
operationalized as mastery and pleasure, were crucial to a
woman's mental and emotional well-being. The "busiest" women
in the study—those who were employed, married, and had
children—were high in well-being (p. 38); women who were employed, married, and had no children rated highest on mastery
and pleasure of the six combinations. The authors concluded

that "a woman who works hard at a challenging job is doing something positive for her mental health," and "doing and achieving are at least as important to the lives of women as are relationships and feelings" (p. 14).

In one other study, data on women who had been members of the well-known Terman longitudinal study of gifted children were analyzed to determine the relationship between work and life satisfaction (Willemsen, 1980). At the time of this analysis (which included data from the 1972 questionnaires and the 1977 interviews), the majority of the women were at or near retirement. Women who had worked for income were generally more satisfied with their work than women who had been homemakers. Furthermore, "work did not damage a woman's chances for great satisfaction in life, successful marriage, or the joy of family life. What the work experience may have done for these women is enable them to look back over their lives with a greater subjective sense of accomplishment than they would otherwise experience" (p. 131).

We found two studies (Dimidjian, 1982; Farone, 1981) that addressed women's patterns of interaction of work and love as a function of life stage. Dimidjian (1982) conducted a biographical study of the psychosocial development of six female psychotherapists in their thirties. She discovered that "the area of most intense focus and concern" for these women in their thirties was the "relational tie with the Special Other" (p. 32). A second area of focus for these women was "concern with external growth, professional development, and achievement" (p. 34). To these concerns were added "concerns about the relational ties with those the woman nurtured or wished to nurture and concerns about the self" (p. 36). Dimidjian detected a "sequential enlarging of the scope of developmental concerns from (1) relational to (2) work to (3) intrapsychic" (p. 40). She explains that "during their early adult years, all subjects focused most intensely on relational ties with a Special Other as the crux, the center pole in the life-structure. However, during these years they also identified and began preparation for a professional career, later entering working experiences which affirmed their competencies as psychotherapists. During late twenties as the 'work' or the 'love' poles of the life-structure proved sources of stress, subjects began to focus more intensely on internal exploration and self-development. In effect, they began to seek more internally defined answers to the question, 'Who am I and how shall I function in my world with others?'" (p. 40).

Farone (1981) also studied the developmental patterns of women who worked full time throughout the adult years and who had incorporated a primary love relationship at or after age thirty. She found that a highly organized and specific sense of self had evolved through a series of age-related phases. Between the ages of seventeen and thirty the women were devoted to attaining proficiency and mastery in work *and* relationships; the next phase (ages thirty to forty-five) was characterized by the need to make a commitment to a relationship and/or work. In the last phase studied (forty-five to fifty-five) women had a highly developed sense of self, inner-directedness, and greater ability to attain self-satisfaction. Farone's and Dimidjian's research suggests that women attend to both love and work in their development, and that the balance of the two might be achieved by or is perhaps related to the ability to look inward.

Finally, in an article reviewing four dissertations that used Levinson's model to study women's development, Roberts and Newton (1987) draw some interesting observations about work and love in women's lives. Unlike the men in Levinson's (1978) study whose "dream" or vision of themselves in the adult world was occupationally defined, women who were interviewed for the four dissertations for the most part had "split" dreams. "Women's dreams tended to be more complex than men's dreams, consisting of vague images of self in a particular kind of environment or community rather than a concrete image of self in a particular occupational role. The relational emphasis of women's dreams heavily shaped their adult life structures" (p. 162). Of the 39 women across the four studies, 6 "were unable to form a dream of any kind; 6 formed relational dreams; and 7 formed individualistic dreams. The 20 remaining women attended equally to both occupational and relational pursuits" (p. 157).

In summary, it seems clear that work and love are important components of women's psychological development and well-being. It also seems clear that interrelatedness, connectedness, and caring are the lens through which women interpret the world; at the same time, "work" or "working" is important for identity and self-definition. Concentration on one domain at the expense of the other leads to lopsided development, while the integration of the two appears to be related to a "mature" state.

Work and Love in Men's Lives

The study of growth and development in adulthood has been dominated by research with all-male or predominantly male samples (see, for example, Levinson, 1978; Vaillant, 1977; Kohlberg, 1973; Perry, 1981). However, this research is rarely construed in terms of the constructs of work and love and even less in terms of the *interaction* of these two domains in men's lives. As with the research on women, the literature is dominated by a fairly narrow concept of work as being part of the industrial/bureaucratic context and love as being defined by marriage and family. Hence, work and love are often studied in terms of the institutions of family and occupation or career. In a comprehensive review of this research, Mortimer and Sorensen write that "there is considerable evidence, mainly derived from research on men, that work experiences induce psychological change, with important implications for family life" (1984, p. 148). Two longitudinal studies of men, work, and families suggest that work experiences bring about changes in personality that have a considerable impact on other family members' lives. The authors of one of the longitudinal studies, in which 512 men were followed for two decades, observe that "recognition that the wage earner occupies a boundary role — at the intersection of work and family careers — gives rise to extremely important questions. To what extent is an individual's position and functioning in each sphere dependent on what is happening in the other? How does the individual's participation in work influence behavior in the family?" (Mortimer, Lorence, and Kumka, 1986, p. 21).

Research by Piotrkowski (1978) on blue-collar men revealed three patterns of interaction between work and family.

"Negative carryover" occurred when workers experienced stress or suffered from role conflict and overload, boredom, and so on. These workers attempted to distance themselves from other family members, and interactions tended to be tense and irritable. A second pattern of "energy deficit" was also noted. Here, men had little energy left for involvement with family, but the interaction was more withdrawal than negative. The third pattern of "positive carryover" occurred when men were satisfied and challenged by their jobs, with interactions characterized by availability, interest, concern, and warmth.

These studies of men's occupations and the relationship to their families suggest a fair amount of interaction between the two domains. But occupation and family are kept completely separate from each other in some men's lives. Lifton (1986) writes about doctors who worked in Nazi concentration camps and carried on "normal" home lives after work. They coped by sealing off one realm from the other. This same determined separation has been found with some men in careers involving law enforcement, the military, medicine, and syndicated crime.

Research focusing on men's psychological well-being and its relationship to work and love is sparse indeed. Vaillant's longitudinal study of ninety-nine Harvard graduates is somewhat of an exception since his framework for assessing mental health involved measures of working and loving. He hypothesized that mental health involved adaptation to life through the use of defense mechanisms, some of which were more "mature" than others. Despite the fact that the "capacity for intimacy was valued less highly than capacity for success" (1977, p. 31) in the original selection of men for the study, Vaillant found that men with more mature defenses "were far better equipped to work and to love. Friendship and mature defenses went hand in hand" (p. 86). In an effort to identify factors correlated with good mental health, Vaillant compared a subsample of those he identified as the "best outcomes" with a subsample of the "worst outcomes." He concluded that "it is success at working and loving . . . that accompanies mental health" (p. 293). "At both thirty and fifty," he said, "the Worst Outcomes were far less likely to have mastered the task of intimacy. Their marriages and friendship patterns were barren" (p. 350). To the extent that the integration of work and love resembles generativity in midlife, Vaillant found the worst outcomes to be far less generative at midlife than the best outcomes: "The Worst Outcomes were less clearly willing to assume responsibility for other adults. Apparently, they were able to give less to their children; for their offspring could neither achieve their father's level of academic success nor adjust to the world — socially and emotionally — as easily as the offspring of the Best Outcomes. Finally, to the extent that it can be measured in dollars and cents, they gave less of themselves back to the world" (p. 350).

The importance of both work and family in men's lives is underscored in a recent study focusing on men who are functioning well in their work lives. Even though the author felt work to be "more nearly fundamental" than family in men's lives, he found that "men require, if they are to feel their lives are complete, a partner to share their lives, with whom they can establish a home. Most men find that marriage sustains their feelings of security and in addition helps them manage the logistics of their lives. Children provide justification for their life enterprise, even more than do the goals the men pursue in their work. Furthermore, having children helps to make sense out of work, because work now becomes a means for providing for the children. Work and family are the two sectors in which men's central emotional investments are lodged. These are the sectors to which men give most of their time and energy" (Weiss, 1990, p. xvi).

That maturity may be the ability to blend working and loving, separation and attachment, is a theme (similar to what was found with women) that emerges from the sparse research with men. Roznafszky found that men at higher levels of ego development were judged by others to be more "socially perceptive of a wide range of interpersonal cues," and to value their "own and others' individuality and uniqueness" (1981, p. 217). In their well-known study of male development, Levinson and others (1978) found that midlife tasks involved redressing earlier imbalances between the four polarities of masculine and feminine, attachment and separateness, young and old, and destruction and creation. But this study focuses on male development within the framework of career. Relationships such as with a mentor or a special woman become means to achieving one's career "dream." While the polarities exist at all points in the life cycle, during the midlife transition they "operate . . . with special force" (p. 198). Levinson and others discuss the importance of dealing with these polarities: "Every developmental transition presents the opportunity and the necessity of moving toward a new integration of each polarity. To the extent that a man does this, he creates a firmer basis for his life in the ensuing phase. To the extent that he fails, he forms inner contradictions that will be reflected in the flaws of his next life structure" (p. 198).

In contrast to the findings of Levinson and others that career absorbs young men until at least midlife, when interpersonal issues press in, Blumenthal (1981) found that in her sample of forty-three young male physicians (average age thirty-three years), family issues were as important, if not more important, than career. Priority goals were mature love, family security, and self-respect; power was ranked as less important. The greatest sources of satisfaction were in nonprofessional areas. Likewise, in a follow-up study of the men in Terman's longitudinal study of gifted children, Sears found that higher life satisfaction was correlated with both occupational competence and a happy family life, with family life being slightly more important than occupation. Sears comments on this unexpected finding: "There is a widespread belief that middle-class males are obsessed with their work and get most of their life's satisfaction from it. Our data suggest some qualification of the statement. Certainly this group of sixtyish men found it important . . . but life satisfaction from family life slightly surpassed it" (1977, p. 121). Several of the men in our own study spoke of their marriage and family commitments taking precedence over work. Norman, a highly successful professor of political science, for example, told us, "When I went to the doctoral program, we made a commitment that our relationship as husband and wife and as family were primary—everything else was going to be secondary . . . and out of that commitment we found ourselves drawing close together all the time but even more so when the wars on the outside, so to speak, were confronting us." Similarly, in a study of over 12,000 American couples, married, cohabitating, and homosexual, Blumstein and Schwartz found that couples in which *both* partners were relationship oriented versus work oriented were "the happiest and most committed of all those in our study. Couples with one partner of each type fall in between. And at the other extreme, couples in which neither partner is relationship-centered are the least happy and least committed of all" (1983, p. 172).

In summary, the research on the interaction of work and love in men's lives, inadequate though it is, suggests that the development of both arenas is related to maturity, and that for most men there is an interaction between career and family, the institutionalized forms of work and love. Although the adult developmental literature on men does seem to frame ego development, identity formation, success, and so on more in terms of work than love, when the *interaction* between work and love is explored, there appear to be few differences between men and women. This fact becomes even clearer in a review of research involving both men and women.

Men and Women: Comparative Studies

The centrality of work and love in adults' lives is played out in two arenas: externally in the workplace and even in the home, and internally within the psychic development of the individual. Whether they view work and love sociologically or psychologically, those who investigate these domains suggest that the two phenomena are intricately related and mutually interactive for *both* men and women. We can draw this conclusion despite the fact that sex-role socialization seems to place work at the center of men's lives and love at the center of women's lives.

In a review of the literature on work and family, for example, Mortimer and Sorensen write: "It is now well recognized that work and the family are linked together and dependent upon one another in numerous ways, despite their institutional separation. Moreover, there is substantial evidence that their relationship is highly reciprocal; work not only influences family life, but the family also influences behavior in the workplace. While some of these effects are contemporaneous, for example, events in the workplace often have more or less immediate impact on the family; others, like the effects of vocational socialization in the family, may be lagged over long periods of time" (1984, p. 139). This interaction of work and family turned up in some studies as the notion of "spillover" (Lancereau, 1987; Nieva and Gutek, 1981; Kohn and Schooler, 1982). Kanter comments that "evidence does make a case for the spillover from the emotional connection with work to other areas of life. People with boring work tend to have boring leisure, and people with involving work tend to have higher levels of both leisure and family involvement" (1984, p. 118). A recent survey of Atlanta's American Society for Training and Development (ASTD) members specifically asked about spillover (Bracken and Gier, 1990). When asked their reaction to the statements, "Generally, when I have a bad time at home, it spills over to my work effectiveness," 40 percent of the men and 50 percent of the women in the sample strongly agreed or agreed. When the reverse was asked — "Generally, when I have a bad time at work, it spills over to my home relationships" — 70 percent of the men and 83 percent of the women strongly agreed or agreed. Other questions in this survey addressing work and family (for example, "Overall, I am currently satisfied with my work/family balance," "The more successful a person becomes at work, the more that person's marriage will suffer") were answered similarly by men and women. We found a spillover effect in our study for both men and women. Matt, a forty-year-old minister, spoke of work affecting his home life: "When things were in distress at work, it increased the stress at home. But with the increased stress in the love end, I wouldn't say that the increased stress was bad or okay, but even in the increased stress maybe there's a good in that, too. Maybe it was the way Elaine and I would go about labeling things. We would talk more, we would talk more about serious things. Our conversations would probably have more anger in them during those times." Similarly, Monica, a fifty-two-year-old nurse, recalled the time when she was working on her master's and the effect that had on her family: "I did it part-time and I was working full-time. My children were school-age. I also had a Girl Scout troup so I was pretty heavily stressed out during those three years and I guess relationships kind of took a back seat. My husband was also very busy during that time so it was just one of those times when we weren't as close as we generally are."

While there is clear evidence of spillover for both men and women, a couple of studies with women suggest that a few may try to separate the two phenomena. Lancereau found that some women choose to erect a boundary between work and love: "Looking at their self-reports, it appears that some of the respondents are determined not to allow interpenetration between home and work. Those women who have a more self-contained view of achievement seem to be the most intent on not allowing their home lives to penetrate into their work lives. It may be that any encroachment of the relationship on work is experienced by these women as an infringement on their sense of identity" (1987, p. 200). Nieva and Gutek comment that one way women handle role overload is "to clearly compartmentalize roles with an effort toward not letting one role interfere with another" (1981, p. 49). In a study of marital satisfaction of dual-career couples, Nicola and Hawkes found that while in general both spouses were satisfied with their marriages, "wives' high career commitment showed a high negative association with marital satisfaction of both husbands and wives, whereas husband's career commitment showed no significance." They attribute the wives' dissatisfaction to "career and family conflict or sheer work overload" (1985, p. 52). While maintaining one's work identity and/or dealing with role overload may explain the separation of the two arenas, type of work may be another explanation. Just as some men in certain occupations like law enforcement feel they can function better by disassociating their work lives from their family lives, the same may be true of some women in certain occupations.

Many questions about the interaction of work and family remain to be answered. Mortimer, Lorence, and Kumka suggest that "there may be optimal levels of work involvement for the family." Both boring and routinized work and "excessively involving and demanding occupations may have similar effects" on family (1986, p. 24). Kanter poses still other questions: "Does the family world serve *compensatory* functions for emotional deprivations suffered at work, or *displacement-or-aggression* functions? Does the family get the best parts of a working member's energy or commitment when these are not called for at work, as some research hints, or does it get only the parts left over from an emotionally draining job? Do people orient themselves to the family emotionally in the same way they come to approach their work?" (1984, p. 118).

From the psychological perspective, the development of both work and love or identity and intimacy are linked to maturity for both women and men. In Kacerguis and Adams's (1980) study of the relationship between intimacy and identity in eighty-eight young adult men and women, advanced ego identity correlated with advanced intimacy development for men and women. They also found that occupational identity predicted intimacy development for *both* men and women. In another study of intimacy and identity, Raskin (1986) examined the relationship between the two components with fifty men and women between twenty-two and thirty-five years old. She found support for a strong relationship between identity status and intimacy in young adults. There were no gender differences other than that the order of dealing with each of these issues varied for younger women and men, but "no such gender differences were found for older subjects" (p. 179).

Finally, in a comprehensive study of psychological well-being at midlife, Hinand looked at work and love patterns of 100 men and women between the ages of forty-five and fifty-five. She defined work as "the state of being involved in the meaningful endeavors of one's society, whether financially remunerated or not" and love as the "state of being relationally connected with other persons" (1984, p. 6). Hinand asked how work and love contributed to psychological well-being. She found a significant positive relationship between psychological well-being and the integration of love and work. She turned up a "high correlation between women's psychological well being and their work life"; also, the expectation "that men would place a greater emphasis than women on the work status . . . was not borne out" in her study (p. 208). She concluded that for men, love is as essential as work in contributing to well-being, just as both work and love are essential to women's well-being.

Summary

Work and love have been studied in terms of psychological well-being or maturity, and as manifestations of the social institutions of work and family. We can make several summary observations with regard to the research reviewed in this chapter. First, this research is based on traditional assumptions that locate work outside the family context, and on conventional definitions of work and love. We know little about their interaction in a family-owned business, in a work-at-home situation, or in communal living arrangements, for example. Second, until very recently, men's primary identity has been seen in terms of work, while women's has been seen in terms of relationships. Gilligan (1982) in a sense inadvertently contributed to this segmentation by discovering that women's development follows a path of connectedness and responsibility versus the male model of separateness and justice. Her urging men and women to recognize the importance of both and attend to the development of both often goes unheard. Some research does suggest that love or family plays a greater role in women's lives (Josselson, 1990; Blumstein and Schwartz, 1983), as does work in men's lives (Levinson and others, 1978).

However, we found a large number of studies that suggest the two arenas are equally important to both men and women. This conclusion emerges from the literature whether or not studies were conducted with only one sex or with both men and women. Vaillant's study of the Harvard men, for example — despite choosing a sample based on career variables rather than intimacy measures — found the best predictor of mental health to be "sustained relationships with loving people" (1977, p. 337). Likewise, Baruch, Barnett, and Rivers's (1983) study of women's patterns of love and work found that optimal well-being occurred in women who balanced working and loving.

Finally, studies that have investigated the interaction of work
and love in both men's and women's lives have found few if any
gender differences. For various reasons, some men and some
women choose to keep their work and family lives separate. For
others, there is a great amount of interaction, or spillover. Only
a few studies support the notion that men emphasize career
rather than family, or that women devote themselves to relationships at the expense of developing a satisfactory work life.
Perhaps the situation is changing and men and women are more
consciously attending to both arenas; or perhaps the stereotype
of men being work-driven and work-defined and women being
driven and defined by love was never really as rigid as popular
culture would have us believe. As Daniels and Weingarten observe, "It no longer makes sense to view love as women's essential and exclusive work, and work as man's essential and exclusive love. For both men and women, both love and work are
means of taking care" (1982, p. 7).

CHAPTER THREE

At the Intersection of Work, Love, and Learning

We have reviewed how the capacities for work and love develop, and how they manifest themselves in adult life. This is not to imply that reaching adulthood equals being mature. Rather, it seems that maturity is a continually evolving process. The experiences we encounter in our daily lives shape the way we think and the way we interact with future life experiences. The key to understanding this process is to understand the learning that adults are continually engaged in, and how this learning is related to work and love.

Ask an adult if he or she has been engaged in a learning activity recently and most will think in terms of what classes they have attended. And formal education is certainly widespread for adults of all ages. In a recent "Dear Abby" column, Margaret M. Hill of Victoria, Texas, wrote to say she could top those who returned to college in midlife. "At 60," she says, "I went to school evenings and during the summer. Shortly before my 65th birthday, I received my college degree and teaching credentials. I taught kindergarten until I was forced to retire because of age requirements. I immediately went to work as a medical insurance clerk. I will be 80 on my next birthday and I'm already looking for places to work as a volunteer when I retire." Margaret closes her letter asking Abby to "please continue to encourage older people to keep on learning. It's never too late" ("Dear Abby," 1990, p. C-2).

Margaret and thousands of adults like her have discovered that learning does not have to end with high school or college, nor is it bound by age or stage in life. In addition to the more formal, institutionally organized learning opportunities that people are increasingly taking advantage of, nearly all adults engage in informal, self-directed learning projects as a part of their daily lives. Informal learning is a lifelong process where values, skills, and knowledge are acquired from everyday experience as well as from other educational influences or settings. Whether learning is formal or informal, work, which is broadly defined as task-oriented activity, and love, which can be broadly defined as relationship-oriented, affective experiences, motivate and shape this learning. In this chapter we examine how work and love structure learning, how these factors distinguish adult learners from children, and how life-experience learning actually takes place.

Work and Love Motivate Learning

Adults have very busy lives. Most work at least eight hours a day and spend as many hours attending to family and community responsibilities. Indeed, love- and work-related activities absorb our time and structure our lives. They also stimulate a great deal of both formal and informal learning. There are many people like Margaret who go back to school for a degree; there are many more who take an occasional course offered by their local adult school, church, library, or hospital; still others participate in training sessions offered by their employer; and then there are those who set out to learn something on their own. Learning on one's own is most often referred to as *self-directed learning,* and it usually involves learning projects adults identify in the course of their daily lives. Nearly all adults have probably directed their own learning at one time or another. But what motivates someone to study for a college degree at sixty? Or to acquire new career skills at forty? Or to learn how to repair furniture or organize a community protest? Not surprisingly, the motivation to learn in adulthood is most often directly linked to an adult's life situation, and that frequently is related to his or her work domain.

Work plays a central role in the concept of adulthood in our society. All adults are expected to be productive members of society, to be workers. Certainly most adults are working, looking for work, or seeking to change their work situations. The triennial surveys of participation in adult education conducted by the National Center for Education Statistics (NCES) show that work provides major motivation for learning for both men and women. A full 64 percent of participants in the 1984 survey indicated that getting a new job or advancing in their present job accounted for their participation in formal adult education activities (U.S. Department of Education, 1987). Cross comments on work as a source of motivation for learning:

> People who do not have good jobs are interested in further education to get better jobs, and those who have good jobs would like to advance in them. Women, factory workers, and the poorly educated, for example, are more likely to be pursuing education in order to prepare for new jobs, whereas men, professionals, and college graduates are more likely to be seeking advancement in present jobs. Men are more interested in job-related learning than women are, and young people are far more interested in it than older people are. Interest in job-related goals begins to decline at age 50 and drops off sharply after age 60. Those who are not currently participating in learning activities (most often the economically disadvantaged and poorly educated) are even more likely to express an interest in job-related education than are their more advantaged peers, who can afford the luxury of education for recreation and personal satisfaction [1981, pp. 91-92].

Learning related to work occurs in many settings, including of course the workplace. In fact the amount of employer-sponsored learning activities is staggering. In a study conducted for *Training* magazine, it was estimated that in 1986, 30.5 million adults received formal employer-sponsored training consisting of 1.3 billion training hours (Gordon, 1986). Further, "employers deliver learning to more people than does the entire U.S. higher-education system" (Carnevale, 1989, p. 27). The financial investment in this type of learning is also staggering. One source estimates training to be a $210 billion business, compared with the $238 billion per year spent for elementary, secondary, and postsecondary education combined (Carnevale, 1986).

While work-related learning is extensive and well documented, the love domain is also the locus for significant learning. A study that focused on the "why" of participation (Aslanian and Brickell, 1980) clearly showed that work *and* love are motivating factors for learning in adulthood. Aslanian and Brickell speculated that it was the transitions in adult life that motivated adults to seek out learning experiences. They found that 83 percent of the learners in their sample could describe some past, present, or future change in their lives as reasons for learning. Transitions were categorized into seven types. Fifty-six percent of the learners were learning because of some work-related transition, and 16 percent were involved because of a family-related transition, such as going through a divorce, the birth of a child, and so on. The other transition areas and the percent of learning activities were as follows: leisure (13 percent), art (5 percent), health (5 percent), religion (4 percent), and citizenship (1 percent). They also classified the specific events that "triggered" the transitions and found that 56 percent of the triggering events were career-related and 36 percent were family-related. "To know an adult's life schedule," they concluded, "is to know an adult's learning schedule" (pp. 60–61).

In addition to the more formal learning activities reflected in workplace training and in Aslanian and Brickell's study, work and love stimulate a good bit of informal, self-directed learning. The first comprehensive study of self-directed learning was conducted by Allen Tough (1971), a Canadian adult educator who suspected that adults were engaged in a lot more learning than surveys of formal participation revealed. He interviewed sixty-six individuals in depth about what he called their "learning projects." He defined a learning project as "a highly deliberate effort to gain and retain certain definite knowledge and skill, or to change in some other way. To be included, a series of related learning sessions (episodes in which the person's primary intention was to learn) must add up to at least seven hours" (1978, p. 250). These learning projects could be (and were) about anything from learning to build a greenhouse, to foreign-language learning, to raising children, and so on. Tough (1978) found that 90 percent of his sample was engaged in at least one learning project per year, and that the typical learner conducted five learning projects of 100 hours per project. He reported that "a great many of these learning projects are related to the person's job or occupation" (p. 33) and to "managing a home and family" (p. 35).

Tough's study has been replicated numerous times with a variety of populations ranging from farmers to physicians to mothers with preschool children. Estimates of participation range from 70 to 100 percent depending on the groups interviewed and how the study was conducted. A national study of the phenomenon by Penland (1979) involving 1,501 respondents yielded a participation rate of 79 percent. Penland found that "almost 80 percent (78.9) of the population of 18 years and over perceive themselves as continuing learners whether in self-planned or formal courses" and "over three-quarters (76.1 percent) of the U.S. population had planned one or more learning projects on their own" (p. 173). The subject matter for these projects was also documented. The two most popular topics for study — personal development and home and family concerns — reflect the broad definition of love used in our study. Reasons given for undertaking these learning projects centered on wanting the freedom and flexibility to structure one's learning to suit individual needs.

Work and love motivate adults to engage in learning, but so do love of learning itself and the social interaction that is part of most learning activities. These motives were discovered by Houle over thirty years ago. He conducted in-depth interviews with a select sample of twenty-two adults "conspicuously engaged in various forms of continuing learning" (1961, p. 13). He asked about their previous experiences with learning, the reasons why they were learning, and their views of themselves as learners. He found that some adults are primarily *goal oriented*, that is, they use learning as a means of achieving some other end such as a new job; others were primarily *activity oriented* in that they participated for the social interaction inherent in the activity; still others were primarily *learning oriented*, seeking knowledge for its own sake. For Houle, the goal-oriented learners were easiest to understand since "the need or interest appeared and they satisfied it by taking a course, joining a group, reading a book, or going on a trip" (p. 18). Activity-oriented adults liked to be doing something and sought out the social contact. Learning-oriented adults had the "itch to learn. . . . The fundamental purpose which lay back of all their considerable educational activity was quite simply the desire to know" (pp. 24–25). Certainly the goal-oriented learners can be linked to the broad concept of work as goal-oriented activity, and Houle's activity-oriented learners can be linked to the broad definition of love as social, people-oriented adult life concerns.

These three orientations to learning have been well supported in subsequent investigations of adults' motivation to learn. The most work has been done by Boshier and Collins (1985), who compiled the results of numerous studies using the Education Participation Scale (EPS) developed by Boshier to assess adults' reasons for participating in learning. Using data from over 13,000 learners worldwide, they concluded that three orientations exist, although they suggested some refinements. The learning-oriented approach is characterized by the factor "cognitive interest," and the goal-oriented approach they call "professional advancement." Activity-oriented learning is, in their analysis, "multifaceted and composed of items normally labeled Social Stimulation, Social Contact, External Expectations, and Community Service" (p. 125). Our broad definition of love is captured by the social dimension of these activity-oriented factors.

Thus studies that have documented formal and informal learning and those that have investigated what motivates adults to learn suggest that both work and love stimulate learning in adult life. They also show that motivations can and do overlap and often change in the course of the learning activity. For example, a person may enroll in a woodworking class for the enjoyment of the activity itself, discover that there is a market for this skill, and thus begin to work toward employment in this area. Adults returning to college to acquire work skills often discover that the interaction with others in the learning environment and/or the excitement of learning for its own sake augment their original reason for getting a degree.

Motivation to learn is a complex phenomenon that psychologists and educators are continually trying to better understand. In adulthood, motivation is linked to the needs and interests inherent in an adult's life situation. Kidd explains that "one of the reasons that adults continue to learn well . . . is that they concentrate their learning in the areas of experience in which their interests also lie. Thus their motivation is substantial and, as everyone knows, wanting to learn is the greatest aid to learning" (1973, p. 91).

How Work and Love Distinguish
Adult Learners from Children

What differentiates learning in adulthood from learning in childhood? An entire field of practice — adult education — is based on the assumption that there are in fact differences, differences that mandate special attention to instruction, programming, and counseling. These differences center on an adult's life situation and the fact that adulthood is a qualitatively different experience from childhood.

To begin with, adults are adults because they are responsible for managing their own lives. In contrast to children, who depend on others for their welfare, adults are defined by being independent and self-sufficient. This factor affects the nature and goals of learning. For children, going to school is a full-time job. In school and at home, children learn to be adults; in both settings, what they learn is determined by others who have decided what they need to know to become responsible members of society. But "adults . . . typically add the role of learner onto other full-time occupations. The learning that adults do arises from the context of their lives. . . . An assembly-line worker whose job is taken over by a robot will need to retrain for other employment. Likewise, a nurse will need to keep up with changes in practice and technology. Zoning and tax laws, waste disposal management, and so on that affect citizens' lives in communities lead to new learning. Thus learning in adulthood is characterized by its usefulness for immediate application to the duties and responsibilities inherent in the adult roles of worker, spouse, parent, citizen, and so on" (Merriam and Caffarella, 1991, pp. 303–304).

The social roles of adulthood are vehicles for the expression of the fundamental forces of work and love in our lives. As Smelser notes, "The adult years mark the development and integration of cognitive and instrumental capacities that enable people to reach whatever heights of purposeful, organized mastery of the world they are capable of reaching. Too, the adult years are those in which people are able to reach their maximum of mutually gratifying attachments to other individuals" (1980a, p. 4). The nature of these social roles changes as we age. The role of parent, for example, is different for someone with preschoolers versus someone with teenagers, and different yet for parents whose children are young or middle-aged adults. Adjusting to these changes in social roles and functions is a strong impetus for learning.

Many psychologists and educators have documented love- and work-related role changes in adult life. Nearly fifty years ago Havighurst delineated specific tasks for different stages of life. According to Havighurst, developmental tasks "are those things that constitute healthy and satisfactory growth in our society. They are the things a person must learn if he [or she] is to be judged and to judge himself [or herself] to be a reasonably happy and successful person" (1972, p. 2). Most young adults, for example, are faced with the love-related tasks of deciding on a partner and starting a family, whereas midlife adults are preoccupied with raising teenage children, and many older adults will have to adjust to the death of a spouse. In the work-related arena, young adults need to get started in an occupation, midlife adults strive to maintain their economic standard of living, and those in late life must adjust to retirement. While these tasks have been criticized as being somewhat outdated as well as restricted to middle-class adults, they do illustrate how social roles and functions can change as we mature. Havighurst also related the tasks to learning, in noting that the emergence of these tasks provides the "teachable moment" for learning.

Other writers speak of transitions and life events that are characteristic of adulthood and that require adjustments — adjustments often made through formal or informal learning (Schlossberg, 1984; Knox, 1977; Fiske and Chiriboga, 1990; Kimmel, 1990). It might be recalled that Aslanian and Brickell (1980) found that 83 percent of adult learning could be attributed to coping with a life transition, and a full 72 percent of these transitions were work or family related. In discussing the informal learning projects adults design, Tough also points out their connection to changes in adults' lives:

> Some learning projects are initiated because of certain changes that occur in the individual[s] as [they] move through the life cycle. They marry and have children. Their interests change with age, and they engage in new sports or leisure activities. As they achieve one goal, they move on to another. As their savings increase, they buy a house or a new car. They receive a promotion because other people in the company retire or die. They receive new responsibilities on the job as their experience and competence increase. These changes and stages in the person's life, and the learning projects they spark, would occur even in a completely unchanging society. . . .
>
> Some learning projects are necessary to help the individual to *adjust* to changes in knowledge, processes, technology, values, and social organization. These changes affect them on the job, in the home, and elsewhere [1971, p. 40].

Adults differ from children based on their life situations and the social roles characteristic of adult status. They also differ from children in terms of life experience and its potential as a learning resource.

By and large, "adults have *more* experiences, adults have different *kinds* of experiences, and adult experiences are *organized differently* than those of children" (Kidd, 1973, p. 46). Not only does the accumulation of experiences separate adults from children, it differentiates among adults themselves. As we age we accumulate experiences that form our individual, unique identities; the older we become the more pronounced our individuality is. With regard to learning, this "growing reservoir of experience" functions as "a rich resource for learning" (Knowles, 1980, p. 44). Adult learners can utilize their past experiences to facilitate their learning; adults can also be resources for the learning of others.

The accumulation of experience functions in other ways in learning. Clearly, "the need to make sense out of one's life experiences is often an incentive for engaging in a learning activity in the first place" (Merriam and Caffarella, 1991, p. 307). Researchers also think that the actual interaction of past experiences with new learning is different for adults than children. Recently several writers have argued that adult learning is characterized by the *transformation* of experience rather than the accumulation of knowledge (Boyd and Myers, 1988; Mezirow, 1990; Daloz, 1986).

Others have suggested that an adult's life experiences may be the source of "mature adult thought," which has the potential to be "qualitatively different from the thought of adolescents or very young adults" (Allman, 1983, p. 112). "Experience," Flavell writes, "is in fact a far more promising source of interesting adult cognitive changes than are biological events. . . . One can imagine some of the major categories of experimental settings which could provide occasions for really significant and enduring changes in an adult's cognition. There are programmed ones, like psychotherapy and adult education, which some adults encounter. There are also unprogrammed ones, such as marriage, child rearing, occupational activities, grandparenthood, retirement, widowhood, and so on, that many or most adults encounter. . . . Most adult cognitive changes probably concern . . . changes in the individual's implicit theories regarding the self, others, and the human condition generally" (1970, p. 249). Some researchers such as Basseches (1984) have already proposed that adults develop a dialectic form of thinking that makes it possible to tolerate the ambiguities and contradictions characteristic of adult life.

The nature and extent of cognitive changes in adulthood need further documentation. However, it is clear that adults are more than grown-up learners and that children are not just little adult learners. Adults are involved in social roles and tasks different from those of children, and most often engage in learning in response to the changing demands and expectations inherent in being an adult. The breadth and depth of accumulated experiences and how those experiences influence learning and/or are transformed in the learning process further differentiate adult learners from children. By way of summarizing the differences between adults and children, Lynch and Chickering offer the following list of distinguishing characteristics of adult learners:

- A wider range of individual differences, more sharply etched
- Multiple demands and responsibilities in terms of time, energy, emotions, and roles
- More — and more varied — past experiences
- A rich array of ongoing experiences and responsibilities
- More concern for practical application, less patience with pure theory, less trust in abstractions
- Greater self-determination and acceptance of responsibility
- Greater need to cope with transitions and with existential issues of competence, emotions, autonomy, identity, relationships, purpose, and integrity [1989, p. 20].

How Learning from Life Experience Takes Place

We have reviewed how work and love structure learning in adulthood, and how the related social roles and transitions of adult life distinguish adult learners from children. Since so much of adult learning is tied to life experiences and since this link is crucial to understanding how maturity, or the capacity to work and to love, is a lifelong process rather than an end state, it is important to review how learning from life experience takes place. That is, how is experience rendered meaningful? And, how does life experience learning facilitate development?

The philosopher and educator John Dewey provides some of the most thoughtful observations about the educative power of experience. He is best known as the originator of the progressive movement in American education, a movement characterized by an experiential mode of learning in the classroom. His insights into the nature of experience and its role in learning transcend classroom walls, however, and offer a foundation for our understanding of informal learning.

In *Experience and Education,* Dewey examines the "organic connection between education and personal experience" (1938, p. 12), although he is careful to note that not all experience educates. Experiences that educate lead to the growth of further and richer experiences, and they must be connected meaningfully to other experiences. Dewey describes how experiential learning works: "To 'learn from experience' is to make a backward and forward connection between what we do to things and what we enjoy or suffer from things in consequence. Under such conditions, doing becomes a trying; an experiment with the world to find out what it is like; the undergoing becomes instruction—discovery of the connection of things" (Dewey, 1961, p. 140). The phrase "experiment with the world" is telling. It is almost as though Dewey sees experience as giving us problems to be solved, and his suggested method is essentially scientific in its approach.

Kolb (1976, 1984)—an educator whose particular interest is in the training of adults in business and management—builds on the foundation laid by Dewey, since he understands learning in terms of the engagement of personal experience and sees adult learning as being intrinsically connected to problem solving. He proposes a four-stage cyclical model of learning: (1) the learner is confronted by the experience itself; (2) this is observed and reflected on; (3) abstract concepts or generalizations are then formulated; and (4) these concepts are tested in new situations, which in turn give rise to new experiences. The cycle is continuous.

More recently Jarvis (1987a, 1987b) has proposed a model to capture the relationship between experience and learning. Like Kolb, he believes that learning involves the transformation of experience into knowledge. For him, "life is about experience; wherever there is life there are potential learning experiences" (1987b, p. 164). Not all experience leads to learning. In his model there are nine possible responses to experience, three of which are categorized as *nonlearning*. For example, a person may be too busy to attend to a potential learning experience or may even refuse to learn from it. Jarvis categorizes three other responses as *nonreflective learning*. Here he includes practicing a skill, memorization, and contemplation. His third category (also consisting of three responses) is called *reflective learning*. This is where an adult attends to and reflects on an experience with the intention of learning something.

While Dewey, Kolb, and Jarvis, among others, describe the relationship between learning and life experience, others focus more on how learning from life experience leads to personal growth and development. An assumption underlying our study is that the development of the capacity to work and to love is an ongoing process involving an ever-widening perspective on one's self and one's position in the world, and that learning is the catalyst for this movement.

The person who probably best represents the connection between personal growth and learning is Carl Rogers, who was both a noted psychotherapist and an educator. He understood therapy as a learning process, and the client-centered form of therapy that he founded is directed toward creating a supportive, caring environment in which personal learning can be facilitated. He published a set of tentative principles about learning that grew out of his practice. These principles tell us much about learning and development:

> We cannot teach another person directly; we can
> only facilitate his [or her] learning.

> A person learns significantly only those things which [she or] he perceives as being involved in the maintenance of, or enhancement of, the structure of self.
>
> Experience which, if assimilated, would involve a change in the organization of self tends to be resisted through denial or distortion of symbolization.
>
> The structure and organization of self appears to become more rigid under threat; to relax its boundaries when completely free from threat. Experience which is perceived as inconsistent with the self can only be assimilated if the current organization of self is relaxed and expanded to include it.
>
> The educational situation which most effectively promotes significant learning is one in which (1) threat to the self of the learner is reduced to a minimum, and (2) differentiated perception of the field of experience is facilitated [Rogers, 1951, pp. 388–391].

Rogers does several things here. First, he connects the process of learning to the structure of the self, an entity that has both protection and enhancement as goals. And second, he defines learning as the assimilation of experience within the structure of the self. He also makes two assumptions that are now commonly accepted: that the ability to learn is innate and that life and learning are directed toward growth. In addition, his principles help explain why certain life experiences do not produce learning, a situation identified in Jarvis's model. Further, Rogers identifies what conditions are necessary before learning, and hence growth, can occur.

The most developed theory to date that attempts to explain how learning from life experiences takes place, and how this learning is related to development, has been advanced by Mezirow (1981, 1990). Mezirow suggests that all human beings function within what he calls *meaning structures*. These structures contain our personal beliefs and values as well as norms and expectations acquired from the sociocultural context. They mediate and give coherence to experience. Meaning structures function as a lens or filter through which personal experience is mediated and by which it is interpreted. When an experience is congruent with the structure and thus with past experiences, it is assimilated into that structure. If it is not congruent, one of two things happens. The experience can be rejected and thus loses its potential to be a learning experience. In Jarvis's model this was called nonlearning. Or, if the experience is too big to reject, it becomes what Mezirow calls a *disorienting dilemma,* triggering the formation of a new meaning structure that can incorporate the discordant experience. This explanation for the ways in which life experiences become learning experiences is not unlike Rogers's explanation of how the organization of self resists or assimilates experience.

Mezirow calls this process of change *perspective transformation,* which he defines as "the process of becoming critically aware of how and why our presuppositions have come to constrain the way we perceive, understand, and feel about our world; of reformulating these assumptions to permit a more inclusive, discriminating, permeable, and integrative perspective; and of making decisions or otherwise acting upon these new understandings" (1990, p. 14). Perspective transformation can occur suddenly and constitute "an epochal transformation" of meaning systems, such as is experienced in religious conversions or in consciousness raising. Or it can happen gradually, which is more common.

We believe that life experience, learning, and development are linked as follows: A person encounters an experience in the form of a life event, transition, or social-role task. Such events, transitions, or tasks are likely to arise from the work- or love-related dimensions of our lives. The experience is assimilated into our meaning structure, or is rejected either because it is too foreign to be accommodated within our meaning structure or because it disrupts our assumptions, beliefs, or values. This disruption sets in motion a sudden or gradual perspective transformation resulting in a new meaning structure that "permits us to deal with a broader range of experience, to be more discriminating, to be more open to other perspectives, and to better integrate our experiences" (Mezirow, 1990, p. 14). We would add that such perspective transformations might also be understood as the process of maturing, resulting in an enhanced capability to work and to love.

Summary

We have tried to show that much of the motivation for adult learning stems from the central forces of work and love. Work has been well documented as a motivating factor for participation in learning. National studies reveal that at least half of adult learners are involved in education for job-related reasons, as are those who are engaged in self-directed learning projects. Family-related concerns are a close second.

The social roles that adults assume — worker, spouse, parent, citizen — are clear manifestations of working and loving. The tasks related to these roles, and the changes and transitions people undergo in these roles, often require new learning. Experiences in these adult roles not only motivate learning, but help us to differentiate adult learners from children. Our accumulated life experiences shape who we are and who we become as adults. Some think that learning in adulthood is characterized by the transformation rather than just the accumulation of these life experiences. Others think that adult life experiences lead to cognitive development in adulthood that is qualitatively different from what takes place in childhood.

In the final section of the chapter we explored the essential link between experience and learning. Dewey and Kolb suggest a process in which experience is grasped and transformed, leading to the solution of problems. Jarvis builds on their work to propose a model that encompasses all possible responses to experience, to include situations of nonlearning, nonreflective learning, and reflective learning. Finally, Rogers and Mezirow demonstrate the relationship between learning and personal growth and development by showing how the learning process is connected to the structure of the self.

CHAPTER FOUR

Tracing the Patterns
of Adulthood

It used to be thought that, like a butterfly emerging fully formed from its cocoon, at about age eighteen a person became an adult and remained unchanged until the dying process set in. The major, important changes in life were presumed to occur in childhood or adolescence or old age itself. It was not until the 1960s that psychologists, sociologists, educators, and others became interested in the adult years. The growing interest in adulthood is due to several factors. First, there are more adults in the population than ever before. Second, the average life expectancy of each adult has nearly doubled since the beginning of the century, from approximately forty-seven to seventy-five years. Theoretically, then, the average person will spend approximately fifty years, or half a century, being an adult versus a few short years as an infant, child, or teenager.

The social situation that today's adults find themselves in has also changed. A global community, worldwide economic shifts, and fast-paced technological developments are forces that affect everyone's daily lives, forces that earlier generations did not begin to envision. Thus more adults are living longer and are affected by, coping with, and/or adapting to changing social conditions. Finally, social scientists have become more sophisticated and more creative in figuring out how to examine something as complex as adulthood.

The study of adulthood is characterized by the tension between uncovering commonalities of experience and at the same time preserving the uniqueness of individuals. Smelser writes that "at the very least . . . the study of adulthood calls for a certain amount of conceptual ordering" (1980a, p. 21). In searching for a basic order or pattern of the life course, we should not lose sight of "those variables that make for disruptions or that impose new directions or change in adult lives" (p. 22). Further complicating the study of adulthood is the fact that it is difficult to sort out the source of change in any person's life. To what extent are the changes in our lives due to the biological process of aging? Or to the behavioral norms and expectations of the society in which we live? Or to the occurrence of historical events such as war, depression, or industrialization?

The search for patterns that help us understand what adulthood is all about has resulted in several frameworks for viewing adult psychosocial change. The most common means of organizing change in adulthood is through stage or phase theories such as those proposed by Erikson (1963), Gould (1978), Levinson and others (1978), Loevinger (1976), Sheehy (1976), and Kohlberg (1973). According to this approach, adults of roughly the same chronological age or in the same life stage such as young, middle, and older adulthood encounter similar tasks or crises that they must deal with in order to successfully move on to the next stage or phase of development.

An alternative framework for understanding adulthood, and the one used for this study, is the concept of life events. Life events are noteworthy occurrences or "benchmarks in the human life cycle" (Sugarman, 1986, p. 131) that usually involve change in a person's activities. Also called marker events, milestones, change events, transitions, or developmental tasks, life events can be individual or cultural. Individual life events such as birth, marriage, graduation, illness, or job loss or promotion are the "punctuation marks" that shape and direct a person's life (Neugarten, 1976). Societal and historical happenings such as political assassinations, the advent of the computer age, natural disasters, social movements, and so on are cultural life events that influence the context in which individuals live. The impact of cultural events on individual lives varies, as do the ways in which people respond to individual life events.

Though usually viewed as occurrences or markers, life events may also be seen as processes beginning before the actual event happens and sometimes continuing well beyond the event. Divorce is a good example. A movement toward divorce occurs well in advance of the actual event itself; after the event, time is needed to assimilate and make sense out of the occurrence as well as to adapt to a new life-style. When viewed as processes, life events are often equated with the notion of transitions. Schlossberg in fact defines transition as "any event or nonevent that results in change" (1984, p. 43). Events can be anticipated (graduation) or unanticipated (a car accident); nonevent transitions "are those an individual had counted on but which did not occur, thereby altering his or her life, such as the marriage that never occurred, the promotion that never occurred, the child that was never born" (Schlossberg, 1984, p. 46). Bridges links transition to growth, since transition is "the natural process of disorientation and reorientation that marks the turning points of the path of growth . . . with this growth involving periodic accelerations and transformations" (1980, p. 5). As will be discussed in the next section, we used a life-event framework to uncover patterns of work and love in adulthood.

Several assumptions about adult development and learning underlie our study. First we assumed that work and love encompassed the central social and psychological forces of adult life, that these forces were interactive, and that quite possibly there were identifiable patterns of this interaction. We also assumed that life events, as either occurrences or processes, would give us a way to define or operationalize the arenas of work and love. Finally, we assumed that there was an intrinsic connection between work, love, and learning. The same events that defined a person's work or love pattern were both sources of learning themselves and stimuli for other learning. In this chapter we will detail how we designed a questionnaire to map patterns of work and love in adulthood, and how we collected and analyzed the data generated by the questionnaire and by supplementary interviews. Readers are referred to Resource A, "Notes on Methodology," for a more technical discussion of the research methodology employed in this study.

Designing the Questionnaire

The genesis of this study can be traced to the senior author's invitation in 1987 to address participants in a career development workshop held at the University of Wisconsin, Madison, and supported by the Kellogg Foundation. Participants consisted of approximately twenty faculty in the field of adult and continuing education from the United States and Canada. The topic was loosely defined as adult and career development. This invitation was seen by the author as an opportunity to explore in more depth her fascination with Freud's dictum that maturity was defined by the capacity to work and to love.

Since role modeling by more senior faculty in the field was one of the workshop's objectives, the author decided to begin exploring working and loving by mapping out her own life events in these two domains. Life events were used in the same sense of what Kimmel calls *milestones*. He defines a milestone as "an *event* (not a general goal) that stands out in one's memory, or in one's future plans, as a significant turning point, marker, or personal reference point" (1990, p. 9). Beginning with the year 1971, which contained a major event in each domain (obtaining a master's degree in the "work" domain, and birth of a daughter in the "love" domain), major events were listed side by side by year under column headings of work and love. There were some gaps, since not every year had an event in each column. Other than noting what major life events had been significant enough to be recalled, a person could not determine much about the interaction of the two domains just by looking at the lists of events. The author then thought that the years could be assessed for each domain as having been a "good" year, a "bad" year, or an "okay" year. For example, for the year 1971, the work domain was rated a good year, as was the love domain. For the year 1980, however, the work and love domains were rated "bad" due to an unsettling job change (work) and divorce (love). While this rating helped the author to better see an interaction of the two arenas by year, it was still difficult to see if there were any overall pattern. She decided to try graphing the two domains using years on the horizontal axis and good, okay, and bad on the vertical axis. The result is sketched in Figure 4.1. Clearly there is a parallel pattern here in which one domain's movement is mirrored by the other domain. The pattern of alternating periods of stability and change was also interesting. This graph generated many questions for the author: Will others have the same pattern? Are women's patterns different from men's? Does one domain drive the other? Are there periods when one feels more productive, when more learning takes place? and so on. She decided that this exercise would be interesting to do with workshop participants.

The exercise stimulated much discussion and many questions about the interaction of work and love. The author was invited back in 1988 for another workshop with different participants, which provided another opportunity to explore the potential of the questionnaire for answering some of the questions about the interaction of work and love. Participants in this workshop volunteered to distribute questionnaires if there were interest in turning the exercise into a larger research study.

The fall of 1988 was spent refining and pilot testing the questionnaire in preparation for large-scale distribution that winter. Several alternative schemes for evaluating the years were experimented with; most suggestions involved making finer distinctions using five, six, or seven categories. However, these proved to be more difficult to use than the original categories of good, bad, and okay. Most people harbored a general impression of a particular year as having been good, bad, or okay with respect to their work and love activities. Thus it was decided to retain the original rating scheme. Work-specific life events were defined as "noteworthy work experiences, paid or volunteer; formal education." Love-related events were defined as "interpersonal relationships, family events; social life; leisure activities." A time span of twenty years (1969–1989) was deemed a reasonable period of time within which to capture interaction patterns of adults of various ages. Participants who were not at least eighteen years old in 1969 were instructed to begin with the year in which he or she had turned eighteen.

In addition to attempting to capture the interaction between the work and love arenas, we wanted to explore the con-

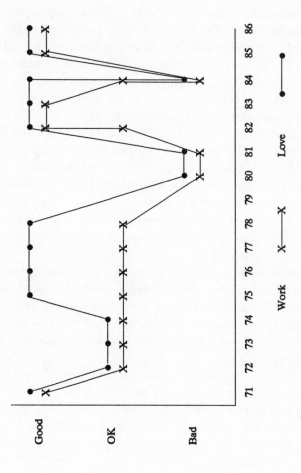

Figure 4.1. Author's Work-and-Love Pattern.

nections between work, love, and learning. We were curious about the amount that adults felt they learned from life events, whether more learning occurred in one domain or the other, and when more learning might occur. In other words, are we more likely to be involved in active, systematic learning when things are going well in our lives? Or does more learning take place when one arena is out of sync with the other? We were also interested in trying to understand why certain learning is considered more significant than other learning we do in our daily lives. To obtain this information on learning, we added a section on a second page asking respondents to identify significant learning events and the year of occurrence, and to note what made the event significant for them. The actual instructions for this part of the questionnaire were as follows: "In reflecting upon the major love and work events in your life, identify formal, informal, or personal learning experiences that were especially meaningful, significant, or intense for you. Briefly describe the learning, when it occurred, and its significance for you."

Other questions on the second page of the instrument asked the respondent's age, sex, race, occupation, and level of education. A final section left room for respondents to make comments ("Please share any reflections you have related to the experience of completing this activity, or comments of any kind") if desired. Exhibit 4.1 is a copy of each page of the instrument. Instructions for creating a chart modeled on the questionnaire can be found in Resource B for those who would like to determine their own work-and-love pattern. (For a fuller discussion of the questionnaire and its limitations, see Resource A.)

Precedents for Graphing Life Patterns

Our scheme for visualizing the interaction of work and love through first listing major life events in these domains, then rating the years as good, bad, or okay, and then graphing the results on the bottom of the first page of the questionnaire proved quite workable. We were able to identify three major interaction patterns through an inductive data analysis procedure discussed in the next section of this chapter. While this is the first

Exhibit 4.1. The "Work, Love, and Learning in Adulthood" Questionnaire.

SSN _____
(last 4 digits)

WORK, LOVE, AND LEARNING IN ADULTHOOD

Directions. First, reflect on your life since 1969* and identify the major events from year to year in the areas of work and love. Then determine whether the love and work dimension—as you remember experiencing it at the time—was good, bad, or OK. Finally, plot those points on the graph below, using the symbols given for the two dimensions.
*If you were not at least 18 years old in 1969, start with the year in which you turned 18.

	WORK			LOVE
	(noteworthy work experiences, paid or volunteer; formal education)			(interpersonal relationships, family events; social life; leisure activities)
Year		Rating*		
1969				
1970				
1971				
1972				
1973				
1974				
1975				
1976				
1977				
1978				
1979				
1980				
1981				
1982				
1983				
1984				
1985				
1986				
1987				
1988				
1989				

*G = Good, OK = OK, B = Bad

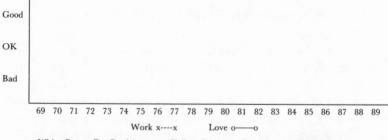

Good

OK

Bad

69 70 71 72 73 74 75 76 77 78 79 80 81 82 83 84 85 86 87 88 89

Work x----x   Love o——o

White Copy—For Participant   Yellow Copy and Final Page—For Researcher

Exhibit 4.1. The "Work, Love, and Learning in Adulthood" Questionnaire, Cont'd.

SSN_____
(last 4 digits)

LEARNING

<u>Directions</u>. In reflecting on the major love and work events in your life, identify formal, informal, or personal learning experiences that were especially meaningful, significant, or intense for you. Briefly describe the learning, when it occurred, and its significance for you.

Year(s)	Learning Experience	Significance

<u>Identifying Data</u>

Age_____

Sex: (1) Male_____ (2) Female_____

Race: (1) Black_____

     (2) White_____

     (3) Asian_____

     (4) Hispanic_____

     (5) Other_____

Occupation_____

Education Level:

     (1) High School Graduate_____

     (2) Some Postsecondary_____

     (3) College Graduate_____

     (4) Some Graduate Work_____

     (5) Graduate Degree (specify)_____

<u>Comments</u>

Please share any reflections you have related to the experience of completing this activity, or comments of any kind.

time a visual representation of these interactions has been undertaken, there are precedents and suggestions for studying adult development in this manner. Over twenty years ago, Back and Bourque (1970) developed a technique called *Draw-a-Graph* for visualizing a person's life over time. The horizontal axis represented age in ten-year segments from zero to eighty. The vertical axis was a measure of happiness, that things were going well. Individuals of all ages were asked to draw a lifeline "with its characteristic dips, peaks, and plateaus. The higher the graph, the happier the individual is assumed to see himself [or herself] as being or having been at the age in question" (p. 250). Although data were collected cross-sectionally, the authors make the point that this technique has "some of the virtues of a longitudinal method" since a person visualizes his or her past, present, and future (p. 250). Analysis of the life graphs of a weighted sample of over 3,000 showed that "most persons see life as gradually improving until it peaks at 55 years at which it gradually declines" (p. 251). It seems to us that the "ups and downs, level periods, rises and declines" (p. 250) that respondents were asked to graph are somewhat analogous to the annual ratings of work and love as good, bad, and okay on our questionnaire.

In a later writing, Back (1980) calls for creative approaches to the study of the life course. Using decision points in one's life as a unifying thread, he writes that

> going from one decision point to the next, we can investigate a sequence of decisions, and the relationships between them, and build up in that way a kind of life cycle. . . . From schooling to leaving home to first job to marriage, having children and finally, the various stages of dissolution of relationships during old age — these choice points describe the parameters of demography as well as of the social psychology of development and of achievement; they define a person's position in a personal or social space.
>
> With some justification, many people claim that this is not all of what we know of human life.

> They are supported by the biographer and the
> novelist, who try to fill out the missing parts, the
> transitions between the different decisions — the real
> meaning which these experiences have for the in-
> dividual [p. 163].

Back goes on to observe that while the language of the
artist, poet, or novelist gives us particularly rich insights into
an individual life course, the language of the scientist gives us
a "public" look at many lives. The challenge for social scientists
is to "contrive a scientific language capable of dealing with the
complexities of the human life course" (p. 165). He proposes
developing a *geometry* of the life course, a geometry of forms that
is more natural than an "arithmetic of numbers" (p. 166). Drawing from "fuzzy subsets" and "catastrophe theory" of mathematics,
he proposes *life-cycle curves:* "Each human life is a unique curve,
defined by its important determinants. Some are similar enough
to form, grouped together, what are called families of curves,
distinguished only by individual parameters, which we may call
personality or social background. Shifts in these curves may be
sudden and extreme reorganizations, which represent real crises,
or they may be just apparent shifts, within a regular curve, which
are unreal crises. The combination and classification of these
forms can become a science of the life course" (p. 168).

What Smelser (1980a) calls *life contours* are similar to Back's
concept of life curves. Life contours can be plotted on a lifeline
for sociocultural functions such as work role, family and marital role, physiological features such as muscular strength and
reaction time, and psychological dimensions such as ego strength.
Individual life contours will of course show variability representative of "a person's journey through the life course. . . . Inso-
far as a person's life has ingredients that are inevitable, irreversible, tightly scheduled, and normatively dictated, to that extent
[the contour] is predetermined, leaving little room for choice.
But . . . not all contours possess all of these restraining features,
and each personal history is not determined entirely by biological and sociocultural agendas. Furthermore, we may expect individual differences in the ways people come to terms with the

inevitable, irreversible, and binding features of the life course" (p. 12).

We found a few instances in the literature on work and love that incorporated or suggested the use of graphs for better understanding the phenomena. As part of the data for her study of the developmental patterns of career-committed women, Farone (1981) used a lifeline of chronologically arranged marker events on which each subject demarcated phases of her life. As an example, one women wrote "graduate from high school and first job" for age eighteen, "new job, higher pay" for age twenty-six, "meets husband" for age twenty-eight, "married" for age thirty, "Illness of mother" for age forty, and so on (p. 170). Similarly Sangiuliano (1978) had the participants in her study of women's identity formation draw a line representing their lives. Small circles indicated important events and the years they occurred. Each event was given a plus or a minus to indicate whether the participants considered the event to be positive or negative. Farone's and Sangiuliano's time-line exercises are very much like ours, except that in our study, work and love events are listed separately.

Rohrlich (1980, p. 233) also proposes plotting work and love activities on a graph to reveal the dynamic tension between work and love. With love on the horizontal axis and work on the vertical axis, a position in the upper left-hand corner would indicate a work addict (high on work, low on love), whereas a point in the upper right-hand corner would reveal a person balanced (and high) in both work and love. Finally, Lancereau (1987) illustrates the findings of her study on work and love through diagrams consisting of six circles representing the domains of occupation and marriage, the modes of working and loving, and the developmental tasks of identity and intimacy. She illustrates a work-dominated pattern of interaction by overlapping the working and loving circles and drawing arrows from the occupation, marriage, identity, and intimacy circles to the working circle. In her love-dominated pattern, arrows point to the loving circle that overlaps with the working circle. These figures represent the two "predominant patterns" of interaction, in which "some people turn their work into a loving experience while others turn their love into a working experience" (p. 204).

Thus while the particular type of graph our questionnaire generated for displaying patterns of interaction between work and love has not been used before, the idea of graphically visualizing life processes and patterns has some precedent. Furthermore, the visual representations of data through graphs, charts, diagrams, and models is common practice in all types of research (see for example Miles and Huberman, 1984). As mentioned earlier, the graphs in this study produced very usable data that were easily analyzed for patterns of working and loving.

Collecting the Data

Participants in the 1987 and 1988 faculty development workshops were contacted about distributing the "Work, Love, and Learning in Adulthood" questionnaire described earlier. Over 500 copies were distributed with instructions for administration by professors of adult and continuing education to adults in graduate or continuing education courses in North America. The instructors distributed and collected most of these questionnaires during class sessions and returned them to the researchers. A few questionnaires were not distributed at all, due to lack of class time or because classes were smaller than originally anticipated. In a few situations instructions were given to the respondents to mail the completed forms directly to the researchers. For the most part, these questionnaires were not returned. Approximately another 80 questionnaires were completed by adults in community organizations, cooperative extension workshops, and church groups and returned to the researchers. Of the 457 questionnaires returned to the researchers, 410 had been completed in enough detail to be used in the analysis. For the most part, participants enjoyed filling out the questionnaire. One wrote in the "Comments" section that "this has been a meaningful activity although a rather draining one. . . . The experience has been personally enlightening in that I have seen 'patterns on paper' that I had never truly discovered earlier." Another said that "this exercise made me realize how much the *whole* person is involved in what we do."

A few respondents had difficulty recalling significant life events. One fiftyish male said that he concentrates on the present and did not remember enough to complete the task. Clearly, a sense of personal history is necessary to fill out the form. Some others found it difficult to evaluate a particular year as good, bad, or okay. One respondent said that in the same year her mother had died and she had gotten married. Another wrote in the "Comments" section that "I found myself frustrated by having to 'average out' a given year's extremely good and extremely bad experiences to get an 'okay' rating." Our instructions for this situation said to try to define the overriding impression of that year and rate it accordingly; if people were unable to do that, they were told to leave the rating for that domain in that year blank.

Overall the vast majority of respondents had little if any difficulty in filling out the questionnaire. We suggested that people not dwell on particular years or particular events, that what we were after was their subjective recall and emotional assessment of the impact in any particular year of major life events. As it turned out, the patterns that emerged were so defined that a change in any particular rating would not have affected the overall pattern.

The final sample consists of 405 adults (the five graphs we were unable to categorize by pattern were eliminated from the study; see the next section on data analysis). The age range of our sample is 20 to 62 with the average age of the participants being 37.6 years. Of the total sample, 112 or 27.7 percent are men and 293 or 72.3 percent are women. The sample is predominantly white (81 percent). Ten percent of the sample is African American, 5 percent is Asian, and 1 percent is Hispanic; 3 percent of the respondents did not indicate their race on the questionnaire. Our respondents are well educated (88 percent are college educated, and of that number, 39 percent have a graduate degree). The majority of our participants are employed in education-related occupations or are full-time students. Teacher, principal, instructor, administrator, counselor, nursing educator, consultant, and trainer account for nearly half of our respondents. This is not particularly surprising given that the majority of the questionnaires were distributed to adults in continuing education classes. Most of the rest of our respondents listed either business-related occupations such as management, human resource director, and sales or human service occupations such as nursing, ministry, medical technology, and social work. Three respondents listed homemaker as their occupation. There were several unique employment situations, such as museum director, interpreter, diplomat, landscape contractor, and historic preservationist. Overall, in terms of gender, race, age, education, and socioeconomic status, our sample reflects the typical participant in adult and continuing education. National studies of participation in adult education indicate that between 14 and 31 percent of adults are engaged in formal learning activities, and that upwards of 90 percent are learning something on their own (Merriam and Caffarella, 1991). So while our sample is certainly biased, it does reflect the typical adult learner in our society. Furthermore, since one of our objectives was to explore the intrinsic connection between work, love, and *learning,* this sample proved to be particularly fortuitous (see Resource A for a fuller discussion of sampling).

In addition to distributing and collecting the "Work, Love and Learning in Adulthood" questionnaires, we conducted nineteen in-depth interviews with men and women of varying ages. When the questionnaires were distributed we asked respondents to indicate by giving their name and telephone number whether they would consent to being interviewed. We then contacted nineteen people for interviews according to their pattern. Fourteen of the inteviews were conducted in person and five were conducted by telephone. All interviews were tape-recorded and transcribed. Table 4.1 presents a profile of the nineteen interviewees. The "Work, Love, and Learning in Adulthood" questionnaires that they had completed formed the basis of the interviews. The purpose of the interviews was to enrich our understanding of the particular pattern of interaction between work and love. We asked interviewees to comment on what they saw in their graph of work and love, the interaction of the life events that they had listed above the graph, the ratings they had given each domain for each year, and the ways in which learning intersected with work and love for them. Data from the interviews are used to better describe and illuminate the patterns of interaction

Table 4.1. Participants Who Were Interviewed.

Name	Sex	Age	Occupation
		The Parallel Pattern	
Thelma	F	51	elementary school teacher
Barbara	F	46	college administrator
Peter	M	32	educational consultant
Nathan	M	38	nurse-practitioner
Ann	F	45	college professor
Ed	M	47	librarian
Sandra*	F	39	counselor
		The Steady/Fluctuating Pattern	
Matt	M	40	minister
Reggie	M	39	county agent
Vivian	F	62	adult literacy teacher
Norman	M	58	college professor
Karen	F	48	college dean
		The Divergent Pattern	
Katherine	F	37	trainer in business and industry
Don	M	54	college professor
Ellen	F	46	human resource consultant
Nadine	F	57	homemaker
Frank	M	50	insurance executive
Brendon*	M	43	engineer
Monica*	F	52	nurse

*These participants are not profiled in Chapters 5, 6, or 7 but are discussed in Chapter 9.

presented in the next three chapters. Our study thus uses both qualitative and quantitative data generated by the "Work, Love, and Learning in Adulthood" questionnaires and qualitative data generated by the interviews.

Analyzing the Data

The major purpose of the study was to uncover patterns of interaction of work and love and to assess how these patterns are related to learning in adult life. We considered the information provided by the questionnaires to be closely akin to journal- or diary-type data, and thus treated them as qualitative data. Our first step in analyzing these data was to examine the graphs for common patterns. We used the *constant comparative method* of data analysis (Glaser and Strauss, 1967). This involved comparing one graph with another and sorting similar graphs into piles. Three separate piles began to form as we compared each graph with ones before it. In this early stage of analysis we used a technique called *investigator triangulation* (Denzin, 1970) to ensure the validity of the emerging patterns. Investigator triangulation is the use of multiple investigators in the inductive analysis of data. A data analysis session was scheduled in which four doctoral graduate research assistants were each given a random set of approximately thirty-five graphs. The assistants were instructed to sort, if possible, their set of graphs into patterns or categories and to give names to the patterns. Each worked independently of the others. All four assistants came up with the same three basic patterns, though they used different images to describe the interactions: One used dance steps, for example, while another used astronomical constellations.

In the next stage, we developed prototype descriptions of the three patterns and criteria for deciding which pattern type to place each of the graphs in. For example, for graphs that seemed to exhibit different patterns the criterion was to assign whichever pattern characterized more than half of the graph. A panel of three raters (the two of us and a research assistant) then independently assigned a pattern type to each of 410 graphs. (For a fuller discussion of this process of analysis, see Resource A.)

The three broad patterns of interaction between the work and love domains are as follows. There is a *parallel* pattern in which work and love conditions move together; change in one domain is reflected by change in the other. One hundred fifty-eight of our sample exhibited a parallel pattern. The second pattern, consisting of 107 adults, we call *steady/fluctuating*. Here one domain remains steady while the other fluctuates. The third pattern, of which there were 140 in our sample, is one of *divergence;* if one domain is rated good, the other is likely to be rated low, and the results seem to flow independent of or in opposition to each other. We discuss each of these patterns in detail in the next three chapters.

We then undertook several analyses to see if these patterns differed by gender or life stage. Life stages were formed by collapsing chronological age into three categories: young adulthood (twenty to thirty), the thirties (thirty-one to forty), and middle age (forty-one to sixty-two). The results of these analyses are incorporated into the discussion of the patterns in Chapter Eight.

We further examined the graphs of respondents in the two older age groups (the thirties and middle age) to determine the extent to which each person's pattern had remained the same since young adulthood. It may be recalled that one criterion for sorting graphs having more than one pattern was that more than half of the graph had to exhibit a single predominant pattern. We also discovered in our life-stage analysis that the parallel pattern was more prevalent in young adulthood, the divergent pattern was more prevalent in the thirty-year-olds, and the steady/fluctuating pattern was more prevalent in the middle-aged group. We were thus curious to know if people's patterns change as they age. Since the graphs for our middle-aged respondents spanned twenty years (1969–1989), we were able to view the data as quasi-longitudinal in the same way that Back and Bourque (1970) used their life-graph data. The results of this analysis of change and stability of work/love interaction patterns are also presented in Chapter Eight.

To explore the relationship of learning to work and love patterns, the number of significant learning events was summed for each respondent. This was done to determine whether a particular work/love pattern generated more significant learning than any other. In addition to summing the learning events, we coded each learning event for each respondent as to its occurrence on the work/love graph. For example, the year that a significant learning event occurred might have been when work was rated good and love was rated okay. There were nine such permutations (work-good, love-good; work-good, love-okay; work-good, love-bad; work-okay, love-good; work-okay, love-okay; work-okay, love-bad; work-bad, love-good; work-bad, love-okay; work-bad, love-bad). To determine when more learning is likely to occur, we also calculated the number of learning events for all respondents for each of the nine work/love permutations. In addition to determining how many, what type (work or love related), and when significant learning occurred, we spent time determining what made the learning events "significant." We did this by sorting the significance statements that accompanied the listing of learning events on the second page of the questionnaire into categories. Finally, as part of our interviews we asked respondents to reflect on the learning that occurred in relation to their particular life events and their pattern of work/love interaction. We present the results of these analyses in Chapters Nine and Ten.

Summary

This chapter has outlined the background and development of our study of work, love, and learning in adult life. The design of our questionnaire evolved over a period of two years and proved to be successful in capturing patterns of work/love interaction. We have reviewed precedents for studying adult development in this way, and have described the procedures we used to collect data with the questionnaires and through interviews with selected respondents.

We conducted analyses of our data in several stages, beginning with deriving three major patterns of interaction of work and love from the graphs on the "Work, Love, and Learning in Adulthood" questionnaire. The fact that four other investigators arrived at the same three patterns, and the high rate of agreement among three independent codings of the graphs, led us to feel confident that these three patterns do in fact describe the interaction of the work and love arenas for our participants. Interviews with nineteen men and women provided further insights into the nature of these interaction patterns. We then used the patterns in statistical analyses to determine if they revealed significant differences in terms of gender and life stages. We also analyzed the results to determine the stability of the patterns over time.

To examine the connections among work, love, and learning, we calculated the number of learning episodes, whether they were work or love related, and when they occurred with respect to each person's work-and-love graph. We also categorized the reasons people gave for labeling a learning event "significant." Our understanding of the place of learning in adult life was enriched by data from the in-depth interviews. We present the results of all of these analyses in the following chapters.

CHAPTER FIVE

Moving in Tandem:
The Parallel Pattern

When we began our study of the interaction of work and love in adulthood, one pattern we expected to find involved a close connection between the two arenas. As we described in the previous chapter, when we were developing our questionnaire we tried it out first on ourselves, and one of us produced a pattern in which work and love were closely related. This pattern did turn out to be the first to emerge clearly from our study.

In what we have called the *parallel* pattern, the work and love arenas appear to move largely together; change in one is usually followed by a similar change in the other. While this does not necessarily produce a uniform or lock-step agreement, it does give rise to an overall sense of congruence. We are reminded of the unusual image the English poet John Dunne used in "A Valediction: Forbidden Mourning" to describe the relationship between two lovers:

> If they be two, they are two so
> As stiffe twin compasses are two,
> Thy soule the fixt foot, makes no show
> To move, but doth, if the'other doe.
> (1930, pp. 36–37)

He compares the lovers to a compass, the instrument we use to draw circles. Because the two legs of a compass are joined at the top, neither can move independent of the other. Donne suggests that two lovers are linked in an analogous way, united by their love for each other. In a similar way the domains of love and work appear to be linked in this pattern, resulting in movement together in the same direction. See Figure 5.1 for an example of a typical parallel pattern.

As you can see, there is some variability in this pattern, but it is limited. The vectors can be superimposed, with work and love given the same rating, as they are at the beginning and at the end of this example. Or they can be separated, though usually only by a single rating, as they are here for the years that love is rated okay while work is rated bad, followed by love becoming good and work rising to an okay rating. The important point for the overall pattern is that the two areas move largely in tandem; change in one is either immediately or soon after followed by change in the other in the same direction.

When we look at our total sample, we see that the parallel pattern occurred most frequently. Out of 405 questionnaires, 158, or 39 percent, were classified as parallel. There were no significant differences in the numbers of women and men having this pattern; they were about equally represented. The only difference we found concerns life stage: Young adults made up a disproportionately large segment of the parallel group.

While information on the distribution of this pattern is interesting, it still leaves us with other questions. For example, we were interested in knowing about the character of the linkage between work and love. What did it mean? Was one arena controlling the other? Or were the two consciously balanced in the person's life? To answer these and other questions, we conducted in-depth interviews with a number of people who had this pattern. Their discussion of how they experience work and love gave us significant insights into the meaning of the parallel pattern. We will examine each of their stories in turn, then assess the commonalities among them.

Movement in Tandem

As we have seen, this pattern is characterized by a parallel relationship between work and love. But the picture is more

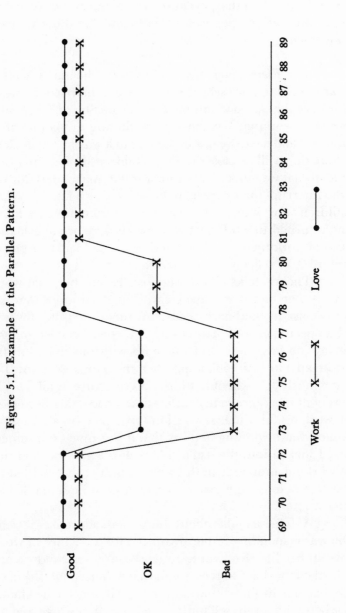

Figure 5.1. Example of the Parallel Pattern.

complicated than that, because our six interviews revealed that there are various possible explanations for this characteristic movement.

The Elementary School Teacher. Thelma is a fifty-one-year-old elementary school teacher who is married; her two children are adults now and on their own. She and her husband are both working, but they are beginning to plan for their retirement and have dreams of moving to a small town in Colorado where they will be closer to their children. In her interview she traces what we think of as a rather traditional pattern for women who interrupt their careers to begin raising a family. When her children were infants she remained at home to care for them; she returned to work part time when they began school, then started working full time when they were older. Her graph (see Figure 5.2) reflects these changes.

Thelma talks about these oscillations between work and love in her life; they have clearly involved more than simply a response to child-care needs: "At that time I did not feel that I had been done out of anything. . . . I was at a stopping point in my job anyway. . . . I made do with making good friends and read a lot and took naps when the baby took naps. I didn't have much of a schedule in life, no structure at all. . . . It was sort of nice because in my earlier time I had either been in school or working full time. It was kind of a nice break. . . . After a while I was beginning to think that it was time I did something, and I looked into the usual, like volunteer work, and that led to working as an aide in the school library, and that led to taking classes to get my teacher's certification, and that led to getting a job."

As Thelma talks about this period, she makes it clear that she was responding to her own need for a balance of work and love in her life. Returning to work once her children entered school enabled her to reestablish that balance, and she describes the benefits of that situation for herself and for her family: "I felt better about myself for having been somewhere and having something to talk about at the end of the day. I think it complemented on the whole. . . . It was much better when we all

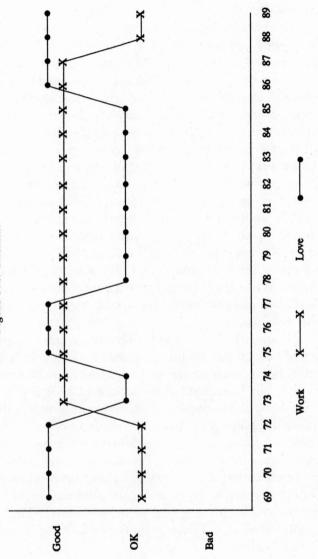

Figure 5.2. Thelma.

had things to report. The children had their things going. My husband had his, and then I was glad to have mine at that time to contribute."

The balance struck here between work and love benefited both Thelma and her family. There were times, however, when conflict between the two arenas developed, particularly when the children were teenagers and Thelma started taking graduate courses toward her master's degree while she was teaching full time. She describes the difficulty of balancing work and love during that period: "I was bringing stuff home because I had a lot of schoolwork to do and the children were getting older and they were having more crises of dating and all. Seems like we were getting where we had to have a lot of emotional attention with the children and we were sort of at odds for a while, the whole family. There was a period in here where things got to be a little too much." She continued to keep both arenas in balance, though, maintaining the family life as okay for these years while her work and school also demanded considerable attention. When her children left home for college, the love arena moved from okay to good. Her overall pattern gives evidence of this balance.

In looking at this graph, Thelma summarizes this pattern and talks about her ongoing need for balance: "I have had times of being restless, dissatisfied, and bored at home and at work too, but I can kind of see a back and forth that I would beef up doing things outside of the house for a while until I kind of reached a point with that and then kind of pulled back and be back at home. . . . Now my children are grown and it's just my husband and I at home. I've sort of plateaued at my job and I've enhanced my interest by going back [to school] and doing other projects which are really stimulating and give me a new interest and a new goal to work toward. I kind of question 'what now?' . . . I don't want to just lollygag around in the job until I retire."

Even as she looks into the future, Thelma seeks a balance point between work and love in her life. For her this need for balance seems to be a personality trait, one that is evident even across shifting life circumstances. And we see how proactive she is to maintaining that work/love balance; she makes a conscious effort to do this. Our next example is a variation on that same theme.

The College Administrator. Barbara is director of a large continuing education program at a community college on the West Coast. She is forty-six and a single parent; her son is now twenty years old. A self-identified workaholic, for years she used her work to compensate for the absence of a significant other in her life. In her graph the two arenas show some variation but remain parallel (see Figure 5.3).

Barbara's marriage began to deteriorate shortly after her son was born, but she did not divorce her husband until 1974, when she discovered he was having an affair with one of her friends. It took her years to recover from this traumatic experience. Because her ex-husband refused to provide any support at all, she had to work at two jobs to maintain herself and her son. She describes how both her son and her work sustained her during these years: "When [the divorce] happened, I was devastated and would have taken my life if it hadn't been for Billie. All I knew was that I had to live, that money was necessary for survival. . . . My son kept me going in that respect . . . and gradually I was offered positions of more and more responsibility. . . . Women divorced like myself, raising a child alone . . . you sort of plunge yourself into your work and it becomes your raison d'être, as well as, of course, your subsistence . . . but it's also where you get your gratification rather than your relationships when there is a divorce."

That work involved teaching high school French and Spanish, then becoming a principal, all the while teaching adult education courses in the evenings. In 1986 she became director of an adult education program, where she remains. On the love side there was little to report in the years after the divorce. She dated little and obtained emotional support largely from her mother and women friends. Her mother's death in 1985 was a major loss. Things improved dramatically two years later, however, when she met an old boyfriend from her childhood and fell in love. They have bought a home in the country together

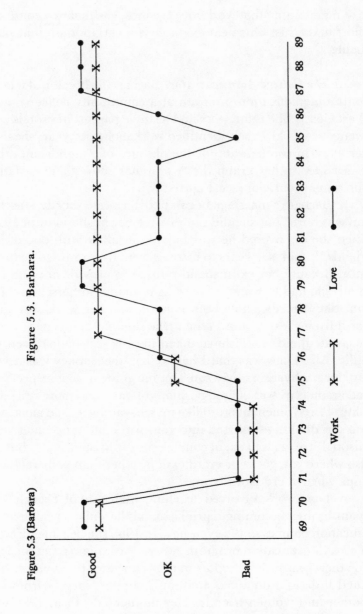

Figure 5.3 (Barbara)

Figure 5.3. Barbara.

Work X——X   Love ●——●

now and they talk about marrying, though she is hesitant to take that step; clearly the wounds from her divorce are not fully healed.

In Barbara's case work has been primary, but it has that position almost by default. The scales seem to have been out of balance because of her circumstances. Once there is a significant other in her life, the balance is restored. She discusses this difference: "I find that when I become involved with someone [things are different]. Right now I'm involved with a guy I met when I was thirteen. . . . I remet him three or four years ago. He's divorced and he also has one son, and it's been wonderful. And what I find is, work be damned! When there is a love interest, and there is someone at home or elsewhere, my vigor and my zest for this job goes down. I don't care as much." She describes her life as being in balance now: "We bought a country home together. We leave on Friday and come back Sunday night, and those three days I don't think about anything at work. There's a very nice balance that exists. I'm going to concerts, movies for the first time, things I have not done in years. For me it is very satisfying and also very balanced."

Barbara speaks of balance while at the same time keeping the two arenas very separate: "I view them as totally different. Once I'm at work, I don't think of home, and when I'm home I don't think of work. They are very distinct." She notes only a minimal impact of one domain on the other. The only exception is a change she sees in herself at work now: "I have more of an emotional equilibrium. . . . Things that would have upset me even more, like criticism from another employee or an over amount of work, are taken down a peg because there is this other part of my life. So [improvement in the love area] has helped me a lot. Where it hasn't helped is that I'm producing less. I don't care as much, where I was much more driven before."

We can see that Barbara experiences balance somewhat differently than Thelma does. Thelma adjusts her emphasis on work or love as her inner needs change. For Barbara, balance is more a matter of compensation, as she showed when she was without a significant love relationship and used work to balance that loss. However, when she is in a relationship again, she begins to attend to both arenas, finding satisfaction in both and seeking an equilibrium between the demands each presents. While they understand and achieve balance differently, for both women it represents a conscious effort to achieve personal satisfaction. Our next example demonstrates yet another variation on this theme of balance.

The Educational Consultant. Peter is an affable thirty-two-year-old who is building a successful career as a trainer and consultant for a firm in the Southwest. He and his wife are both committed to their careers, but they are also establishing a family; they are both devoted to their five-year-old son and hope to have more children. Peter's graph (see Figure 5.4) reflects this dual commitment.

This graph is even more tightly parallel than Thelma's. Peter's work domain is largely steady. He spent the earlier years in college, with a year off as a Senate intern in Washington. He completed his bachelor's degree in 1980 and immediately went to work with the consulting firm that he still works for. His responsibilities have grown steadily; he is now in charge of a large region in the state, and his prospects for continued advancement are excellent. In 1987 he finished his master's, and the following year began work on his doctorate.

His love arena fluctuates a bit more than work does. His college years were happy; he dated a lot and established a wide network of friends. In his senior year, however, his father died suddenly and that loss affected him for the next year. In 1984 he married, and in the following year his son was born. This new family is very much at the center of his life and he devotes a lot of energy and as much time as he can to them.

Peter describes himself as being "in the front end of a marriage and the front end of a career," a combination that creates a high level of stress in his life. He talks about his efforts to balance the two: "Now I face a situation that I'm pulled by my family wanting my time, my young son, you know — I've been married for five years, which is still a relatively young marriage. My work has now evolved because of location change that now

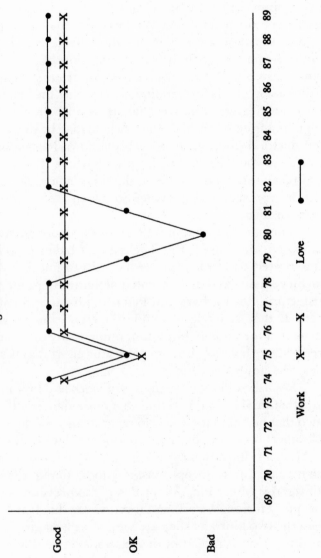

Figure 5.4. Peter.

I am driving 800 miles a week and I'm on the road. And I do feel torn now. . . . I'm trying to get home . . . but the demands on my job necessitate that I'm not there. . . . So, they're pulling on each other now. . . . We focus on quality time and we try to fit schedules. We hope it's short-lived, that it's kind of an intermediate stage in the career, that sort of thing." Adding to the tension is Peter's involvement in graduate school, and his discussion of this further dimension makes the balance metaphor even clearer: "I do feel that stress on both sides because I'm pulling from one or the other. School may be the kicker. . . . That doctoral program is probably kind of like the nth thing I do . . . so you have to steal from somewhere. . . . Even if you stop to play with your child, you should be studying. If you stop to study, you should be playing. So, yeah, the stress — you can add it all to it."

Thelma, Barbara, and Peter all speak of balancing work and love in their lives. For Thelma that balance point seems to be located within herself, as she tries to find the right mix of achievement- and love-oriented activities to attain personal satisfaction. For Barbara and Peter, the balance point is more external; they struggle to divide their energies between two arenas that are equally important and equally demanding. All three achieve balance through conscious effort that is sustained across the adult life course.

We asked Peter if the arenas of work and love influenced each other, and he said yes. But even more significantly he mentioned that he found it difficult to separate the two domains from each other: "It is real hard to separate my family and my personal relationships from my work. . . . My work is so interlaced with my life; I'm in a people business and it ties in tremendously with the rest of my life." What Peter is expressing is a kind of conceptual fusion of work and love, where the distinctions between the two blur and they are viewed as a single reality. For him this fusion is rooted in the relational style that characterizes his behavior in both areas and that is fundamental to his identity. We will see this theme of conceptual fusion again in this pattern.

In addition to deliberately trying to achieve a balance between work and love, Thelma, Barbara, and Peter are also similar in the fundamental stability they experience in their lives. There are few dramatic changes in their circumstances; they tend to stay with things for sustained periods of time. Our next example of this pattern will test these commonalities further.

The Nurse-Practitioner. Nathan is a thirty-eight-year-old African-American man who has two careers as a family nurse-practitioner and a minister. He has been married seventeen years and he and his wife have two children. His graph (see Figure 5.5) is almost perfectly stable, with both work and love rated good.

The one exception in the stability of Nathan's graph is when he and his wife lost their newborn son to Sudden Infant Death Syndrome (SIDS). He describes his response to that tragedy: "I lost a son in 1979, which was a traumatic experience . . . but what I've tried to do in life was to even things out that were unpleasant. I tried to convert them into a positive attitude. As a result of the death of my son, I was able to become a SIDS counselor and counsel other families that experienced SIDS. In life I've found that even though you might be hurting mentally . . . there was always someone with a more difficult time. [I remember] one particular family that I counseled; they lost two children to SIDS. . . . Then I look at my difficulties and look at theirs and it doesn't really hit me." The tragedy that occurred in Nathan's personal life became a resource in his professional life, and that aspect of his work in turn helped him deal with his own loss.

This close connection between work and love involves more than the impact of one arena on the other; the two are essentially fused in Nathan's mind. This conceptual fusion is similar to what we saw with Peter, who had a relational style that was expressed in both arenas, but for Nathan it is more than a matter of style. He describes his orientation toward helping others as basic to how he understands his life: "That's the way my life has been . . . I have always been able to go in directions where I saw that there was a need. Basically, well, it's people oriented. Having grown up in the church, the Southside

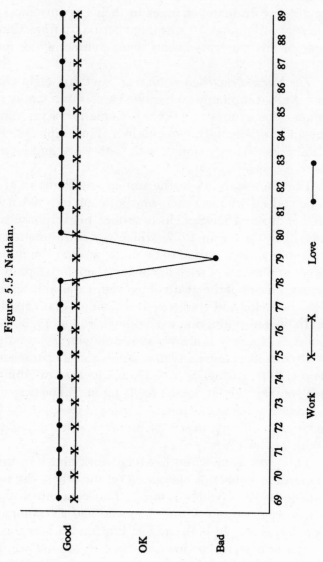

Figure 5.5. Nathan.

Church of Christ . . . ever since I was eleven I would have a profound love for people — helping people and providing instructions, etc. And I have always had a good support system, which I think is probably one of the most precious things that I have seen as a part of my life. With it you can connect, and that has been with common people and professionals." It is this orientation toward people that led him to become a nurse and to enter the ministry, and he has worked in both capacities since 1974. He notes that "I could have gone other places and have been offered other jobs to do other things and could make more money, but [what makes me stay is] the love that I have for the job and for what I do." He goes on to assert that "love is basically the foundation in any arena we are in."

Another aspect of Nathan's life that encourages conceptual fusion of work and love is his spirituality. He talks about this in regard to his marriage: "When my wife and I started out . . . we proposed within our hearts or within our minds that we were one with the Lord first, then put ourselves and our families second, and then we put our job third. . . . We started at the very beginning with that type structure, and when either one of those gets out of alignment, we have to put it back into alignment. And I think that has been one of the successes in terms of our marriage. We have maintained that, we go back to the agreement, and we have been one on purpose."

Nathan gives us more insight into the character of this fusion of work and love. His story suggests that there is an underlying factor that unifies them, and that that factor can be located in different areas. In his case the unifier is his religious beliefs, while for Peter the unifying factor is his relational style. Wherever it is located, the effect of the conceptual fusion is the same: The person does not dichotomize work and love but understands them as one reality. Our next example illustrates another kind of relationship between work and love.

The College Professor. Ann teaches history and sociology at a college in New York. She is forty-five, married, and the mother of two teenagers. Her life has been very stable in both arenas: She and her husband recently celebrated their twenty-

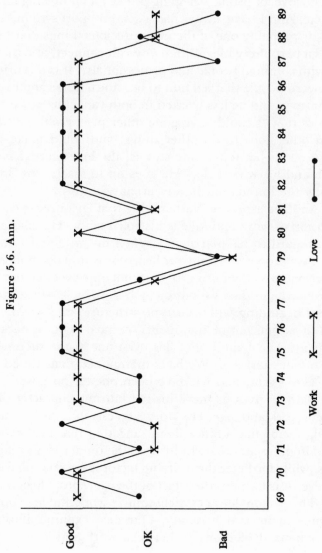

Figure 5.6. Ann.

fifth wedding anniversary, and she has been on the faculty of her college for fifteen years. While her work and love vectors show some fluctuations, they move largely in tandem across the twenty-year period (see Figure 5.6).

For Ann work and love are closely related, but she stops short of fusing the two. Instead she speaks of a spillover effect of one on the other. By spillover we mean that work and love have an impact on each other but yet remain conceptually distinct. That impact can be beneficial or costly. As an example of this, Ann talks about the impact her graduate studies had on her family: "In 1981 I entered the Ph.D. program in history and took about fifteen hours at the same time I was working full time. I did fine, I made my three A's, but it was too much. At this time my daughter would have been about ten or eleven, just going into puberty. . . . I was writing a paper one evening and I found out she needed to talk to me. And I found myself saying, 'I don't have time to talk to her.' And I didn't want to. It was sort of like, you know, one of those moments that are etched in your memory. I mean I can remember what color [she was wearing]. I walked out of the room and said, 'I'm quitting school.' What it was is I was taking too much time away from my family."

In this case Ann's work situation created stress in the love arena. But spillover can also have a positive effect. Ann notes that when she completed her master's degree and began teaching, "I felt a sense of professional accomplishment; at the same time I think that sense of accomplishment spilled over to relationships in the home." In both instances, the arenas remain distinct even though they influence each other.

Ann also illustrates two other ways in which work and love can be kept separate. First, a person can make a conscious choice to keep them apart to achieve a particular goal. She talks about recovering from her father's death: "[When my father died] I could get back to the work and . . . at work I could think about work. . . . Yet there was still the grieving process that [went on] when you got home and alone and things were quieter." Here Ann seemed to consciously locate the grieving process in the love arena. But working apparently enhanced her ability to deal

with her father's death; it helped give her the strength she needed
to cope with her loss.

Second, Ann describes a time when work and love were
separate because one was particularly energizing. In 1987 her
father-in-law died, and she and her husband had the additional
responsibility of caring for both their mothers. She rates this
year as bad for the love arena, yet the work rating is good for
that year. She describes why work was so separate at that point
in her life: "This particular year I really enjoyed. I worked with
[a professor in another department] and we developed a new
course. . . . She teaches reading and I teach sociology. We developed team teaching where the ten people she taught in reading I also taught in sociology. There were other people in my
class, but what we did was we developed a program to reinforce her reading skills with what I taught in sociology. . . . It's
just really been exciting because we saw some progress. . . . We
met on a daily basis and it really turned out to be a good thing.
[What was happening at home did not have an impact] because
this was so stimulating. . . . It still didn't make things that much
better when you got home. But at work I could get my mind
off of it because I had to do that. We had contracted to do it,
and I had to do it."

In Ann we again see the conscious effort to balance work
and love that we saw in Thelma and Peter, but with a difference. For her it is the positive or negative impact of one arena
on the other — what we have called the spillover effect — that
serves as the balance mechanism. Ann appears to be sensitive
to this interrelationship rather than to the demands of either
work or love on her time and energy, as is true of Peter, or on
her level of personal satisfaction, as is the case for Thelma. Ann's
efforts to balance work and love are more nuanced in that
respect.

Ann demonstrates some of the complexities of the relationship between work and love in the parallel pattern. In our
next example we will see another kind of relationship entirely.

The Librarian. Ed is a librarian at a vocational school
outside Chicago. He is forty-seven, married, and has a twenty-

two-year-old daughter. He has had two careers, initially as a college librarian for thirteen years, then in the area of forestry for ten years. He became dissatisfied with the second career, however, and happily took a library position again in 1986. His wife is also a librarian, though she works at one of the universities in the city.

Ed's graph reveals a high degree of stability (see Figure 5.7). The love arena is usually rated good; the dip from 1984 to 1986 marks the protracted illness and then death of his mother. Fluctuations in the work arena reflect his changing level of satisfaction with his career; it is during the low period in 1984 and 1985 that he loses interest in forestry and begins to think about returning to library work.

When we asked Ed to describe the relationship between work and love in his life, he gave a definitive response: "They're totally different. I wouldn't see a connection in them in day-to-day living." For this reason he was surprised to see that the domains largely paralleled each other. Yet it became clear, as he talked, why this was true. Overall he talked far more about work than he did about experiences in the love arena, and when we asked him if work was primary in his life, he admitted that it was: "I find my job very satisfying. . . . I think I've read that it's more important for men than for women to be satisfied with their jobs, that they get more satisfaction out of their jobs or something, than they might compared to marriage, but I think it is a primary thing that I like my job."

This primacy of work in Ed's life was clearly revealed when he had a chance to become a librarian again. The new job was in another part of the state, which meant that he was separated from his family during the week for almost a year. His description of that period brings out the dominant role work plays in his life: "I was really bored with [the job I was in] and I was not happy with it the last couple of years I was in it. . . . And then this job opportunity came along in 1986, and I think that when I changed it did affect my marriage a little bit, that my wife hated my being over there. I liked the job, and still it meant a real stressful situation in my marriage. . . . I'm not sure what would have happened to my marriage if I'd continued to work

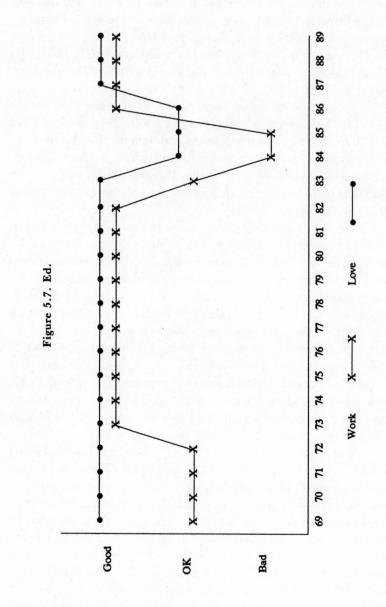

Figure 5.7. Ed.

over there. . . . I felt that I was happy with the job change, I really liked my job over there. And I didn't mind the separation as much as she did. . . . I was happy with the way it was going, but I think she needed more emotional support from me than she was getting, probably, at that time. I didn't quite need as much of it."

The stress Ed describes in the marriage was clearly his wife's rather than his; later in the interview he describes his marriage as "very stable," and from his perspective it is. While the marriage is obviously important to him, he shows that he largely takes it for granted. His primary focus is on work, and his experience in that arena appears to have limited impact on the love domain. He goes on to note that "there's really nothing in the love domain that impacted my job at all," further emphasizing the predominant role of work in his life.

This same theme was echoed during his mother's final illness. He talks about feeling guilty that he was not close by during that time, yet notes that his work and marriage were unaffected: "My folks lived in Montana and we didn't see them very much. . . . My mother started having strokes and was in a nursing home for a period of time, and then finally my sister and brother-in-law moved onto the farm, where my parents lived and where I grew up, to take care of my mother. . . . I think I felt guilty about not being there and sharing some of this havoc, although if I was there, I'm not sure what I could have done. . . . So I felt guilty about that at the time, though it didn't seem like it was of *that* much significance to my job or my marriage, to be quite honest."

In short, work and love exist independent of one another in Ed's life. This is unlike anything else we have seen in the parallel pattern so far. Rather than demonstrating balance, Ed's experience shows that one domain can be dominant over the other, effectively carrying that secondary domain in its wake. While in Ed's case work is dominant, we believe the reverse situation can also occur. This is a very different explanation for the parallel movement of the domains from the balance or conceptual fusion that we saw in the other interviews.

Having studied six examples of this pattern individually,

we will now adjust our perspective to see what overall picture this pattern offers.

The Parallel Pattern: Discussion

Our first question about this particular pattern focused on the tandem movement of the two arenas. Not surprisingly, we discovered that there was more than one explanation for this pattern. In fact, we heard three different explanations: (1) a conscious effort to keep work and love in balance, (2) a conceptual fusion of the two, and (3) one arena dominating and thereby "carrying" the taken-for-granted arena. We will examine each of these alternatives in turn.

Conscious Effort to Create Balance. The most common explanation for the movement of the domains in tandem is the conscious effort to balance them. We have seen this expressed in four different ways. Thelma seems to balance work and love in her life according to an internal sensor: She adjusts the emphasis on one or the other to achieve a personal balance or satisfaction. Remember how she spoke of being restless after a few years of full-time child care, whereas at first she welcomed the break from her nine-to-five job. She is sensitive to her own needs here. Peter, on the other hand, appears to respond to an external sensor. He feels outer forces pulling on him, demanding his time and attention: work, family, school. His balancing is done among these competing interests in his life, and he would like to be able to satisfy them all. Ann has elements of both internal and external factors; she withdrew from her doctoral program because her children needed more of her time, but she also credited her work with increasing her self-esteem and her sense of personal capability. What Ann adds is the idea of spillover from one arena to another, meaning that events in one have an impact, positive or negative, on the other. That impact acts as a force that helps create a balance between the two arenas. Perhaps the best example in Ann's story was her choice to terminate her doctoral program. Certainly working full time and carrying fifteen hours of graduate coursework (itself a heavy load for a full-time student) constitutes an overload for even the most ambitious. The impact this had on her family, more specifically on her daughter, caused her to bring her life into more reasonable balance. Barbara demonstrated a fourth approach when, earlier in her life, she used work to balance the loss of a significant relationship in the love arena. This was essentially a compensatory strategy. While somewhat different, all four of these strategies balance work and love through conscious manipulation, and, as we have seen, each is effective.

Conceptual Fusion of Work and Love. The second explanation for the tandem movement of work and love is what we are calling conceptual fusion. In our study, this occurs only in the parallel pattern. By fusion, we mean that these people do not distinguish between work and love in their lives; when asked to do so in our interviews, they reacted against making what they believe to be a false dichotomy. Instead they see a fundamental unity between the two domains. Remember Peter saying that "it is real hard to separate my family and my personal relationships from my work. . . . I'm in a people business." Remarks like this have made it clear to us that people who fuse the two domains do so because they approach both work and love in a relational manner. For these people, relating to others in a meaningful way is as important in work as it is in love.

Peter and Nathan are our best examples of this conceptual fusion of the arenas. Recall how relational by nature both are. And for Nathan this is augmented by a religious belief system that effectively unites both domains. Fusion of work and love may be more likely to occur among those in human service professions like teaching, nursing, or the ministry — the professions represented by Peter and Nathan. The relational connection here is obvious; less clear is whether this conceptual fusion precedes or follows their choice of career. These people may conceptualize love quite broadly as a concern for others, and they may see work as a way of operationalizing that concern. It is also interesting that, among those we interviewed with this pattern, both examples of conceptual fusion of work and love involved men. While our sample is far too small to allow any conclusions about gender differences in this regard, this question invites further research.

   Dominance of One Arena by the Other. The third explanation for the parallel movement of the work and love arenas is that one arena can dominate the other. In this case the second domain is given less attention than the first, and because of this differential attention, that taken-for-granted arena appears to simply be carried along in the wake of the primary or dominant one. We saw this only once in our interviews and that was with Ed. For him work is primary. It is not that he does not love and value his wife and family; clearly he does. But he largely takes them for granted and gives most of his attention to his career. He showed this most dramatically when he took a job in another part of the state and had to live apart from his family for a year. The separation was not stressful for him but it was for his wife. The library position he currently holds became available and resolved the situation, but he notes that he did not know what would have happened to his marriage if the separation had gone on much longer. Notice that he gives no indication that he considered giving up the job he liked in order to resolve the problem; work obviously came first. What is important here is the dominance of one arena over the other. While in Ed's case the dominant domain is work, love could also take precedence. Thus we see that the parallel pattern can be created by the centrality of one arena, not just by the careful balancing of both.

   Other aspects of the parallel pattern besides these explanations for the movement of the arenas in tandem are of interest. One is how people who have this pattern conceptualize work and love. Except for those few people we interviewed who fuse them, most of our respondents distinguish between work and love. There is a range in their sense of separateness, however. Certainly Barbara and Ed distinguish between work and love more sharply than the others do. The degree of separateness can also change, as Ann illustrates. She notes that she sometimes draws the distinctions more clearly to achieve a particular goal, like grieving for her father when at home but putting that aside while at work. They can also be more separate because one domain is particularly energizing, as her experience of team teaching one semester shows. Overall, then, we can say that for most people who conform to the parallel pattern, the domains of work and love are distinct.

Most of the people we interviewed value the two arenas equally. This is reflected in the concept of balance that predominated in our interviews. Only Ed names one arena as primary. Barbara appeared to also give work primacy in her life, until she developed a significant love relationship again, at which point things began to move into balance for her.

Finally, we can point to one aspect of the parallel pattern about which there is unanimity. All six people we interviewed with this pattern demonstrate a high degree of stability in both arenas. All but Barbara are in their original marriages, and she was married nine years before getting her divorce. Their careers are likewise long term. Even Ed, with his change of careers, spent ten years in forestry before returning to library work. Their lives are marked by continuity overall, a feature that we do not see to the same degree in either of the other patterns.

In many respects, the parallel pattern appears to be simple and straightforward, but our interviews reveal that it represents a complex and multifaceted reality. We turn now to the second of our three patterns to see how it differs from what we found here.

CHAPTER SIX

One Stable Force: The Steady/Fluctuating Pattern

If we had to give a single impression of the interaction of work and love in adult life we would probably say without hesitation that the relationship is characterized by *change*. As our data accumulated we were struck by the overwhelming variability in people's lives, both in terms of changes in their life situations and in their evaluation of those events. However, when we examined our results more closely we discovered an exception to this general trend. That exception became the key element of our second pattern.

This pattern is different precisely because one of the vectors does not change; it remains steady, or largely steady. But the other vector does change, exhibiting exactly that variability absent in the first domain. We have called this pattern *steady/fluctuating* in an effort to depict that split character. It is important, though, to understand this pattern as a unified, not a "schizophrenic" phenomenon. An apt analogy might be a complex piece of music like Pachelbel's Canon in D, in which one hears both an intricate melody and a steady rhythmic baseline. This is what musicians call the ground, defined by one music dictionary as "a theme which recurs over and over again while the music proceeds independently above it" (Demuth, 1964, p. 42). The steady/fluctuating pattern of work and love reflects the same kind of interrelationship.

The arena that is steady in this pattern can be either work or love, but in our study it was usually work. Interestingly, the steady domain was rated good in almost all cases; less than 5 percent of the steady/fluctuating patterns in our sample had the steady domain rated okay or bad. Figure 6.1 is a typical example of this pattern.

We also found a variation on this theme in which the steady vector reverses itself midway through the pattern. Love, for example, might be steady at first, with work fluctuating, then work stabilizes and love becomes variable. Figure 6.2 provides an example of this reversal. Occasionally both vectors were steady, creating a period of parallel movement, but this was always brief.

Of the 405 questionnaires we received, 107 or 26 percent of them were classified as steady/fluctuating. There were no significant differences by gender in this pattern; women and men were equally likely to have it. We did find a difference by life stage, with our middle-aged group being disproportionately represented. While these statistics give us an overall sense of the distribution of the steady/fluctuating pattern in our sample, they cannot answer other questions we wanted to pose, especially questions of interpretation. We were particularly intrigued by the steady domain. What did it mean to have one arena remain constant? What function does it serve for the person? And why is that domain almost invariably rated good? To answer questions such as these, we conducted in-depth interviews with several people who had this pattern. We will consider each in turn, then look across all five to see what themes are shared.

Five Windows into the Steady/Fluctuating Pattern

As was true of those with the parallel pattern, each person with the steady/fluctuating pattern that we talked with had different life experiences, but the interaction of work and love in their lives was similar. Their stories help us grasp the nature of this pattern of work and love.

The Minister. Matt is a forty-year-old pastor of a rural parish in the Midwest. He has been married twenty years. He

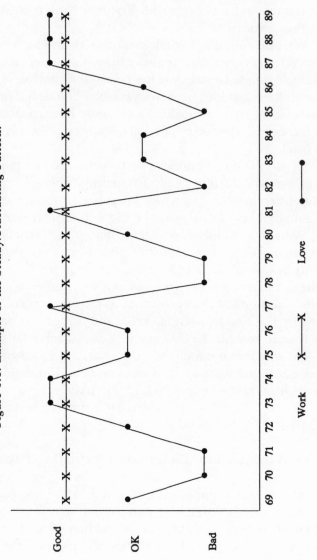

Figure 6.1. Example of the Steady/Fluctuating Pattern.

Work X———X   Love ●———●

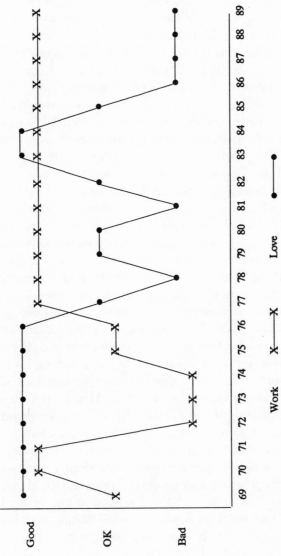

Figure 6.2. Sample Reversal of the Steady/Fluctuating Pattern.

and his wife have not had children, but they fulfill their parenting needs to some extent by working with some of the poorer children in their community, and they have not given up hope of adopting a child of their own. Both are also working toward doctorates at a nearby university. Matt's pattern of work and love has love as the steady arena (see Figure 6.3).

In reflecting on this, Matt says without hesitation that love is primary for him: "The most important thing in my life is my marriage, and if my marriage had children, then I'm sure it would have included the children." Work is a distant second: "My good works have never been as good as my average marriage." This primacy seems to be a consistent theme for Matt, and while work and love are definitely separate for him, his marriage is obviously the stabilizing force in his life.

Matt and Elaine married when they graduated from college. He had always done well in school (he was his high school valedictorian), and he started graduate school with high hopes. He was disappointed with his studies, however, and did not do well; these years are reflected in the first dip in the vector for work. He tried changing his major to recreation, building on his lifelong involvement in sports, but this did not help. He finished his master's degree but describes these years as his "first encounter with failure" and a time of loss of confidence. Things improved somewhat when he began teaching high school, but it was only when he decided to enter the seminary that his work vector moved from okay to good. His discussion of that decision reveals significant ambivalence: "Maybe the minister thing was sort of a cop-out or wrong decision probably. Sounds like the most radical but in some ways it was the safest. . . . Maybe being a coach might have been something really worthwhile for me, except smart and successful people with high expectations just didn't do that. . . . I'm not good at knowing what I want."

The years in seminary were happy ones for both Matt and Elaine, though; she was a student as well, completing her master's degree during that time, and both worked their way through school. She was not convinced that the ministry was the best choice for them, but she accepted the idea and worked to develop her own career as an English teacher. Things changed

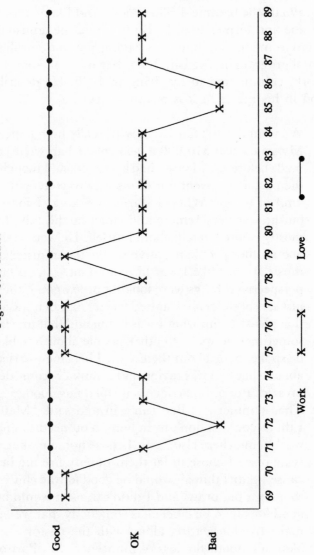

Figure 6.3. Matt.

for them both when Matt was ordained and got his first job as
an associate pastor in another state. At first he liked the church,
but gradually he became disillusioned. And Elaine missed their
old home and former friends. By the time she adjusted to the
new environment, finding a satisfying job and enrolling in a
doctoral program in English, things began to fall apart for Matt
at work, culminating in his firing in 1986. He describes this
period in his life as "a loss of innocence":

> We went to First Christian with really high hopes.
> My salary was $10,000 a year more than what I'd
> made before. . . . I never had a mentor and I thought
> the pastor . . . went out of his way to convey that
> kind of image. When I started working, I found
> out he was very remote and when he did talk, he
> mostly wanted to talk about himself. He would talk
> about other people negatively, like the minister of
> music. It was like I was his confidant. . . . In my
> perspective, things were looking pretty good, then
> just sort of suddenly I started feeling that Ben wasn't
> that pleased with what I was doing and that maybe
> sometimes he spoke to other people about me like
> he spoke to me about them. . . . I became worried
> about what Ben was saying and I think I became de-
> pressed. But our marriage was still doing good. . . .
> That summer . . . Ben came in and said, "Matt,
> I think you just don't fit in here. You need to find
> work somewhere else." . . . I chose not to make an
> issue of it. I chose to let them quietly fire me be-
> cause I didn't think it would be good for the church
> to have a big brawl and I didn't think it would be
> good for me to be labeled as somebody that would
> make trouble getting along with the pastor. . . .
> You talk about the loss of innocence. . . . Part of
> church is teaching people who don't fit in to be
> productive together. I had trouble understanding
> the church running around to find people they liked.
> I felt that a lot, quietly; Elaine was just hostile. She

still swears that before we leave this area, she's going to tell Ben off, and I cannot let her do that.

After the firing Matt enrolled in a doctoral program himself and invested heavily in his studies. The next year he became pastor of a small rural church in the same state, but by
this point it was clear to him that "work is work" and that his
major goals did not lie in that area: "I guess the one thing I
think I've decided more than once, and that's been reinforced,
is that what I live for is not to get done some accomplishment
in the area of work. . . . Now I've decided that I'm not going
to be either rich or famous even with all that great success I
had at school, like 'most likely to succeed' and all that stuff. It's
harder to say I will make that. I'm accepting success as being
there, holding on to the values that I feel are most essential in
life, and accepting that as being what I'll ultimately be judged by."

Throughout all these work-related oscillations, the stabilizing force in Matt's life was his marriage. This is clearest when
he describes times of particular stress, like being fired:

> When I lost my job, or when I started the process
> that led to losing it, it created more turmoil in my
> family, but we went to each other for a lot of sup-
> port. It was sort of a loss of innocence for both of
> us. We had seen the world as being more fair than
> it really is up until that point. . . . Working through
> difficult times makes you grow more. The bad in
> my life didn't bring the family down. In fact, I
> would say here that that's the first time in my life
> that I could probably without any reservation say
> my wife would stick by me through anything. Up
> until that time I would have given lip service to that,
> but way down inside I would say, "Well, how do
> I really know?" When I just thought the bottom was
> gone, she was there, and that's kind of comforting.

When Matt talks about their marriage, he is careful not to ideal-
ize it, though. It is clear that it is not without its turmoil:

When things were in distress at work, it increased
the stress at home. But with the increased stress in
the love end, I wouldn't say that the increased stress
was bad or even okay, but . . . there's a good in that
too. . . . We would talk more, we would talk more
about serious things. Our conversations would
probably have more anger in them during those
times. But I think that other emotions — those years
of personally sticking with me and caring together —
that those feelings would compensate. Was the nature of the relationship the same? No. When things
were going good, we'd just roll along. When things
were bad in work, it changed what we talked about
and put stress in the house. We would get mad and
walk out on each other more. Probably some of our
best sex was during the down times of intensity;
it was strange even how often we did it. . . . I don't
want to picture Elaine and me as having some ideal
marriage where everything is happy [all the time]
because we don't do that good.

Matt makes it especially clear in this passage that his ranking
of the love domain as consistently good does not mean that things
were always going well; external events had their impact. But
internally for him the marriage remained unvaryingly supportive
and satisfying, despite its outward ups and downs. It is the
benefit that he derives from the marriage that remains constant,
and that is what the uniformly good ranking of this arena reflects.

The love arena provides more than support and security
for Matt; it also is the source of his identity. He contrasts his
own development with Erik Erikson's model, in which identity
is shaped in adolescence and precedes the development of the
capacity for intimacy. Many researchers, such as Gilligan (1982),
now suggest that women follow a different sequence, developing intimacy first, and Matt sees that pattern in himself. "There
are people who argue the male/female side of [identity forma-
tion] and in some ways I would fall more into the female rather
than the male pattern. . . . So I'm saying I didn't do Erikson's
thing, I didn't gain an identity before I did intimacy. I did in-

timacy before. Identity is real complex and I did gain a lot of my sense of identity in a broader sense which literature doesn't cover very much, enough to keep our marriage strong when work wasn't going as ideally. But identity is framed in our culture through knowing what work you want to do."

That Matt would draw his primary support from the arena in which he locates his identity is hardly surprising. Further, his lack of satisfaction in the work arena would make it unlikely that he would locate his identity there. To see if this is a general characteristic of those who have the steady/fluctuating pattern, we turn to some other examples. Using Matt's experience as a kind of baseline, we first look at another man who is both similar and different in the way he articulates this particular pattern.

The County Agent. Reggie works for the Cooperative Extension Service in a rural area in the Southwest. He is thirty-nine years old, has been married twice, and he and his second wife have two children. He has worked at the same place since graduation from college, and has been promoted several times until now he is director of his office. Reggie expresses fundamental satisfaction with his life in both work and love, but for him, as was true in Matt's case, the love domain is largely stable, while work fluctuates (see Figure 6.4).

The one change in the otherwise stable love arena occurred when his first marriage broke up. Reggie's description of this experience reveals a lot about how this arena functions for him: "I married my high school sweetheart . . . and we were just wrapped up in each other. . . . We went to the university and she got a job and I went to school and we did real well. . . . I had a chance to get a Ph.D. but I was tired of school; I wanted to go home. So we went home . . . and she established another beauty shop and I worked as an extension agent, and little by little we just fell out of love with each other."

When Reggie describes the actual decision to end the marriage, his investiment in it becomes clear:

> She told me probably six or eight months earlier
> that she wasn't happy. And I said, "Let's work this
> thing out. Christmas is coming up, let's go through

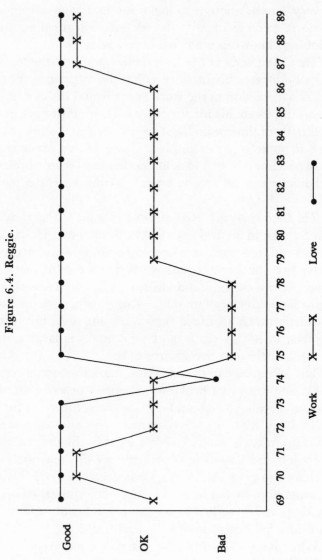

Figure 6.4. Reggie.

that, that's a happy time of year." And we never did talk a whole lot more. The whole time we were going through the love process — we were husband and wife, go to church, make love, you know, on a regular schedule. Nothing ever fell apart in the bedroom. And then after Christmas I thought things got a little bit better. . . . And then she dropped the bombshell on me about February. . . . She said, "You know, this thing is not working, and I'm going to file for divorce." I didn't know it but she had been seeing someone else. I was true blue, I was just as true blue as true blue could be. I wouldn't even think about looking for somebody. . . . But that part didn't bother me, the fact that she had a boyfriend. . . . I think she said this on Monday or Tuesday, and she said, "I'm leaving Friday." . . . On Friday afternoon we both came home from work and she backed her car up to the door and started loading up stuff. . . . And we had a big scene, you know, a big cry [and I was] begging her not to go. And she drove off and then I said to myself the craziest thing. I didn't really say to myself, "What am I going to do?" You know what fool thing I thought of? "What am I going to tell my Mama and Daddy?" I had not lived in their house since I was eighteen and there I was, twenty-five years old.

Reggie did go to see his parents that night and was surprised to hear that they knew for some time that the marriage was floundering. He spent the night with them, then the next day he says "I just got in the car and drove back to where I was working and stayed there and hit the ground running, so to speak."

Like Matt, Reggie seems to use the love arena as the center of security in his life, but unlike Matt he has a tendency to take it for granted. His surprise at his wife's unhappiness in their marriage and his efforts to cover it over reveal this, as does his instinctive return to his parents' home once she leaves. And this taken-for-granted security in the love arena seems to continue into later life. He married again two years after the divorce, and he describes his relationship with his second wife in a way that reflects basic satisfaction: "It's comfortable, it's very comfortable to me. . . . We have not had any major problems with parents or anything like this, my children have been healthy, there's not been any real hard, hard times, so I reckon we've stood the test of time. . . . We try to do things together, we try to vacation, we try to maintain a certain spice of life, as much as you can after twelve or fifteen years of marriage."

Yet this domain is not without the possibility of disruption, and Reggie talked about that when he began musing about midlife crisis, what he called "the middle-age crazy": "There's something else that I think might be significant: the middle-age crazy. I feel that I'm probably going to go through that darned thing; I'm going to have to deal with it. . . . I'm not really looking for it, but I see other people my age it hit and I know they're not any different than I am. . . . I don't know how it's going to affect me, but I feel like it's going to happen."

He links these thoughts to awareness of his own aging process and associates that with possible sexual experimentation: "You look into the mirror and you see your head getting bald. You know there are some things you can't do as well as you used to, and you want to prove to yourself that, yes, you can do them. And maybe if the right lady comes along and shows an attraction . . . the biology or chemistry or whatever . . . I may have to experiment with that thing, even though I don't want to."

We asked Reggie how the thought of this impending crisis made him feel and he replied, "Bad. Because I know it's going to come and I'm not sure how I'm going to deal with it." The thought of this domain being threatened is very unsettling to him. It remains the arena in which he finds his security, and it is here that midlife issues get worked out.

In contrast to the largely stable love domain, Reggie's work domain experiences a fair amount of change. As was true in Matt's case, the fluctuations reflect changing external circumstances. For Reggie that was the movement from junior college to university to graduate school, then — the low point on his graph — his first years in his job. Those were difficult years for him because of a power struggle between two strong personalities in the office, a situation that affected him but that he could do little to change. Things improved finally when one of them retired and Reggie was promoted to that position. His work domain then rose to good in 1987, when he received a statewide award accompanied by a $5,000 stipend for professional development.

To underline this observation that the fluctuations reflect external rather than internal factors, Reggie comments on the limitations of the graph: "I would think my work relationship is better than the graph shows. The graph doesn't show the fact that I was happy with what I was doing. I am happy no matter what I am doing. . . . If you told me I had to quit my work tomorrow and go to work for somebody else doing something totally different than what I am doing now, I could find satisfaction in that." He goes on to recall that the phrase "my duty is my pleasure" appeared beneath his picture in his high school yearbook: "That really captured me and it made a difference in my life. I think about that thing at least once a month as I go along — 'my duty is my pleasure.' . . . I reckon I do enjoy my duty, no matter what it is."

Reggie also speaks about seeking change or stimulation. It is something he does not seek in the love domain; when he talks about his marriage he says clearly that "I'm not looking for any change; I'm perfectly happy." But work is another matter, and he is ambivalent here. He might want a change: "I'm kind of at a turning point with this job. . . . I've been there fifteen years. . . . I may need a stimulus." But then again, maybe he does not: "I may be looking at a new position as a kind of shot in the arm . . . I don't know. I don't know if I need a shot in the arm. I may have reached where I need to be in life." What Reggie appears to be affirming is a continuation of the same steady/fluctuating pattern of work and love in his life, suggesting a stability in that work/love relationship that we see in the other examples of this pattern as well.

For Matt and Reggie, love is the steady arena, and while Reggie is less explicit about locating his identity in that arena, for both it is a source of fundamental stability. We turn now to someone whose experience is significantly different and for whom work is the steady dimension.

The Adult Literacy Teacher. Vivian is a sixty-two-year-old retired special education teacher who is anything but retired. She and her husband, married forty years, have four children and seven grandchildren. They are natives of Tennessee and now live in a rural part of that state. Vivian was a special education teacher for most of her career, but in 1980 she became interested in adult literacy and worked as a volunteer in that field while continuing to teach in the public schools full time. She took early retirement from teaching two years ago and is now devoting her full attention to her adult literacy work.

In Vivian's pattern of love and work, the work area is steady (see Figure 6.5). As we saw with both Matt and Reggie, the fluctuating arena reflects changing external circumstances; in Vivian's case these are mostly family crises like illness and death. However, the way Vivian experienced this pattern shows some significant differences from what we have seen so far.

For Vivian, work is the constant domain, and when she talks about it, she emphasizes that it serves as the stabilizing force in her life. This is especially obvious when there are fluctuations in the love arena, such as when her father died: "In 1974 my father died. He had been sick for several years, but between September and December, the beginning of a school year, I had a particular need for a class in special ed at that time. . . . He had had much surgery, he had emphysema, he had heart problems, he had, well, just about everything he could have, and they just all went at once. . . . I expected his death . . . but that was just such an emotional thing that . . . when it actually hit, it was just a down time with me, and also being the only daughter . . . it also hit me with the fact that my mother was now going to be the one that was going to depend on me and I would feel responsible for her and I guess I was a little bit overwhelmed right at that time. . . . But also I wanted to keep my stability with my work."

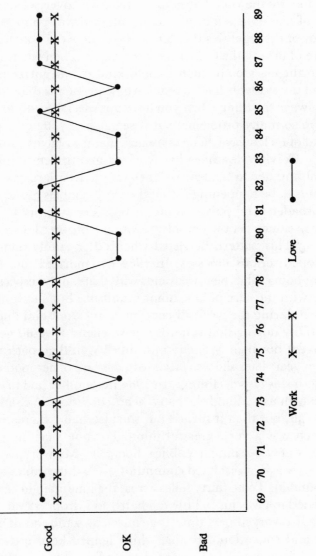

Figure 6.5. Vivian.

She goes on to describe how her teaching contributed to her stability at that time: "Well, he died the day before Christmas and so by the time Christmas break was over we had made a lot of decisions about where my mother was going to be, and a lot of the legalities that had to be done were able to be taken care of during the Christmas break. . . . Then when I got back into the classroom, then I could kind of categorize my mind. And my students had so many worse problems than I did. This is always the thing when you have got special ed students — they have so many problems that it seems like your own problems kind of melt away when you realize that they have problems too."

Vivian describes her work as giving her "stability" and enabling her to "categorize" her mind. In a larger sense what seems to be happening is that the work enables her to maintain a broader perspective on life; it provides stability by allowing her to situate her own problems within a broader human context.

This pattern persisted when other family members developed serious illnesses. In 1984 her married son developed lymphoma. She spent weekends with that family, especially helping with the care of her infant grandson, but she continued to teach during the week. "I continued my work and that was the stability during that time. Every weekend I would get real involved, but then Monday morning I would go back to work." Two years later she was faced with the care of her mother, whose health was also declining: "In 1986 my mother had to come and live with us . . . and she had a heart condition. We thought that was all, but then it turned out she also had pancreatic cancer, which was a very stressful thing. For one year here I had to drop out of teaching in public school. . . . My workplace [at that time] was in an isolated community . . . thirty miles across the mountain. To be thirty miles across the mountain in case mother needed me was just a little too hard, so I dropped out. . . . [Instead] I worked part time at a church as senior adult coordinator and education director, which helped keep me going."

Vivian took a leave of absence for a year from a job that was too far away to enable her to meet her obligations to her mother, but she needed to take another job to meet her own needs during that period. This shows just how important the work arena is as a source of support in her life.

We have seen so far in this pattern, identity seems to be located in the steady arena. This was clearest for Matt but also true, though less explicit, for Reggie. Vivian further validates this observation, while at the same time extending our understanding of it. Like most women of her generation, she assumed a role in relation to her husband, locating her identity there. That role was even more clearly defined for her than for most women because he was a Baptist minister. When he changed jobs, becoming a regional administrator rather than a pastor, that had profound implications for her. Vivian's description of that experience gives us a dramatic picture of this process:

> In 1979 there was a big change for me. My husband had been a pastor through all our married life — a little over thirty years — and all of a sudden he was not a pastor. He was asked to be a director of missions for the mountain area, which meant we had four Tennessee counties in the mountain area. As a pastor, he had one church and I was his only wife, and I was the pastor's wife. So I had my role. Now when he became director of missions, he had to earn his place because he had no official relationship with the churches; he was just placed there as a support and help, and the churches could either accept or reject him. And so . . . he had zero identity. And it was a real struggle for me at first because in the mountain area most of the people are very suspicious of you unless you have long-term roots . . . but I was a city girl. . . . We had to earn our own place, and I had to find out who I was. . . . I was at a low point and I had to decide "Who am I and how can I work out my ministry?" I think each of us as Christians have to find out how we are going to follow the Lord in some kind of ministry. [At this time] I found myself at a minister's wife retreat. The lady that was giving the devotionals . . . used every example from adult literacy because that was what she did as her ministry. [That was how] I was introduced to adult literacy . . . and as soon

as I found out about it then I started trying to find
a way that I could get involved in it even though
I had no way to train. I had to wait until the next
year before I could even get some training. At least
I had a glimmer that maybe I was a person.

Vivian convinced her denomination to develop adult literacy programs in their churches, and quickly went on to assume
a leadership role in adult literacy in her state.

Vivian's discovery that "maybe I was a person" brings into
sharper focus the connection between the steady arena and identity in this pattern. Being the pastor's wife was another aspect
of work for her; when she no longer had that role, she forged
a more personal identity within work of her own choosing. The
steady character of the work arena in her life may well have
helped make the change a smooth one for her.

Vivian gives us a more nuanced understanding of the
meaning of the steady domain in this pattern and how it relates
to identity. Our next example sheds more light on how people
experience the steady/fluctuating pattern.

The College Professor. Norman is fifty-eight years old. He
and his wife have been married thirty-two years and they have
three adult children. He is a professor of political science at a
major university in the northeast, where until recently he was
chair of his department. He decided to resign as chair and limit
his academic duties to teaching so that he could resume his work
in ministry on a part-time basis. Ministry had been his first
career before he entered academic life in 1967. He now happily combines both careers.

Norman's pattern of work and love is predominantly
steady/fluctuating; for him work is largely constant, while love
fluctuates (see Figure 6.6).

In 1969 Norman was completing the coursework for his
doctoral program and working at his first job in his new field.
He rated that year as both good and bad because the values
of the institution in which he was working were different from
his own, and he took another, more congenial position the next

Figure 6.6 (Norman)

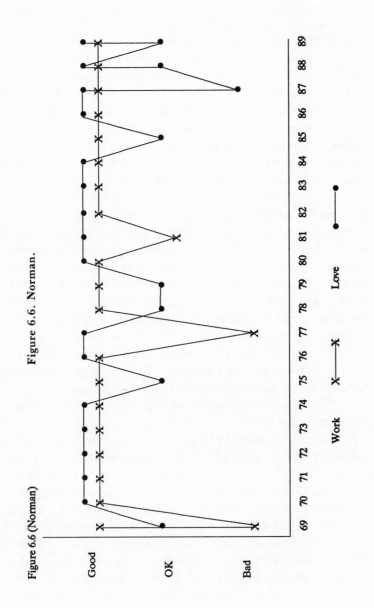

Figure 6.6. Norman.

year. The decision to obtain his doctorate and to become an
academic was made together with his wife, and it indicates the
primacy of the love domain for him: "When I went into the doctoral program it was a joint decision between my wife and myself. We made that decision at a missionary dedication service
during the singing of the hymn, "Once to Every Man and Na-
tion Comes the Moment to Decide," and basically that was the
first major decision that we made, that both of us made together,
outside of having the children, since we had been married. [He
was already a minister when they married.] That was what in
a large measure sustained us over a period of time."

He acknowledges that this emphasis on the love arena is
unusual, but he credits it with sustaining their marriage through
difficult times, most notably the graduate program itself: "We
have seen friends of ours, you know, their love was strong for
a while and then it was gone, and their families have broken
up. For instance, there were twenty-five of us couples who were
in the graduate program together, and two of us stayed together.
The other couple said to us, 'Well, we're the only two who stayed
together and you all stayed together because you love each other,
and we stayed [married] because we're committed to giving each
other a hard time.' Basically that has been very very much
primary as far as our life together is concerned."

He also made subsequent decisions about his career together with his wife.

Norman worked in education-related institutions for several years before getting an academic position in a university,
his goal since deciding to get his doctorate. Yet, even when not
able to attain that goal, he rates his work domain as good. The
two further exceptions (in 1977 work was bad, and in 1981 it
was rated okay) reflect times of political upheaval in his state-
funded institution when his job was in jeopardy. He understands
his work in spiritual terms, and this accounts for the overall satisfaction he derives from it. "It's the constancy of a call, whether
it's to do preaching in parish ministry or to do education, or
if it's to do a combination of the two, or whatever. It's like there's
a beating of a different drum that's going on all the time that
drives me . . . not drives me in the sense that I'm a driven type

of person, but in the sense that it sustains me. That's what's going on; that's what excites me. I can be tired beyond words sometimes, but the next morning or a couple of mornings later, I'll be raring to go again."

It is interesting that this sense of call carries him through stressful situations at work, such as when he became department chair and had to deal with strong opposition among some of the faculty to his leadership. Rather than using the more collegial style of decision making that he prefers, he found it necessary to assert his power at an early faculty meeting, to the point of summarily adjourning the meeting when his opponents insisted on changing the agenda. He describes this as "one of the most distasteful decisions I ever made" but locates the strength to make this and other harder decisions in that same sense of call:

> When I was confronted with doing various things that may have been distasteful in some sense, nevertheless it was internally what I felt, "this I need to do." Same thing when we decided to go into a doctoral program. Family and friends basically told us we were nuts, but we stuck together and simply said, "this is what we have to do." And we did it. It was difficult. We had two children with the third one on the way. We moved from a seven-room house to a two-room apartment, but when that internal sense of "this is what you need to do" comes to that point, you're ready to do it. Same thing last year when the Lord began speaking to me again. After four years I hadn't been preaching because I was chair at the time and the work load was about even, so I didn't pursue the clergy stuff at that time. Then I got the nudge a year ago now, and well, I've learned there's two ways I respond to what the Lord tells me to do: one is, I obey what He tells me: the other is, I wish I had!

In discussing the love arena, Norman is careful to note that the fluctuations reflect particular family crises, not changes within the marriage. Dips in that vector included (in order) a family move, the illness and then death of his father, his mother's death, the involvement of his youngest daughter in drugs, and the illness and death of his mother-in-law. He responded to these crises with the same religious faith that informs his actions in the work arena, though he does not use the concept of call when he talks about the love domain.

When he was asked how work and love interact, he noted that fluctuations in either arena make the family even more cohesive: "We found that in the times of stress . . . we drew close together. . . . We found ourselves drawing close together all the time but even more so when the wars on the outside, so to speak, were confronting us." Those "wars" could occur in either arena; the result would be the same.

Norman's experience of the steady/fluctuating pattern is similar to the others we have seen in that he locates his identity in the stable arena, which he conceptualizes as a spiritual call, and that steady domain provides fundamental stability in his life. Unlike the others, however, he names the fluctuating arena as primary. Our final example of this pattern explores these themes further.

The College Dean. Karen, forty-eight years old and in her second marriage, is dean of a small liberal arts college in the Southwest. She has worked in higher education throughout her career and has steadily achieved in that arena. In her case, work is largely steady and love fluctuates (see Figure 6.7).

As Karen talked about her life, it was clear that she has experienced a lot of interaction between the domains. It began with her first marriage: "When I was first married in 1967, I had a job and then actually left the job to care for a stepchild, and my whole career pattern at that point was distorted and off-track as a result of that decision, which was directly related, of course, to the love domain. And I found that, as my marriage ended . . . , a concern for my own autonomy and independence became paramount. In fact, that became a big motivating force in how I approached my work. So it was a sense of loss in the personal life that started my career going, despite

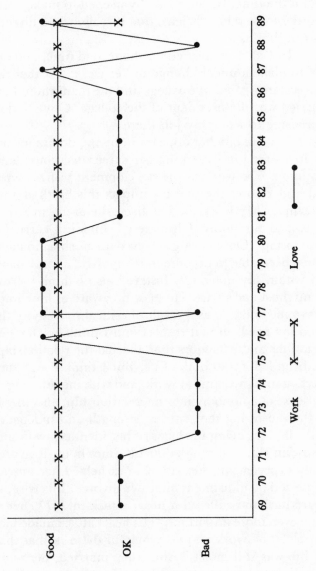

Figure 6.7. Karen.

that interruption. I remember asking for my very first promotion at the time, because I really needed to make more money in order to be self-sufficient, that it really was a direct relationship in that aspect."

In 1980 she married for the second time, and once again had to make a major change in her work: "At that time I was an assistant dean at the college and the man whom I eventually married was the president of the college. Our relationship required me to leave my job there."

In spite of what appears to be the dominant position of the love arena in governing her career decisions, Karen gives prominence to work in the development of her own identity, and underscores the positive impact this has had on her relationships: "My work life has been the arena in which I have developed autonomy. Ultimately I think it is carried over into relationships. Once having achieved a sense of autonomy, I think I have been able to become much more of an independent person within my marriage, fostered also I think by an attitude on my husband's part. He became aware of how important it was to me and . . . as a result of critical reflectivity, he understood my needs in that respect and I think he changed his expectations and behaviors that affected the relationship. So this has been helpful to both of us. But I think it was the domino effect, starting with me at work, and with me bringing my growing sense of autonomy into the relationship, affecting him, and he then fostering the sense of strength and independence."

Besides being the locus of her identity, work also helped to sustain Karen through difficult times in the love arena. Certainly experiencing success at work helped her move through the period of adjustment after her divorce. Likewise, when her future husband suffered a heart attack in 1977, her work became even more important: "His heart attack made me feel vulnerable. The work was very helpful there in that that part of my life was still intact." After they married, her work helped her adjust to having stepchildren: "I was adjusting to having to share the other part of my world with two new people in my life, and things were less mine here at home than they used to be. So the job had a different dimension at that point. It was something that was exclusively mine in a way. That helped me at that time; I was not allowing myself to be eroded. I was not able to deal with the adjustment in a totally positive way; sometimes it really bothered me that I had these responsibilities. And the job was a real good—I hate to say the word 'escape'—but a balance of things."

When we asked Karen if work was the source of stability for her that it was for the others we interviewed with this pattern, she made an interesting distinction: "The notion of stability—I don't know if I could really use that word comfortably. Drive would be more accurate for me. . . . I think it's been the source of a steady drive. Despite what I said about the growth of capability and autonomy, I'm not so certain I have ever relinquished feelings of insecurity. I get nervous about work; I work very hard at what I'm doing, probably as a reaction to concerns about insecurity. . . . I just don't know how I would survive without [this drive] but I don't see it as necessarily a positive or negative thing." Later in the interview Karen illustrated this point when she discussed her adjustment to the doctoral program in which she is currently enrolled part time: "When I entered the program, I came in with an enormous anxiety, I just was petrified. Anxiety was something I could feel physically. I think it had to do with whether I could do the work, then when I realized that I was capable of doing the work, it shifted to 'will I have time to do the work?' But somehow or other I confronted a level of insecurity that I really didn't think I had left. Irrespective of any success at work, which is also head-work, I was still really terrorized. I'm still struggling with that. The first learning experience was to learn I had that kind of terror about this kind of experience." The drive that sustained her in her studies was the same force that enabled her to be productive as an administrator. This parallels that sense of spiritual call that sustained Norman in his work, or the support Matt experienced in his marriage. All demonstrate the stabilizing character of the steady arena in this pattern.

Like the others, Karen also notes that she evaluates the steady arena differently from the fluctuating one. She speaks of the complex reality of work, noting that "an awful lot goes

on in that domain . . . the hard work, the challenges, the nature of the work environment which is extremely fluctuating and
fluid, and what that means for coping." But in spite of these
variable elements, she derives a consistent benefit from this domain: "The consistent benefit is a sense of excitement, intellectual commitment to it, status, salary." It is that consistency that
results in the steady vector.

We asked her if, as in Matt's case, the negative or stressful times in her love arena seemed to reinforce this stable character of her work domain. She responded emphatically: "I would
say that the dips in the love domain definitely reinforced the
work domain, definitely. [The steadiness of work] takes on more
of an importance [in those times], I think." Her experiences of
the divorce and her later adjustment to new stepchildren would
support that assessment.

We have already seen how identity in this pattern tends
to be located in the steady arena, and Karen's development of
autonomy in work would further confirm this. She talked about
moving toward a more integrated sense of identity formation,
however, noting that "gradually over time I'm feeling more
together as an identity," and her discussion of her growing sense
of autonomy in her relationships supports that claim. She also
said that for her the two domains were equally valued, though
"if I were forced to choose, I would choose my family under
all circumstances."

Having looked through five separate windows into the
steady/fluctuating pattern, we now look across all five to determine what themes they share.

Common Themes in the Steady/Fluctuating Pattern

We begin our analysis of this pattern by noting that what
sets it apart is the presence of a stable arena, a feature seen in
no other pattern. We are now in a position to explore the meaning of that stability and to understand its relationship to the fluctuating arena that complements it.

Arenas Evaluated Differently. Perhaps the most striking
thing we see in our five examples is that the two arenas are evalu-

ated differently. The fluctuating domain reflects shifting external factors: a job change in work or a family illness in love, for example. Reggie underlined this for us when he pointed to the changes in his work arena but emphasized that those fluctuations reflected shifting circumstances, not changes in his degree of happiness. Remember that he is the one whose duty is his pleasure. Others, like Matt, would not go that far; certainly his fluctuations in work reflect both external circumstances and his measure of happiness or unhappiness with them. But the important point is that all four consistently list external events when plotting this arena.

They interpret the steady arena differently, though. It is not that things do not happen in this domain; there is always a lot going on. Recall Matt's realistic description of his marriage or Norman's difficulties as chair of his department. If external circumstances were being reflected, this arena would be anything but steady. Clearly something else is going on here, and we hear it in the way these people talk about the steady arena. Here their evaluations are of an internal reality, one they experience as consistently beneficial, hence the uniformly good rating they give this area of their lives. This feature is consistent across the interviews, suggesting that in this pattern the two vectors reflect very different things. In a sense there are two frames of reference here: an external frame for the fluctuating arena, and an internal frame for the steady arena. The presence of these two frameworks accounts for the dramatic difference in the vectors and hence for the pattern itself.

Another similarity among the interviews is the location of identity in the stable domain. Some interviewees are clearer about this than others, but all demonstrate it. Most revealing is the picture given by Vivian, who experienced a shift in her identity during the twenty-year period, moving from her ascribed role as pastor's wife to the achievement of her own identity as an adult literacy teacher. Significantly, her graph shows no fluctuation during this important transition. Perhaps that is because the experience was a positive one for her. Others, for example Reggie when his marriage broke up, show a break in the steady domain when the experience is negative. But all maintain their identity in this stable domain rather than shifting it to the fluctuating one. Karen, speaking of a more integrated sense of identity, demonstrates how changes forged in the steady arena influence behavior in the other arena.

Function of the Stable Domain. Given this connection with identity, it is no surprise that the stable domain provides the element of security or stability for these people. Some, like Vivian, even call that domain their "stability" in life. She describes that stability in two ways: as a way of coping with stressful situations in the other arena, and as a way of situating her experience within a larger context. Matt makes a similar point when he talks about his marriage. Karen gives us a more dynamic conceptualization of this element, calling it a steady drive that sustains her. While each person articulates it differently, this element is present in all we interviewed with this pattern.

One other thing that is particularly interesting about this pattern is the interaction of the two arenas. Dips in the fluctuating arena do not appear to create stress in the stable domain. On the contrary, at those points the supportive character of that stable domain is reinforced. Remember Matt's comment about the effect the loss of his job had on his marriage; it drew him and his wife even closer together and reaffirmed their commitment to each other. Possibly we could even understand the fluctuations of one arena as contributing to the stability of the other.

People with this pattern clearly consider the two arenas to be separate realities and make no effort to fuse them. Some, like Matt and Norman, go so far as to name one as primary; others, like Reggie, Vivian, and Karen, imply that they value the two equally. And, as we saw with Norman, the steady arena is not necessarily the one that is named as primary. It makes sense that the two arenas be separate since very different things are being evaluated, namely internal and external realities.

Finally, it is interesting to note how men and women differed in this pattern. Of the people we interviewed, those for whom love was the steady arena were men: Matt and Reggie. The two women interviewed, Vivian and Karen, had work as their steady arena, as did the other man, Norman. However, in our total sample there were no significant differences between women and men in terms of which domain they held steady. Work, for example, was the steady arena for 64 percent of the men and 68 percent of the women who had this pattern. Our results in this regard must therefore be understood as an anomaly attributed to the smallness of that group; our total sample of 405 gives the true picture, and it reflects no difference by gender.

Our analysis of the steady/fluctuating pattern reveals, as was true with the parallel pattern, that the outward simplicity of this pattern belies an inward complexity. We turn now to our third and final pattern type, where we will find still another way that work and love interrelate in adult life.

CHAPTER SEVEN

No Order Here:
The Divergent Pattern

When we conducted our interviews for this study, we usually began by asking participants their impressions of their particular pattern. Those whose patterns were largely parallel and those whose patterns could be characterized as steady/ fluctuating had an easy time of it; the basic pattern was obvious. The others, however, were often puzzled. One person even exclaimed, "There's no order here . . . it's all a mess!" What appears at first glance to be that "mess" constitutes our third and final pattern.

We decided to call this pattern *divergent* because rather than being in an ordered relationship, work and love seem to exist at cross-purposes to one another. Much like the partners in a contemporary dance who move independently, sharing only a common dance floor, the vectors in this pattern seem to move in opposition to each other. That very oppositional status itself constitutes a relationship. The arenas can diverge in two ways: They can intersect frequently as they shift and move in opposite directions, and they can move in the same direction but at the farthest possible distance from each other. Both of these possibilities are illustrated in Figure 7.1. Graphs were also coded as divergent if they had segments of all three patterns, giving an overall sense of divergence.

In our total sample of 405 people, 140 or 35 percent had the divergent pattern. Here, as in the other two patterns, there were no gender differences; neither women nor men were more

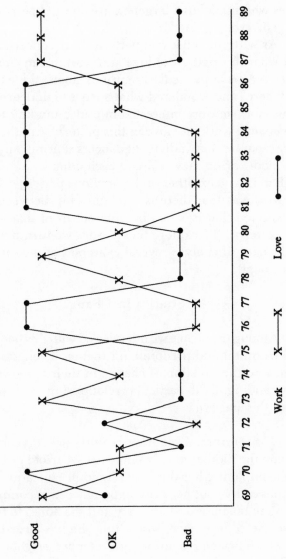

Figure 7.1. Example of the Divergent Pattern.

likely to have this pattern. The only significant association was with life stage, and in this case it was those who were in their thirties who made up a larger-than-expected percentage of the divergent group.

As with the other two patterns, our concern is to understand what this pattern of love and work means for those who live it. We were particularly curious about the extreme variability here, and wondered what such a high degree of change meant. And we were interested in understanding the relationship between work and love in this pattern. Are the two arenas totally separate, like individual dancers sharing only a common dance floor, or do they relate to each other in a more complex way than is true in either of the previous patterns? Our hunch, of course, was that there is a relationship between them, but we suspected that it would be different from that found in the other patterns. To explore those issues we turn now to our interview data to analyze several examples of the divergent pattern in depth.

Studies in Change

Among the people we interviewed with this pattern, change was a common and predominant theme. Their stories give us insight into the function of change in their lives, as well as an understanding of the particular relationship between work and love in this pattern.

The Trainer. Katherine is thirty-seven years old, married, and the mother of a dynamic two-year-old girl. She is currently completing her doctorate in adult education at a Canadian university, but her prior experience is in communications training in business and industry and she hopes to teach in that field at the college level, something she has already done and liked. Her husband is a history professor at a neighboring university. They have been married fourteen years, and are committed to maintaining their dual careers. Their daughter has been a pleasant addition to a marriage that has had its ups and downs; they both wanted the child and they do their best to share the responsibilities of child care.

When Katherine looked at her graph with us, she talked first about the variability in it: "I sort of had this chaotic dance and then this even period in my life . . . like a military march in the middle where my life is more orderly . . . then another chaotic dance but with a different kind of tune. I predict that if I was going to a new level of this chart, my next set [would be] a lot like this middle segment here, which is a little bit more balanced, a kind of stable period."

As she says, Katherine's graph does seem to break into three segments or cycles that are distinct from each other (see Figure 7.2). We occasionally found such cycles, or alternating periods of stability and change, in this pattern, though Katherine's cycles are longer than most. We will focus on each cycle in turn to hear how she experienced the more varied as well as the more stable periods.

In the first cycle Katherine completed her undergraduate degree, went on for her master's, and began working. This period of establishing herself as an adult was particularly conflicted because she had to move against her father's expectations of the proper roles for women: "I started off getting boxed into things I didn't want to do and I would just go through it quickly and then I found ways out. I sort of figured out that education was the way out of a lot of things here. That was a real painful period to reflect on because I didn't like that period at all. . . . My dad said, "All good Catholic school girls become nurses," so I just said, "Sure, Dad," and I was going to become the standard thing. . . . I was too young and stupid not to listen so I listened and obeyed and then it occurred to me halfway through 1969 that I didn't have to do anything he said. . . . It was too late to get out of the school so I switched out of the program and went into liberal arts, much to his disdain. It was the best thing I ever did but it was a slow evolutionary process."

Katherine followed a similar pattern after graduating and going on for her master's degree. Rather than continuing on for her doctorate, she again let herself be thwarted by the expectations of others. This involved both work and love: "I wanted to pursue my doctorate and really did not allow myself for a number of reasons. I didn't get a lot of emotional support from family and friends. My boyfriend at the time was saying, 'What

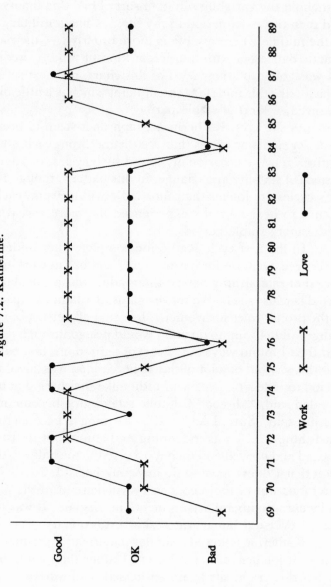

Figure 7.2. Katherine.

the hell do you need this degree for?' and I went against my better judgment at that time and said, 'I think I will succumb and get married.' [I did] what I felt was the proper thing at that time rather than what I really wanted to do. . . . I go ahead and get married and get probably one of the worst jobs that I could have gotten. . . . I got this master's degree in rhetoric and found myself selling advertising; I was totally depressed. . . . It also directly affected the marriage. I probably was very difficult to live with."

In this first cycle, from 1969 to 1976, we see Katherine tentatively making her way in life. Several times she tries to follow the expectations of others, only to realize that she must do what *she* wants if she is to be happy.

She seems to take hold after that low point in 1976, however, and from there moves into a period of stability. She attributes that improvement to a college teaching position that she fought for and won. She was particularly proud to land that job with only a master's degree. As she talks about that time it is clear that work plays a determining role in her life: "From 1977 to 1984 I taught at the university in the speech communications department and it was probably the most fulfilling professional time of my life thus far . . . I felt fulfilled on a personal, emotional level. I felt very stable during that time period and I found that when my life was professionally stable, I could cope with almost any kind of personal crisis or dilemma or the averageness of my marriage. . . . Steve and I were both sort of marching along, both very involved in our careers, knowing that the marriage was just sort of okay. . . . We both were professional together, that was our commonality at that point. . . . I look at that period of time of my life as incredibly stable and I pin that on the fact that I was teaching."

Katherine is careful to note that work is the dominant arena both in stable times and in times of flux; she clearly places her identity there: "A lot of my self-concept is really tied up in what I would call the professional side of myself. . . . "When my professional life is out of whack, my personal life seems incredibly unbalanced. I can't even come to terms with it at all, whether it's friendships, love life, boyfriend, husband, whatever it might be. . . . But the professional side of myself has a very small definition. If it's academically related, if it's something of an intellectual nature, then I'm happy. . . . Teaching, training, any type of what I would call thinking type work makes me feel real stable."

The stability that Katherine describes differs from the stability we saw in the steady/fluctuating pattern. There it was constant; here it is dependent on a job that is personally and intellectually satisfying. When she loses that job, which happened when her teaching position ended in 1984, her world crashes again. She talks about taking another job selling advertising at that point, calling this time "a death period": "This is worse than 1976, so it would probably be lower on the chart if the chart could reflect that. At this point I felt that I knew I was a good teacher, I knew I was in the right field, and I was not there anymore, and it was a really depressing experience. A lot of the stuff that had happened in the okay part was now unmanageable. . . . But what was interesting for me on these charts is that when I reach these low points, I don't stay long."

As Katherine notes, she does not stay down very long, at least not in the work arena. Her third cycle, now a period of change, begins with that bad year, but she manages to improve her job situation by adding training to her duties, and she begins her doctoral work. Her marriage continues to experience stress, however, until the birth of their child. That event brings the love vector to good, in spite of her mother's unexpected death shortly afterward. Katherine discusses the difficulty she had rating that year:

> I had a real hard time classifying this as good and I had to really think about that a lot. That was probably the worst year of my life, yet I would classify that as good. . . . I probably was the most fortunate because when my mother died, we were total friends and really at a peaceful point with each other. And I think that was good because we had kind of a rocky year prior to that. She had come down to visit me and we just put to bed a lot of stuff and felt real

good about ourselves, and she was inviolved with me having the child. Not so much that she thought I should have a child because she was really not that much a pusher for kids, but she said, you know, "Katherine, this is something you need that is just going to be for you, and I only like things that are for you." I thought that was a real neat thing to say and then she died right after that and I thought that in a way it was a good year because it could have been different in lots of ways.

The resolution of Katherine's relationship with her mother outweighed the loss she experienced at her death. That and the birth of her daughter combined to make this a good year.

There is no question that the work domain is primary for Katherine, and that she locates her identity here. She was surprised herself to see how important work is in her life, and offered an interesting reflection in the interview:

For the most part, probably the thing that has taken larger precedence in my life is the professional life, and I think that's because it's the one area that I feel I'm in control of for some reason. I think that's why there is very little interaction [of work and love] at certain points. . . . I'll tell you what I learned in doing this. If you asked me, I would always say that people are the most important thing in my life, and that's obviously true, but I find the only place that I can really be who I am is in my professional life. I feel like with family, friends, the intellectual side is not encouraged. . . . It's the one area that I can pursue and feel comfortable with and it's mine and nobody else's, and that's I think why it's so crucial for me. It's almost that I wouldn't want to separate something called work from personal [life] because the work is me personally. And the other stuff represents my interaction towards people.

This connection between control and the work arena is a theme we will see again in this pattern.

In Katherine's life, work and love appear to operate largely independent of one another; for the most part, change in one arena does not alter the other. The only exception to this occurs when a major decline in work adds stress to the marriage, bringing it down as well. But when work is good, her love situation does not improve; instead she speaks of being able to cope better with the frustrations in her personal life. This is a type of interaction between the arenas that we have not seen in the other patterns.

Katherine sums up her pattern by reflecting on the alternating cycles again, calling the start of each new period her "gatekeeping years." She explains: "I like the term *gatekeeping* because the gatekeeper is the person that sort of edits out or sorts out what people are going to do. Basically, the gatekeeping years are the ones that I'm sorting through my crap and I'm going to shut out things and bring in things and then I decide what these things are going to be, and then I maintain that for a while until it doesn't feel good anymore." This image is a telling one, especially in combination with Katherine's earlier discussion of her need for control over her life. What comes through is a restless searching for a way of expressing herself authentically. For her at least, the divergent vectors seem to be homing in on a dynamic truth that lies within her, and it is hard to imagine that they would ever completely stabilize. The movement suggested here is dynamic and searching, not oppositional and conflicted. We turn now to another person with this type of pattern to see if this characteristic can be generalized.

The College Professor. Don is fifty-four years old, married, and the father of two adult children. His marriage has been troubled on and off for many years, and he and his wife have been living separately for the last four years. This arrangement has improved their relationship, and they have no plans to change it. He is currently teaching journalism full time at a midwestern university, but he has also done some administrative work and for several years he combined both careers. Don's graph reflects these changes (see Figure 7.3).

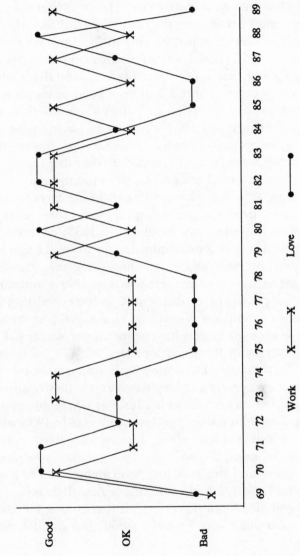

Figure 7.3. Don.

The first part of the graph is somewhat parallel. In that time he had changed jobs twice out of dissatisfaction, and the family had moved to a new city. He notes that the divergence of the arenas began after they had all established themselves in the new setting: "I'm just looking at the dates when they begin to change and I know I was going through some personal counseling then because of the marriage . . . and that's when things began to digress. There I had very good years professionally. In one way, as I reflect on it, I don't know whether compensation is the word for it, but when you're having personal crises, if there are opportunities to sort of excel professionally, I don't know, they sort of put a Band-Aid on the other part of your life."

The rest of Don's graph tracks the ups and downs of his marriage, as well as the oscillations in his career. He suggests that, apart from compensating for each other, work and love have little impact on one another: "In 1983, just coincidentally, I took on this part-time administrative job and I also had major surgery, but even so I rated those as good years because it brought us together and there was a lot of love and caring then. A lot happened there. But it just so happened that I took on this new job which was exciting, challenging, at the same time that I had to go in and have some major surgery. I don't see any relationship there particularly."

In that case, Don rated both arenas as good; two years later work was good and love was bad, yet they continue to have little impact on each other: "This was where our marriage began getting a little worse and was followed in 1986 with a separation which is still in effect. It's not a legal separation; we're still good friends, but we're not living in the same place. At the same time, and this was just coincidental so I'm not sure it's cause and effect, I had come into a new division . . . and was getting to do a lot of travel. . . . It was getting kind of exciting there, and that's why I rated it good. But I'm not sure they're related."

We asked him if he could identify any time when events in one arena affected the other, and he could think of only one instance. In 1982 he was teaching at a university in another state for six months, and his relationship with his wife improved dur-

ing that time. That experience of the benefit of distance clearly
set the stage for their decision to live separately four years later.

Don, then, shows even more uniform separation of work
and love than Katherine does, in that there is seldom a causal
interaction between the two. However, he does indicate that
there can be interactions that are other than causal between the
arenas. For him, good work experiences can compensate for
difficulties in his personal life — a process he describes as "putting a Band-Aid on the other part of your life." Compensation
as a form of interaction between work and love is something
we have seen in each of the patterns. Don goes on to illustrate
another way the arenas can be related, too. For him work involves relationship:

> I like to think that I come across as more of a per-
> son than a professor . . . so that even in my work
> area, so to speak, that it's still the personal me that's
> there. [My focus in teaching is on] the facilitation
> [of learning] certainly, but the relationship is very
> important. I spend the first week of any class mak-
> ing sure [the students] are comfortable with me and
> that they understand where I'm coming from and
> that I know who they are. Then I find that learn-
> ing is a lot easier and it's a lot more fun. So I try
> to break down some of those stereotypes that stu-
> dents have about who [professors] are and what we
> do and let them know that I really care about
> them. . . . I'm interested in their learning, not in
> failing them or making it tough. . . . I think that
> interpersonal relationship is very important in every-
> thing we do.

It is important to note that Don is not tempted to fuse
the two arenas here; he does not say that for him work is the
same as love, something we saw in some examples of the parallel pattern. What he points to is the common element of relationship in both arenas; only in that sense do they overlap
for him.

One of the striking characteristics that we see in the divergent pattern is a great amount of change. We asked Don about the role of change in his life, and he immediately responded:

> You know, I've reached a point in my career where I've done a number of things and I've been doing them for quite a while, and some people might be content to just go on doing them, but my makeup is not like that. I seek change. I feel there are a limited number of things I can do, but when I see an opportunity, I jump in. For example, I teach advertising here. . . . In the mid-seventies I got interested in the freshman survival program, then . . . in 1983 I was asked to come on as associate director. I thought that was a wonderful opportunity, my dean sanctioned it, and I cut down to teaching half time. I did that for six years, [then] I felt it was time to come back to teaching, and that was another change. . . . Now I'm working with the provost here trying to push for a faculty development program. . . . So that's my latest thing.

He also reports a readiness for change in the love arena, though those changes are not as extensive as at work: "I enrolled in some acting courses about two and a half years ago, and I started performing. And I just keep looking for different kinds of things. I think the acting especially was sort of to fill some kind of loss that had happened in the marriage. So, for one reason or another, I welcome new kinds of things."

When Don began reflecting on change in his life, he spoke about not being content with the status quo. This "welcoming of new kinds of things" tends to mark the divergent pattern. In our next example, we will see this quality even more clearly.

The Human Resource Consultant. The third person who illustrates the divergent pattern is Ellen, a forty-six-year-old businesswoman who has established a successful management consulting practice in the Northwest. Her story is similar in many respects to Katherine's and Don's. Like them, she has experienced a high degree of change in her life. And she describes events in both work and love as occurring largely independent of one another. Her particular experience of these elements, however, advances our understanding of what these dimensions mean for those who have this pattern.

Ellen's experience of change is located in both arenas (see Figure 7.4). She began her work career as a public school teacher, moved into retail management in clothing and textiles, then entered the corporate world as a human resource manager. In 1985 she started her own consulting business and has maintained that while completing her master's degree. And she is planning to begin work on a doctorate within the next two years. Her first marriage, which took place right after she graduated from college, was problematic for many years and finally ended in 1979. For the next four years she was involved in an intense and satisfying relationship with a business associate, but when he made it clear that he would not commit, she ended the relationship. In 1985 she married for the second time, in her words, "for security and companionship."

When we asked Ellen if she thought her life had more than the usual degree of change, she responded spiritedly: "Right on! I've said many times, when I listen to other people, 'Did they give all the easy parts away?'" This shows that she perceives her life as not only subject to more change than most but also more difficult as a result. She went on to discuss her experiences of change, as well as her growing understanding of its impact on her life:

> I have always felt like I was fairly adaptable. I grew up moving all over the United States [because] my father worked for Exxon. . . . So I felt like I was a real flexible person just because of that. . . . When I was working on my master's . . . I did this study on change. At that time my whole focus was on organizational change. . . . I started doing a whole lot of research . . . and the more I read the more I was convinced that you really couldn't talk about

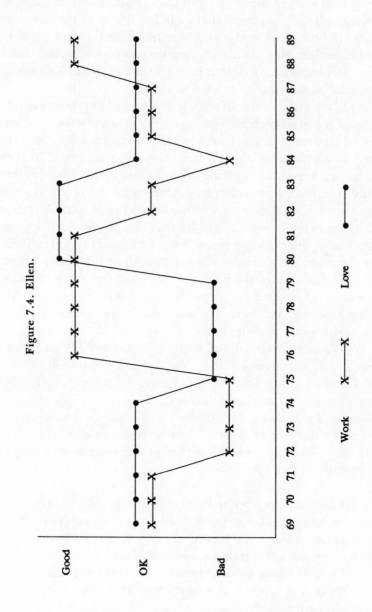

Figure 7.4. Ellen.

organizational change, you had to talk about individuals and how they deal with change. And as I began to delve into individual change, I found it to be an extremely emotional experience because I then looked at how I had dealt with change throughout my life. And I had found that it was sort of difficult for me, that I sort of went through it kicking and screaming! I was sort of dragged through it! . . . I spent a great deal of time searching for what I thought might be meaningful for me to do.

It is interesting that Ellen finds change difficult, especially when we note that she initiates most of the changes in her life. She says clearly that she sees herself as more proactive than reactive. Further, she is aware that these choices have both a benefit and an emotional price. What she calls "searching" is done in reference to an inner sense of what is best for her, and that sense itself is a dynamic reality, a quality we also saw in Katherine. When we asked what triggered most of her changes, her answer was unequivocal:

Pain. I have discovered that I didn't make major changes until the pain was extremely intense. When I got the divorce, it was three months of absolute hell. I had lost a job — I was laid off; my father died; my husband threatened to commit suicide and left; and I'm left with a mentally ill mother. I mean, the pain was incredible! It was those kinds of times that made me initiate the divorce. And then I look at the other changes in my life, like when I decided to end the relationship in 1983, I was in a whole lot of pain for probably close to a year. . . . I was beginning to realize that I really wanted something that he didn't want, there wasn't any parallel there, and he wasn't willing to address the issue. . . . So pain has always driven my change.

For Ellen none of these experiences are precipitous; instead they are marked by careful reflection and deliberate choice.

What we hear in her description of these events is a keen sensitivity and responsiveness to an inner voice telling her what is right for her at any particular time. She also adds another dimension to this process: She suggests that reflectivity is a factor that plays a role in fostering change in her life: "I think if I didn't wonder and think so much, and just accepted things as they rolled by, if I didn't challenge it around why, it would be easier. But I always want to explore it and to learn a lot more about it. . . . It would be so easy to walk away and to follow and to not rock the boat, and when you go in and ask questions of folks, things shift. But I just think that people who don't ask questions, either they ignore it and don't respond to their inner needs, or maybe they never have those questions, I don't know."

Ellen is aware that this reflective quality, focused as it is on her response to changing inner needs, makes her life less predictable and secure. She seems comfortable with this, however, as she shows when she reflects on her current marriage: "I'm looking at the relationship that I'm in real closely, and we're going to counseling every week and trying to work out some of the issues. Both of us know that it's important to work these issues out but if we don't that we certainly won't continue a relationship for years and years and be miserable." She contemplates what her choices might be if this marriage ends: "Would I ever get married again, or would I just continue to cycle in and out of relationships every five to seven years? Because, as a bright woman, where do you get your satisfaction? Do you get it with other bright women, or with men who are not threatened by bright women? I guess I'm looking at redefining what is a satisfactory interpersonal relationship. And I'm also looking very closely at my need for intimacy and what intimacy is and how I define it."

The questioning attitude that Ellen articulates so well is also seen in Katherine and, to a less extent, in Don. This quality may well be common to all those who have the divergent pattern, and it may account for the high degree of change here. Ellen suggests that this characteristic accounts for both the change itself and the person's acceptance of it. Although she describes change as difficult for her, she also cannot imagine herself as a person who does not think and question and therefore change. It seems fundamental to her personality.

When Ellen talks about work and love, she describes them as "more separate than blended." Their impact on one another is not causal, but she goes beyond the compensation that we saw in Don's experience. For her the impact is often facilitative. One example of that is when she changed jobs in 1976, a shift that increased the stress within her troubled marriage: "The work I was doing was in retail. It is something that I have always loved in terms of being very creative. . . . I put myself in that environment and somebody there believed in me, the store manager, and we increased sales 12 percent every year — we were extremely successful. And when my husband at that time saw that, he was extremely resentful about it, . . . he found it threatening. It really caused more and more of a rift between us." When we asked Ellen if this situation helped her make the decision to end the marriage, she replied: "I would say it was definitely the beginning of when I started to think about divorce as an option." Experiencing success and satisfaction in the work arena, therefore, not only intensified the problems in the marriage, it also helped her to assess the situation in a new way and to consider other options.

Work again facilitated her handling of difficulties in the love arena in 1979 when she got the divorce; it was also the year her father died. She credits her good work situation with enabling her to cope: "In 1979 when I got a divorce and when my dad died, those were both very stressful times personally. . . . I had a very stable work environment, and I think that's where I needed to be at that time. It was fairly structured, so I would say that because the personal relationship part of my life was so difficult, it was extremely beneficial for me to have a work environment that was predictable and secure." She goes on to say that her creative efforts in photography also flourished during this time, thanks to her stability at work. In addition, being in that satisfying job enabled her to risk establishing a new intimate relationship the following year.

It is interesting that Ellen, like Katherine, tends to find her stability or security in the work domain. When we asked her how she would explain this, she answered in terms of control: "I think that security or predictability in the work domain is more likely than in the love domain. I think maybe it is [because] I have some control over it, that I actually have some input, and I can push it one way or the other so that it works for me. . . . In personal relationships I feel less in control." Notice how closely Ellen parallels Katherine here. Both speak of control in describing the stability they find in work. Later in the interview we asked Ellen to define what she meant by stability, and the theme of control appears again: "I would define stability as a kind of balance in my life, where I felt comfortable and again felt in control. . . . It all has to go back to a feeling of being in control in that I have something satisfactory going in both sectors; I have some kind of personal satisfaction in a personal relationship and I have some kind of satisfaction in my work." Ellen could not name very many years when she achieved this balance, but it remains important to her.

In Ellen we see an example of someone with the divergent pattern who feels in charge of her life. In the next example, we will look at a kind of divergence in work and love that is not so voluntary, and we will consider whether the source of the divergence alters the experience of this pattern.

The Homemaker. In the other examples of the divergent pattern, work has been the dominant arena. In Nadine we meet someone for whom love has been the dominant life influence. Nadine, a New Englander, is fifty-seven years old, and she and her husband of thirty-five years have two adult children and one much-beloved grandchild. Like many women of her generation, Nadine has had to tailor her own career to her husband's. Whenever he took a new position it meant relocating the family to a new city; Nadine's work career, therefore, reflects these changes in her husband's career rather than changes she initiated. In that sense her love arena has been dominent. Her graph reflects these complex changes (see Figure 7.5).

Nadine discusses the stress that this arrangement entailed for herself and the family: "Some of the more drastic changes . . . are related to geographical moves, and when you have children

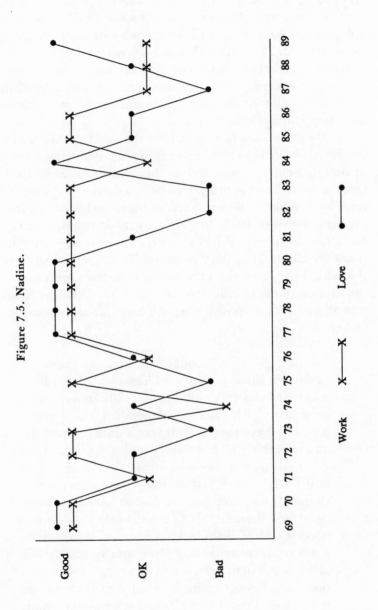

Figure 7.5. Nadine.

and you have a geographical move and if you are a woman of my age you know we always moved when our husbands got a different job someplace. It involves a lot of adjustment and a lot of stress and I would be leaving a good job I liked and there would be a period of adjustment. And my kids would go through making new friends and they are unhappy and everything is really traumatic for them, so that's kind of an unstable time, and then it usually lets up."

Nadine's work history follows the interrupted pattern she describes. While her chidren were growing up she taught in public and parochial schools. When the family moved in 1971 she spent a year doing volunteer work in addition to being a full-time homemaker, then entered graduate school, earning her master's degree in 1973. In 1976 they moved again and she got an administrative position at a nearby university, remaining there for eight years. Her responsibilities grew, and by 1983 she was director of the continuing education program. Her description of the decision to leave that job when her husband was offered another position reveals how important the job was to her:

> I think I gained self-confidence over the years, especially in Burlington when I had a job I really liked and that I did very well in and really moved up in very fast. I felt almost independent and I really hated to leave there. That was a time of great decision making in our family and it was a time of great stress, too — marital stress. So where before that I might have just willingly gone along with a change, I had a lot more soul-searching to do there because I thought, "Do I want to do this? Is this good for me?" But it was. Larry has never taken a job or never gone any place that we didn't talk about it at length before, and they were always joint decisions. I'm not saying he wanted to move on and it was a unilateral thing, because we always made joint decisions and I could see the reason for doing it, and then he made his decision.

We can hear in this passage the different role that work was beginning to play in Nadine's life. She was becoming more autonomous and more confident; her sense of identity was being altered by this positive work experience. Leaving it was costly, and she left with reluctance. In the new city she found another administrative position in education, then began work on her doctorate. That job ended in 1988 and, rather than searching for another job, she took on the full-time care of her grandson for a year, putting her graduate studies on hold.

The oscillations in Nadine's love arena reflect these times of relocation, as well as more particular family crises. The various low points represent adjustment problems that her children were experiencing, or episodic marital conflicts; 1982 and 1983 were particularly difficult years. From 1985 to 1987 Nadine and her husband were faced with the illness and death of her father and the illness of both her mother and her mother-in-law. This family stress was heightened in 1987 when their son became incapacitated and Nadine and her husband had to assume the care of their infant grandson. He has now been adopted by their daughter and her husband, so they no longer have that responsibility. However, Larry recently retired from his firm only to start a business venture of his own, and he expects Nadine's help in this. As was true earlier in her life, family needs have taken precedence over her own.

We asked Nadine what role work plays in her life. She answered by carefully defining work as more than career, and noted that she always derived satisfaction from it: "My career has been an important part of my life, but I never felt a void when I wasn't working in a job because I always had so many things that I wanted to fill that time with." When we asked if work gave her greater control in her life, however, she spoke specifically in terms of her career: "I think work allows you to know your own strengths and weaknesses a little better than other activities might allow you too. I think the economic factor is what gives you a sense of control, because I'm not going to be dependent on somebody else. . . . But I think success in work, aside from the economic aspect, makes you feel more independent because you feel you have more confidence in your own strengths; you become more aware of your own strengths, I believe. I think there are experiences that come up in work that would not come up otherwise that cause you to see certain strengths that you have that you wouldn't see otherwise."

When she discusses the interaction of work and love in her life, Nadine notes that stress in one arena can make functioning in the other domain harder, but she never indicates that that stress will bring the other domain down. She does speak of compensation in familiar terms: "There would have been times when I felt so down and so bad, and you tend to feel 'gosh, do I have any value?' in one area, yet in the other area you know that what you're doing is meaningful. I think it helps. I think that when you're having a bad time in either domain it would help to have success in the other."

Nadine chooses not to name either arena as primary; she values them equally. But she also seeks both kinds of satisfaction in her life: "I would hate to have a good love relationship with someone and not be involved in some kind of work that I felt was meaningful. . . . I would like to see the two in balance." This idea of balance as achieving satisfaction in both arenas is something we also encountered in the case of Ellen.

We were particularly interested in knowing how Nadine responded to change, since it appeared that most of the changes in her life were not self-initiated. However, she affirms the comfort with change that we have seen with others in this pattern: "The career moves, in some sort, were caused by my influence. . . . I always wanted to leave Pittsfield, so when the opportunity came to come to Manchester, I was hot to trot. So that was a positive change for me. . . . The changes have been brought on in a way by Larry's career moves, but I didn't feel that he was dragging me along, until we left Burlington, and he didn't drag me along, I don't mean that, but that was the only time I was reluctant to leave because I did have a responsible job [that] I felt a great deal of satisfaction in. . . . But change has been positive, I see most all of it as positive in my life. . . . I welcome change if I foresee that it's not going to be threatening to me; I'm somewhat of a risk taker."

In Nadine we see the basic themes of the divergent pattern reaffirmed in a somewhat different light: Work plays an important role in her life even though her career is interrupted by family concerns, and she welcomes change in spite of the fact that her control of change is limited. We turn now to our final example of this pattern to test these themes still further.

The Insurance Executive. Frank is fifty years old, married, and the father of a son and twin daughters. A former Air Force pilot, he worked for a time in the aerospace industry before entering the corporate world of insurance in 1971. He has changed jobs several times and is now with a firm in California. His graph shows fluctuations in both domains (see Figure 7.6).

The fluctuations in his work arena reflect the shifting circumstances that characterize the corporate world, and Frank speaks of this absence of control at what he calls the strategic level of his career: "Working in the corporate world, I'm subject to the whims of corporate executives and decision makers, and this doesn't necessarily have anything to do with what I am doing or how well I have done, or anything else. I can point out two very vivid examples of that. In 1970 I lost my job because the company was sold to another company. Just this past year . . . again, my job was eliminated and I spent eight months looking for a new job. And it was again because a decision was made at the chairman-of-the-board level to do some things differently. . . . So I have less control in the corporate world." Frank does have control over day-to-day operations at work, but he would like greater strategic control as well. To achieve that he enrolled in a doctoral program in 1989, and after he is finished he is planning to teach at the college level and do consulting. Formal education for him is a way of obtaining greater control in the work arena. Frank demonstrates a need for control in the work domain similar to that expressed by Katherine and Ellen.

Frank has experienced even greater fluctuations in the love arena, due to varius illnesses and deaths in the family as well as to happy family events like the graduation of his children. The period from 1978 to 1982 was particularly tumultuous: His

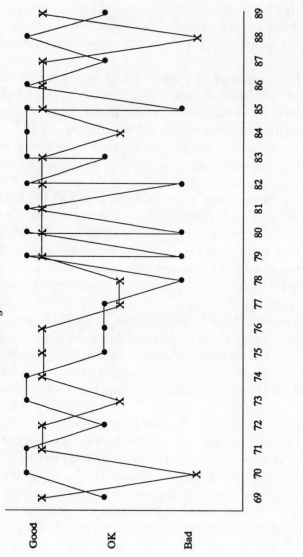

Figure 7.6. Frank.

stepfather, mother, grandmother, and mother-in-law died in those years, and Frank had to assume major responsibilities for his extended family. He also turned forty during this time and experienced a midlife crisis, which he responded to in part by having a brief affair: "There were so many things going on . . . and everything depended on me. . . . My going out and having an affair, that was kind of an escape valve that I had to use to get out from under some of the obligations. I don't want to rationalize but I think that's what it was about." Also during that time Frank's community involvement significantly increased, and he even ran for local political office. As things in the love arena stabilized, these community activities became a regular part of his life; his children are involved in them as well, though his wife seldom shares these interests.

When we asked Frank what impact the two domains have on one another, he said that he keeps work and love separate, a tendency he attributes to his personality. He noted that he might compensate for frustrations in one domain, work, for example, by giving more attention to his family, but one never affected the other: "I didn't let the bad at work spill over and spoil the good things going on at home." When asked if one domain was primary, he made some clear distinctions: "I'd say that work is achievement oriented . . . and feeling good and happiness is in the love domain. Work doesn't make me happy, it makes me satisfied in my achievements. But the love side, that makes me happy. I think those are two distinct characteristics."

Because of his location in the corporate world, Frank's opportunities for initiating changes are limited, just as Nadine's were. Yet he too expresses a basic comfort with change: "I would say that there has been a lot [of change in my life], and that in past years I had less deliberate control of that than I have in more recent years. . . . I'm comfortable with it. That's where my professional life is, in managing change. . . . I can't do anything that is repetitive." Frank goes on to say that when he first learned in his doctoral program about perspective transformation theory, which describes how major changes occur in adulthood, "it was like I was hearing all the thoughts I'd been having finally being put into a theoretical setting." Like the others we have seen in this pattern, Frank shows an affinity for change that seems to be part of his personality.

The way Frank lives out the divergent pattern is congruent with all we know so far about this pattern. The additional insight he gives us relates to the strategies of augmenting control in the work domain, particularly through the use of formal education. We turn now to an overview of the defining characteristics of this pattern of work and love.

Themes Revealed by the Divergent Pattern

When we consider these five examples of the divergent pattern together, there are several common strains or themes that emerge. Perhaps the dominant issue is the high degree of change that occurs in this pattern. Then there is the largely independent movement of the work and love arenas in relation to each other. And finally, this pattern reveals an interesting emphasis on work that is unlike what we found in either of the other patterns. We will consider each of these points in turn.

The Importance of Change. If the divergent pattern can be said to be characterized by anything, it would be change. Work and love seldom stabilize for more than short periods of time. In listening to people with this pattern talk about their lives, we detect a restless questioning, searching, and exploring. This is not an oppositional or conflicted drive; it comes across as positive — as a dynamic that is directed toward enhancing life. And this seems not so much a choice of behaviors as it is a feature of their character. Remember how some describe themselves: Don speaks of not being content to just go on doing the same things, Katherine expresses a need for challenge and intellectual stimulation, and Ellen talks about what it is like to always question things and avoid complacency. Even Frank and Nadine, who have less control over the changes in their lives, mention a basic comfort with change. These people experience a high degree of change in their lives not by chance but by design — the design imposed by their personalities.

There is a further dimension to this factor of change.

Simply saying that it is a function of personality might imply that the changes themselves are accomplished with ease, yet ease is not what we see in our interviews. All of these people struggle with the changes in their lives. Ellen, for example, talks about taking several years to come to the decision to end her first marriage, and she is the one who asked the rhetorical but telling question, "Did they give all the easy parts away?", when discussing the difficult changes in her life. Furthermore, she credits pain with being the greatest facilitator of change. Katherine likewise demonstrates the costs involved with each twist and turn of her life. And Nadine speaks dramatically of the strain of involuntary change, particularly when she had to leave her position as director of continuing education to allow her husband to accept his newest job offer. Though change does not come easy for people who conform to the divergent pattern, they are willing to pay this price because of the benefits these changes bring.

The chief benefit appears to be the enhancement of personal growth. Each person speaks in these terms, though in somewhat different ways. Katherine phrases this in terms of intellectual development, something that for her is coupled with identity formation. Ellen speaks of a sense of needing to grow when she faces a turning point in her life. Nadine discusses her experiences, particularly those she labels as crises, as enhancing her sense of self. And Don reflects on his marital problems as an opportunity to understand himself better. Personal growth, then, is a common theme throughout their discussion of change.

The Independence of the Work and Love Arenas. The second major characteristic of the divergent pattern is the largely independent movement of the work and love domains. Yet it is not sufficient to liken them to two dancers sharing a single dance floor; our interviews do not support the conclusion that there is no relationship between them at all. It is true that there is no causal relationship here: When work or love fluctuates, it rarely affects the other arena. However, we have identified a compensatory relationship in this pattern; that is, events in one arena often compensate for events in the other. Don illustrates this best when he mentions taking advantage of opportunities to excel professionally during times of personal crisis — a combination that he calls "putting a Band-Aid on the other part of your life." Nadine and Frank also talk about this. And, though they do not speak specifically of compensation, both Katherine and Ellen describe the personal satisfaction they derive from their work, something that is highlighted when the love arena is less fulfilling.

In a sense, what is happening in one arena makes it possible to cope with the other. Katherine is the most articulate about this when she describes how satisfaction in her professional life enables her to deal with personal crises or the ongoing "averageness" of her marriage. Ellen has had a similar experience, but she says that the satisfaction of work enabled her to make the tough decision to divorce her first husband. Whether it is to maintain or to change the direction of the second arena, satisfaction in the first arena often makes that action possible in this pattern.

The Centrality of Work. The third significant theme that emerged in the divergent pattern was the emphasis placed on work. While work appears as primary in examples of the other two patterns, people whose lives reflect this pattern talk about work in certain consistent ways. Interestingly, they all tend to locate their identity and to develop personal autonomy in this arena. Perhaps Nadine is the best example, since for her love prevailed over her career choices; yet even for her, identity seems to be forged most strikingly in her work experiences. It was, after all, her extended experience as an educational administrator that enabled her to even question whether she should continue to give precedence to her husband's career. Work, then, is the domain where more personal growth appears to be located in this pattern.

There is one other aspect of the emphasis on work that is striking in the divergent pattern. Several of those we interviewed spoke of control in describing this domain, and linked that control to the achievement of a kind of stability. Katherine and Ellen almost echo one another in this respect. Katherine names work as the one area she feels in control of, and it is work that makes her feel stable. Ellen likewise feels more in control of work, and she goes on to define stability itself as involving control. And Don is changing his career in order to augment his personal control in the work arena. While less explicit, the other interviews also support this reading, making the work arena especially powerful in this pattern.

The relationship between work and love assumes distinctive parameters in the divergent pattern, just as it did for the parallel and steady/fluctuating patterns. Now that we have outlined the three alternatives separately, we will summarize our findings by contrasting the three patterns and then relating these findings to what we know about adult development.

CHAPTER EIGHT

Comparing the Patterns

So far we have examined each of the three patterns of work and love in depth, giving us a sense of their particular characteristics and unique features. It is as though we have taken a microscope to the patterns, using our interview data to look beneath the vectors themselves to discern their underlying meaning. We would now like to broaden our perspective in several ways. First, we will look at the patterns within the context of our total sample. For that picture we have available to us figures on the distribution of the patterns across the 405 people we studied; we also know how the patterns were distributed by gender and by life stage. Second, we will present what we learned about the interaction of work and love from a comparative analysis of the three patterns. The final section of the chapter explores the notion of continuity and change in adult life and how the three patterns reflect both of these constructs. The findings from the total sample analysis and from the cross-pattern analysis will be situated within the context of what we already know about work and love in adulthood. By bringing in previous research and writing, we will be able to see what ideas our study has confirmed as well as what new insights we have gained about the interaction, meaning, and value of work and love in adulthood.

Patterns of Work and Love in Our Study

As we have already explained, three patterns of work and love were derived from an analysis of the 405 "Work, Love, and

Learning in Adulthood" questionnaires we received. In the parallel pattern, work and love largely move in tandem; change in one arena is followed by a similar change in the other. In the steady/fluctuating pattern, one arena remains steady throughout, almost always rated as good, while the other fluctuates freely. And in the divergent pattern, both arenas change but do so independent of and in apparent opposition to each other.

The three patterns were distributed somewhat evenly across the respondents in our study. One hundred fifty-eight (39 percent) exhibited a parallel pattern; 107 (26 percent) had a steady/fluctuating pattern; and 140 (35 percent) were classified as divergent. It is important to keep in mind that all of our findings are based on a limited sample of respondents who are well educated, mostly white, and heavily female. While it is reasonable to assume that these three patterns would be present in a more economically and/or culturally diverse sample, the distribution of the patterns and the factors that shape the interaction of work and love might be quite different.

Once we had identified the three patterns, we were particularly curious as to whether there were gender differences in their distribution. As Table 8.1 shows, there are only small differences in the distribution of the patterns by gender. That is, 44.6 percent of the men and 36.9 percent of the women had parallel patterns, 25 percent of the men and 27 percent of the women had steady/fluctuating patterns, and 30.4 percent of the men and 36.2 percent of the women had divergent patterns. These

Table 8.1. Work and Love Patterns for Men and Women.

Pattern Type	Men		Women		Total	
	No.	%	No.	%	No.	%
Parallel	50	44.6	108	36.9	158	39
Steady/ Fluctuating	28	25	79	27	107	26
Divergent	34	30.4	106	36.2	140	35
	—		—		—	
Total	112		293		405	

Note: Percentages may not add up to 100 due to rounding off.

differences are statistically nonsignificant, that is, they probably occurred by chance. Women and men were equally likely
to exhibit any one of the three patterns.

We were somewhat surprised by this finding. We expected
to see a significantly higher proportion of parallel patterns among
women, wherein both arenas are valued equally and where love
affects work as much as work affects love. Gilligan (1982) and
others have discovered that women define themselves in terms
of relationships that "spill over" onto work. Josselson (1990),
for example, found that "women do not leave their relating selves
behind when they go to work" (p. 183) and that women do "not
make a clear separation between relating and work" (p. 184).
By the same token we expected men to exhibit the steady/fluc-
tuating pattern, in which a stable marriage-and-family situation would allow for development (hence fluctuation) in the
career area. Interestingly, although the differences are not statistically significant, we see a trend in reverse — a greater percentage of women had a steady/fluctuating pattern, and a greater
percentage of men had a parallel pattern. Perhaps our expectations reflected cultural stereotyping of women being more love
oriented and men being more work oriented. This finding might
also be attributed to our sample population. That is, the women
in our study are highly educated and career oriented. It would
be interesting to see if there were any differences in a more
diverse sample. It might be recalled, however, that studies of
work and love involving *both* men and women have found few
differences. Hinand's (1984) study of the work and love patterns
of 100 men and women between the ages of forty-five and fifty-
five, for example, found the development of both arenas important for the psychological well-being of both men and women.
(See Chapter Two for more discussion of this point.)

We also wanted to know if there was a relationship between pattern and age. To determine this, we divided our sample
into three life stages: young adult (twenty to thirty), the thirties (thirty-one to forty), and midlife (forty-one to sixty-two).
We discovered that the parallel pattern was more prevalent
among our young adults than either of the other two patterns,
the divergent pattern characterized the thirties, and the steady/

fluctuating pattern was disproportionately represented in our midlife group. Table 8.2. shows, for example, that 31 percent of the ninety-five young adults had a parallel pattern versus 18 percent steady/fluctuating and 19 percent divergent; likewise, 47 percent of the thirties respondents had divergent patterns, and 44 percent of midlife adults had steady/fluctuating patterns. In this analysis, a chi-square statistic of 11.37 was significant at the .02 level. (This means that the distribution of patterns is probably due to something other than chance, such as one pattern being more characteristic of a particular stage in life than another pattern.)

This finding is most likely due to what is called a *cohort effect.* A cohort is a group of people born about the same time who thus have somewhat similar experiences. Today's emphasis on attending to career as well as personal life for *both* men and women may explain why more of the young adults exhibited a parallel pattern. Likewise, the prevalence of more divergent patterns for the thirties cohort may reflect the pace of change, fluctuations in social norms, and so on that people in their thirties have acutely experienced. Finally, the older adults in our sample may have sought and may value security and stability in the face of accelerating social change, thus explaining the prevalence of more steady/fluctuating patterns for this group.

Findings from a Comparison of the Patterns

Analysis of the quantitative data in our study gave us the distribution of each pattern with respect to gender and life stage. But it was the qualitative portion of the study — the interviews and the open-ended comments on the questionnaires — that helped us understand the particular characteristics of the patterns themselves. Chapters Five to Seven have described each pattern in detail. Let us briefly summarize the features that distinguish each pattern before we present the findings from a comparative analysis of all three.

In the parallel pattern we found a general sense of congruence between work and love; events in one appear to shape the other. These people tend to be equally sensitive and attentive

Table 8.2. Pattern by Life Stage.

Life Stage	Pattern		
	Parallel	Steady/Fluctuating	Divergent
Young Adult 20–30 n = 95	31%	18%	19%
Thirties 31–40 n = 167	38%	38%	47%
Midlife 41–62 n = 143	31%	44%	34%
Total	100%	100%	100%

to both arenas in their lives, and they usually place equal weight on work and love. The tandem movement of the arenas seems to be a function of this approach to life, seen most clearly in those who speak of a conscious effort to balance work and love. For others, a conceptual fusion of work and love accounts for the tandem movement. Less often, it is the dominance of one domain over the taken-for-granted secondary domain that creates the parallel pattern. Overall there is a sense of stability in this pattern, and less evidence of a need for change or challenge.

In the steady/fluctuating pattern, the striking feature is the steady arena. In our study, this was almost always rated good, and it was usually work rather than love. This steady arena functions as a source of security and as the locus of personal identity. It remains steady even when the fluctuating arena experiences dip, and these dips, rather than creating stress, seem to reinforce the stabilizing character of the steady arena. Either domain can be primary and both are conceptually distinct; there is no fusion between the two. Most significant is the different way our respondents evaluate the two domains. The fluctuating domain reflects shifting external factors. While a lot is going on externally in the steady domain, people evaluate it according to an internal sense of the benefit it provides, and that benefit remains constant. It seems to be this differential evaluation that gives rise to the steady/fluctuating pattern.

The divergent pattern is characterized by a high degree of change in both arenas. Much of that change is self-initiated. Furthermore, there is a strong affinity with change in the personalities of these people; by nature they are not content with the status quo. They appear to be characterized by a questioning attitude and a need for challenge. While change does not necessarily come easily, they do find it beneficial, particularly in terms of personal growth. The arenas move independent of one another in this pattern; for the most part shifts in one do not create shifts in the other. But one domain can compensate for the other, as well as provide the psychological resources to cope with stress in the other domain. Finally, work seems to play a predominant role in this pattern, and it is frequently linked with the need to be in control.

In comparing each pattern with the other two, we discovered differences in three areas: domain emphasis, the stabilizing factor, and modes of interaction. Domain emphasis refers to which domain, work or love, is considered primary in the lives of people exhibiting each of the patterns. There is also a source of stability in each of the patterns, which facilitates achieving a sense of balance or harmony. Finally, our respondents described the interaction of the two arenas differently depending on pattern type. Following is a discussion of each of these dimensions presented within the context of what is already known about the relationship of work and love in adult life.

Domain Emphasis. Nearly everyone we interviewed kept work and love conceptually distinct. The only exception we found occurred in some people with the parallel pattern who fused the two domains; that is, they saw their lives as unified and viewed the work/love distinction as a false dichotomy. Except for these few within the parallel pattern, the finding that people think of the arenas as separate seems to contradict Smelser's claim that on a personal level, "the two orientations are often so inextricably meshed that it becomes difficult to distinguish between them. For example, one can love one's work, and one can—indeed, is well-advised to—work at love. What we call 'work' invariably has some kind of expressive dimension and what we call 'love' is never without an instrumental component" (1980b, pp. 105–106). Erlich and Blatt, who conceive of love and work as being and doing, echo Smelser in stating that "at certain points in the course of normal development a synthesis takes place of the two" (1985, p. 69). Furthermore, "the one and same event, act, or situation contains the seeds of both dimensions" (p. 72) and "anything that contributes to the splitting of the two modes from one another, in real life as much as in the treatment situation, is . . . bound to have detrimental connotations and outcomes" (p. 75).

While most of our interviewees thought of the two arenas as separate entities, there were differences by pattern in domain emphasis—that is, in the emphasis placed on work and love. In the parallel pattern, most valued the domains equally, unable to identity either one as primary. Only a few respondents declared one domain primary, and in those cases that dominant domain appeared to "carry" the other in its wake, thereby creating the parallel pattern. In the steady/fluctuating pattern one domain was usually named as primary, but there was no consistency as to which domain (work or love) or which vector (steady or fluctuating) was identified as such. Matt, for example, stated that his steady arena (love) was of primary importance, while for Norman love was the fluctuating as well as the primary domain (see Chapter Six for a fuller discussion). In the divergent pattern work was designated as the primary arena, as in the case of Katherine, who said that "for the most part, probably the thing that has taken larger precedence in my life is the professional life, and I think that's because it's the one area that I feel I'm in control of." These findings are consistent with those from Lancereau's in-depth investigation of love and work patterns of young married professional women. She found that one arena predominates in the way in which women view and organize their experiences. "Some people," she writes, "turn their work into a loving experience while others turn their love into a working experience" (1987, p. 204).

In the steady/fluctuating and divergent patterns where one arena was named as primary over the other, there were again no gender differences in our results. That is, men were as likely to name love the dominant arena as women were to name work. This is consistent with our findings regarding the lack of gender differences in the distribution of the patterns overall (see above).

The Stabilizing Factor. The second major dimension of comparison uncovered in our analysis is what we labeled the *stabilizing factor.* By this we mean that each pattern had a locus of stability that allowed our respondents to feel a sense of organization and control in their lives. This stabilizing factor provides clues to the personalities of those in each of the patterns. Those with parallel patterns derive stability from a sense of harmony and interdependence of the two domains moving in tandem with each other. The rhythm of the pattern itself feels stable. Those with the parallel pattern appear to be less prone to initiate change, more content with things as they are; for them, stability is defined as maintaining continuity in their lives.

Those with the steady/fluctuating pattern obtain stability in a manner that is similar to and yet different from those with the parallel pattern. What is sustained here are not external events; things can in fact change a great deal. The constant factor is the internal benefit derived from the steady arena; this is what serves as the stabilizing force in their lives.

The source of stability for those with divergent patterns differs yet again. For them, change means growth and development; it presents a challenge rather than a threat, and they usually seek it out. Stability, rather than being the absence of change, is linked to control. This in turn is located in work. Stability is something these people create for themselves apart from the variability of external events. Rohrlich's definition of work as "the skillful organization, manipulation, and *control* of the external and internal environments, to achieve a desired goal most efficiently and effectively" (1980, p. 38; emphasis added) speaks to the notion of linking work with control and thus stability. In a pattern where there is so much change, work provides a means of control: "Work is the most visibly defined and bounded arena of our lives. Work goals establish a structure for our experience. Once a goal is conceptualized, and the efficient, linear realization of that goal is our desire, we are within a structure. We have a specific direction. We apply defined skills, established methods, techniques, and procedures to reach our goal. Time provides precise boundaries to our work activity. There are schedules and deadlines which harness and outline our endeavor" (Rohrlich, 1980, p. 52). Interestingly, in her investigation of the development of love and work in career women, Farone (1981) found that a sense of self in work was a stabilizing factor as they worked on problems with heterosexual concerns.

While the literature, including previous research on work and love, rarely speaks to sources of stability per se, it does have quite a bit to say about the notion of balance. To us, these concepts of stability and balance seem closely linked. The stabilizing factor in each pattern allows one to cope with both domains and to strive for a sense of balance and harmony. Adapting to and adjusting to changes in each domain would certainly seem an easier task when one feels in control overall. In fact, it might be recalled that Freud's dictum that forms the basis of this and other research states that a healthy, mature adult is one with the capacity to work *and* to love, not just to work *or* to love. Rohrlich addresses the importance of dealing with both arenas in our lives:

> The poet Robert Browning said, "Take away love and our earth is a tomb." One hundred years or so later, Albert Camus formulated an equally indisputable truth: "Without work all life goes rotten. But when work is soulless, life stifles and dies." There is no question that the vitality of our lives is a function of our capacities to work and to love. Without satisfying work and pleasurable love, life does become a kind of death. . . . The quality of our existence depends on the quality of our work and our love.
>
> But, as Santayana pointed out, "Life is not a spectacle or a feast; it is a predicament." The "predicament" has to do not only with fulfilling ourselves in work and in love, but with resolving the inevitable conflict between them. . . .

The challenge to develop, balance, and harmonize working and loving is with us every day, regardless of the presence or absence of a job or a loved one" [1980, pp. 231–232].

Ignoring one domain at the expense of the other results in "lopsided" development, a fact confirmed in Baruch, Barnett, and Rivers's study of women's emotional and mental well-being. They write that one "who shuts off the emotional side of . . . life and throws [oneself] entirely into activity becomes the workaholic. But we hear less about the other side of that coin" — the person "who only pays attention to the feeling side of . . . life, and who becomes what might be called a 'lovaholic.' The workaholic can wind up overworked, exhausted, and emotionally sterile. The lovaholic risks feelings of worthlessness, dependency, and depression (1983, p. 15). Other studies have found balance related to adjustment and good mental health. Lancereau also speaks of the tension between the need for dependence usually found in relationships, and independence usually achieved through work. She feels there is no permanent resolution to this tension, "no true homeostasis, only a tentative balance" (1987, p. 195). Both Farone's (1981) and Dimidjian's (1982) studies on women's development suggest that women attend to both work and love, sometimes alternately, in an attempt to achieve balance in their lives. Lancereau speaks to this notion of alternation or oscillation: "The individual may attend to one need up to a point of satisfaction or saturation and then gravitate in the direction of the other need" (1987, p. 195). This seems particularly descriptive of our divergent pattern. However, all of our interviewees spoke of dealing with both arenas in various ways, and they emphasized the importance of a source of stability from which they were able to draw energy in coping, adjusting, and balancing the two.

Modes of Interaction. The third dimension of comparison evolved around the modes of interaction between work and love. This was of particular interest to us given the paucity of research focusing on interaction itself. What literature there is presents varying viewpoints on the nature of the interaction.

Mortimer, Lorence, and Kumka ask the basic question related to interaction: "To what extent is an individual's position and functioning in each sphere dependent on what is happening in the other?" (1986, p. 21). They present three models of interaction used to characterize linkages between work and family life. In the *segmentation* model "there is little or no connection; persons adjust their attitudes and behaviors according to immediate situational demands. There is little carryover — participation in each sphere is quite distinct" (p. 21). Nieva and Gutek, for example, observe that in the face of "role overload" and its resulting stress, some women choose "to clearly compartmentalize roles with an effort toward not letting one role interfere with another" (1981, p. 49). A second model is *compensatory* in nature, that is, "work and family spheres are linked by processes of compensation — workers seek satisfaction or activities in one area that are lacking in the other" (p. 21). The third model, and the one that Mortimer, Lorence, and Kumka (1986) subscribe to, is the *generalization* model. Here "attitudes formed in the work setting spill over or generalize to affect the most basic orientations toward self, others, and children; overarching values; intellectual flexibility; and other psychological attributes" (Nieva and Gutek, 1981, p. 21). Numerous other researchers speak not only of the spillover of work onto family, but also of overlap in reverse — that is, of family onto work (Lancereau, 1987; Josselson, 1990; Vaillant, 1977; Nieva and Gutek, 1981). While there is no consensus about these models of the work/love interaction, there is some support for each in current research.

We found some support for all three models in analyzing the modes of interaction in our patterns. The parallel pattern revealed considerable overlap or spillover, which is akin to Mortimer, Lorence, and Kumka's (1986) notion of generalization. Events in one arena directly affected the other, for good or ill. A drop in one arena led to or was reflected by a drop in the other, with the same being true when one domain ascended. Ann illustrated spillover best, both in terms of its benefits and its costs. Working on her doctorate while teaching full time created so much stress within her family that she withdrew from graduate school. Earlier, however, the sense of accomplishment she experienced when she entered teaching had a positive impact on her relationship with her family. Fluctuations in her domains reflected these experiences of spillover.

In the steady/fluctuating pattern we found a mode of interaction unique to this pattern. In this case, when events in the variable, fluctuating domain worsen, the stable character of the steady domain is reinforced rather than being placed under stress. Matt expressed it best when commenting on the experience of losing his job: "The bad in my life didn't bring the family down. In fact, I would say here that that's the first time in my life that I could probably without any reservation say my wife would stick by me through anything." Rather than bringing his love arena down, stress at work served to reaffirm the steadiness of the love domain in his life.

Finally, in the divergent pattern we see evidence of segmentation and compensation. In a divergent, segmented mode of interaction there is no relationship between the arenas; they exist totally separate from and independent of each other. What happens in one domain has no impact on the other, of either a beneficial or harmful nature. We heard this only rarely, and then solely in the divergent pattern. Don was probably the best example of this because he noted the least impact of work and love on each other in his life. He spoke, for example, of the time when he and his wife began their separation, an experience he rated as bad. But things at work were good because he was in a new division and getting to travel more. He saw no relationship between the two.

Compensation, however, was often expressed by those having a divergent pattern and occasionally by those with the two other patterns. Here satisfaction in one arena compensates for stress in the other, and the person is conscious of this process and often capitalizes on it. Ellen mentioned this several times but most dramatically regarding the year she got her divorce and her father died. Work assumed greater importance for her then: "Because the personal relationship part of my life was so difficult, it was extremely beneficial for me to have a work environment that was predictable and secure." Compensation enables the person to cope more effectively with the domain under stress, even to the extent of making decisions to resolve the stressful situation itself. Katherine provided an excellent example of this when she talked about the importance of work in her life: "When my life was professionally stable, I could cope with almost any kind of personal crisis or dilemma or the averageness of my marriage."

Table 8.3 offers a summary of the points of comparison across the three patterns. The work and love arenas are valued equally in the parallel pattern, one arena is named primary in the steady/fluctuating pattern, and the work arena seems to be emphasized in the divergent pattern. The stabilizing factor in the parallel pattern is defined as work and love being maintained together over time; in the steady/fluctuating pattern it is the sustained internal benefit of the steady arena; for the divergent pattern stability is found in control through work. For the modes of interaction, overlap or spillover characterizes the parallel pattern, reinforcement the steady/fluctuating pattern, and segmentation or compensation the divergent pattern. These qualities define the unique character of each of the patterns and distinguish them from each other in meaningful ways. The insights gained from this cross-pattern analysis give us a much fuller understanding of the relationship between work and love in adults' lives.

Stability and Change in Adult Life

In comparing the three patterns we were able to identify a source of stability for each and ways in which the work and love arenas interact. In doing this analysis we were struck by how much the notions of stability and change permeated our findings. Development in adulthood can in fact be understood as the interaction of change and stability over time. With regard to personality, for example, researchers have been interested in the extent to which people change over time. How is it that people change, yet seem to be the same person as they age? Focusing on the life course itself, investigators have tried to determine how predictable adult lives are, how much change can be expected, and if there is a rhythm to the periods of change

Table 8.3. Results of the Cross-Pattern Comparison.

Dimension of Comparison	Pattern Type		
	Parallel	Steady/Fluctuating	Divergent
Domain emphasis	Equal	Work or love	Work
Stabilizing factor	Sustained rhythm	Steady domain	Control in work
Modes of interaction	Overlap or spillover	Reinforcement of steady domain	Segmentation or compensation

and stability. We will examine our data in relation to change and stability for both personality and the life course.

Our results demonstrate a significant amount of stability with regard to the three work and love patterns. The patterns that we uncovered — parallel, steady/fluctuating, divergent — remain stable over time. By analyzing the instruments of adults in our sample who were old enough to have graphed a twenty-year period (that is, at least thirty-eight years old), we were able to assess the stability of each of the patterns. With very few exceptions, the overall pattern, whether it was parallel, steady/fluctuating, or divergent, turned out to be characteristic of the individual as a young adult, a midlife adult, and an older adult. An occasional graph revealed a "false start" in the first years of adulthood. That is, a steady/fluctuating graph may have started out divergent; a divergent pattern may have begun as parallel. However, there is an overall consistency in the patterns — a fact reinforced by the ease with which three investigators were able to classify the graphs (see Chapter Four for a fuller discussion of this procedure).

That the adults in our study exhibited stable patterns of work-and-love interaction may indicate that the patterns are related to personality types. It could be speculated, for example, that "divergent" pattern types thrive on change and activity and are perhaps more crisis oriented than steady/fluctuating persons. Likewise, those with parallel patterns appear to seek equilibrium by attending equally to work and love concerns. If in fact these patterns are reflecting personality types, their stability is not surprising. Research with thousands of adults points to the basic stability of personality (McCrae and Costa, 1990; Costa and McCrae, 1988). Typically this conclusion is drawn after scores on various personality measures (such as extroversion, traits related to self-concept, self-image, and so on) are obtained from the same people over time. Block (1981), for example, collected extensive data on several hundred Berkeley and Oakland residents, first when they were in junior high, then in their late teens, mid thirties, and mid forties. He found a high level of consistency on all measures from the earliest to the final assessment. Costa and McCrae recommend that "instead of looking for the mechanisms by which personality changes with age, we should look for the means by which stability is maintained. Are traits genetically determined, and therefore as stable as genetic influences? Do individuals choose or create environments that sustain the behavior that characterizes them? Are we locked into our nature by the network of social expectations around us?" (1980, p. 81). Others express a need to study both stability and change, for "it must be recognized that each of us reflects, over time, both stability and change. . . . Now that researchers have established beyond reasonable doubt that there is often considerable stability in adult personality, they may be able to move on to a clearer understanding of how we can grow and change, even as we remain the same people we always were" (Rubin, 1981, p. 27).

   We can also look at the patterns from the perspective of the life course. By life course we mean the ebb and flow of our lives as we move from childhood to young adulthood to middle age to old age. Kimmel speaks of this flow in terms of times when our lives are in and out of sync: "Continuity is only a period when the various aspects of one's life are synchronized; discontinuity, or change, is much more frequent since all dimensions of one's life are seldom in total harmony" (1990, p. 408). Research by Levinson and others (1978) found that there was a basic structure, an internal "scaffolding," to men's lives, and that these lives were characterized by alternating periods of structure building and structure changing. A stable or structure-building period was found to last "six or seven years, ten at most" while a transition or structure-changing period was found to last "four to five years" (p. 49). They described transition periods as "a bridge, or a boundary zone, between two states of greater stability" (p. 50). While we could chart alternating periods of change and stability in each of our patterns, we did not find any consistency in the length of either change or stable periods as suggested by Levinson and others. Nor did we see a greater frequency of change over stability (except in the divergent pattern) as suggested by Kimmel.

Our findings with regard to change and stability in the life course are more consistent with what Atchley calls the *continuity theory* of aging. This theory asserts that there is a basic structure to our lives "which persists over time. . . . The basic structure is coherent: It has an orderly or logical relation of parts that is recognizably unique and that allows us to differentiate that structure from others" (1989, p. 183). The three patterns represent three basic structures of work/love interaction. But within each of these patterns no two graphs were exactly alike; each person's graph was unique. These findings mirror much of the research in adult development and aging, where the goal is to uncover what people have in common as they age without obscuring the uniqueness of each individual.

According to Atchley, there are internal and external dimensions to this continuity. "Internal continuity is defined by the individual in relation to a remembered inner structure, such as the persistence of a psychic structure of ideas, temperament, affect, experiences, preferences, dispositions, and skills" (p. 184). External continuity has to do more with the "structure of physical and social environments, role relationships, and activities" (p. 185). All three of the patterns in our study demonstrated both types of continuity, but how this was done varied by pattern. Those with parallel patterns maintained continuity by keeping both internal and external sources of change at a minimum. Steady/fluctuating pattern types seemed to have a strong sense of internal continuity by holding the steady arena constant. Those with the divergent pattern were consistent in being open to change within themselves and in relation to their environment.

Atchley makes the point that continuity is not the opposite of change. Continuity in fact "allows for a variety of changes
to occur within the context provided by the basic structure" (p.
183), and "even substantial changes can occur in life without
causing serious disruption in the stable directional context within
which life's various episodes are played" (p. 184). He compares
continuity theory to a drama in which—though there is "an ebb
and flow to the drama of everyday life—there is also substantial continuity of both character and plot" (p. 184).

The metaphor of a drama in which there is continuity
of both character and plot is a good vehicle for summarizing
our findings with regard to stability and change. It would seem
that the patterns might represent personality or character types
while at the same time exhibiting an ebb and flow or "plot" of
the life course in adulthood. The rhythm and sources of stability and change vary from pattern to pattern. For example, accelerated change is evident in the divergent pattern, whereas
we can detect an effort to keep change at a minimum in the parallel pattern. Stability in the divergent pattern involves having
control in the work arena, but in the steady/fluctuating pattern
it is located in the steady domain (either work or love). What
is striking is that all three patterns of work/love interaction accommodate periods of change and stability while retaining the
essential structure of the pattern.

Summary

This chapter has sought to expand our understanding of
the interaction of work and love in adult life. From the close
analyses of the three patterns presented in Chapters Five to
Seven, we changed to a wider perspective to look at our findings
in relation to the total sample and to the literature in adult development. We found the three patterns to be fairly evenly distributed overall, and also among the men and women in the
study. This lack of gender differences was a surprise, but it is
not inconsistent with much of the recent research on the topic
that is reviewed in Chapter Two. We did find differences by
age group, and this we explained as a cohort effect.

A cross-pattern analysis revealed three dimensions of comparison: domain emphasis, the stability factor, and modes of interaction. Depending on the pattern, domain emphasis varied from equal emphasis, to either work or love being valued, to work being identified as the key domain. There is also a stability factor in each of the patterns, which facilitates achieving a sense of balance. Finally, the interaction of the work and love arenas was described differently by our respondents, depending on their pattern type. We compared these findings with what was known previously about the relationship between work and love. We found some findings to be congruent with earlier work, while other findings have enlarged our understanding of work and love in adult life.

Since an underlying theme in our cross-case analysis seemed to be the twin factors of stability and change, in the final section of the chapter we looked more closely at the presence of these in the three patterns. Continuity could be seen in the stability of the patterns for individuals over time. That is, a person whose work and love domains move in concert with each other (parallel) maintained this pattern over at least the twenty-year period represented by the graph; the same was true of those with steady/fluctuating or divergent patterns. At the same time, there are periods of change within each of the patterns. We suggested that our findings are congruent with the research on personality and life course. All three patterns of work/love interaction display periods of change and stability, yet each pattern retains its essential structure.

CHAPTER NINE

Intrinsic Connections:
The Patterns and Learning

When Freud spoke of maturity as the capacity to work and to love, he obviously understood this as an ongoing process rather than an end state. We believe that learning is central to this process, that it is through learning that we develop the capacity to work and to love across the life span. The intrinsic connection between learning and these two arenas is readily apparent. In Chapter Three we discussed how work and love structure learning in adult life. Transitions in both domains are powerful motivators for participation in education. It makes intuitive sense that learning would permeate the two major dimensions of adult life, since we all must accommodate changing social roles in both arenas as we age. Not to learn is not to grow and mature.

While we know that learning is a vital part of both work and love in adulthood, we know little about how it relates to the two arenas. For example, does more learning occur in one arena than in the other? Is there a difference in the amount and quality of learning when things are going well compared with when things are going badly? Are there particular learning experiences that are common to each domain? These are some of the questions we addressed in our study. In this chapter we will discuss the answers we found.

The connection between the two domains and learning that forms the focus of our study was immediately apparent on our "Work, Love, and Learning" questionnaire. On the first page

176

participants were asked to list memorable events by domain by year and to rate them, and on the second page they were asked to indicate significant learning experiences occurring during the same span of time. There was a distinct overlap between these two sections, since some of the same events appeared in both places. Thus we can conclude that the life events that gave rise to the vectors of work and love are also sources of learning. So even before we analyzed the findings in depth, it was obvious to us that the relationship between the two arenas and learning is an intrinsic one.

In this chapter we will examine this connection from several perspectives. First we will look at how the learning is distributed between the arenas. Then we will address the differences between those learning experiences that occur when work and love are rated good, as opposed to those that occur when times are bad. Finally, we will examine the major sources of learning in each domain and some of the linkages between work, love, and learning that our study revealed.

The Distribution of Learning

As we explained in Chapter Four, we devised a rather straightforward way of generating our learning data. On the second page of the "Work, Love, and Learning in Adulthood" questionnaire, participants were given the following instructions: "In reflecting upon the major love and work events in your life, identify formal, informal, or personal learning experiences that were especially meaningful, significant, or intense for you. Briefly describe the learning, when it occurred, and its significance for you." This task looks far easier than it is; most people seldom think in terms of life-experience learning. This type of learning is so entwined with life events that it becomes difficult to separate it out, which is one reason this type of learning has not been extensively studied. The participants in our study listed an average of four learning experiences; some were unable to identify any, while others listed as many as ten. This variation is probably due to their differing ability to think about learning and their lives in this way, rather than to the actual presence or absence of learning. Even with the difficulties presented by this part of the questionnaire, however, we obtained some very interesting data. A sample of typical responses is given here.

Learning Experience	*Significance*
began teaching word processing	discovered what I wanted to do with my life
making friends	helped me to become more flexible and open
separation from abusive husband	real independence; regained self-esteem
accepted supervisor's job	learned how to deal with people

When we examined the learning events themselves, we noticed that the overwhelming majority of these were not experiences of formal education but rather could be categorized as informal or life-experience learning, a finding all the more striking given the high educational level of our sample (80 percent have done at least some graduate work). For example, one forty-four-year-old woman who is currently working on her doctorate listed six major learning experiences: "master's degree; travel with spouse to Europe; new job in staff development; parenting, balancing graduate school, work, and family; and husband's significant promotion." A twenty-eight-year-old former Peace Corps volunteer listed five learning experiences that were significant in his life: "father's death, living on my own, living in West Africa, the breakup of a serious relationship, and starting graduate school." This proportion of informal to formal learning was the norm in our sample, suggesting that life experience may be the predominant and most valued form of learning in adulthood.

As we examined our results further, we had some basic questions about the occurrence of learning in our sample. Were some people more prone to significant learning than others?

Were there differences by gender? by pattern? by life stage? Our statistical analysis gave us those answers; these are summarized in Table 9.1.

Table 9.1. Significant Learning Experiences.

Average number per person	3.9
For women	3.9
For men	3.7
Average number by pattern type	
Parallel	3.7
Steady/fluctuating	3.8
Divergent	4.2
Average number by life stage	
Young adults	3.0
Thirties	4.2
Middle age	3.9

Each person in our study had an average of about four memorable learning experiences, and the differences between women and men were insignificant. When we examined the average number of learnings for each pattern, again it came to about four learning experiences for people in each pattern, and once again there were no significant differences among them. Only when we divided our sample according to life stage did we see any difference, and it was one that you would expect: Young adults have significantly fewer learning experiences than adults either in their thirties or in middle age. This makes intuitive sense; young adults have lived fewer years in which to have those experiences. But overall we found nothing noteworthy about the distribution of learning across our sample; it was essentially the same by gender, by pattern, and, with the logical exception of the youngest group, by life stage.

The next question we asked was whether more learning was likely to occur in one arena than the other. To get this answer, we categorized the learning events according to the arena in which they occurred: Learning could be work related, love related, or both or neither. Some examples of work-related learning with job training, receiving feedback on work performance,

and getting sales experience, some typical love-related learnings were moving away from home, the breakup of a relationship, and adjusting to stepchildren. For a learning event to be
considered as both love and work related, it had to have aspects
of both domains — for example, learning to work with difficult
people. To be neither it had to manage to fall outside either
domain — for example, recovering from a car accident. Relatively few learning events fell into these "both" or "neither"
categories. Our findings for this question are summarized in
Table 9.2.

Table 9.2. Number of Significant Learning Events by Domain.

	Work	*Love*	*Both*	*Neither*
Women	597	408	122	13
Men	225	141	43	1
Total	822	549	165	14

The interesting result here is the predominance of work-
related learning for both men and women. The differences are
dramatic: A total of 822 learning events occurred in the work
arena as opposed to 549 in the love arena. It is difficult to interpret the meaning of this finding. It may suggest that more tends
to be happening in the work arena, providing more opportunities for learning. Or the finding may be a function of our sample, which consisted of an unusually large percentage of professional, career-oriented people. We might not find the same thing
in a group that is more representative of the general population. Work-related learning events may also be more discrete
and therefore easier to identify than learning that occurs in the
love domain.

There are a number of things we can conclude about the
distribution of learning in our sample. There are no differences
between women and men in the amount of significant learning
reported, nor are there major differences among the pattern types
in this regard. Likewise life stage, with the logical exception of
the young adult group, is not responsible for any meaningful
differences in the amount of learning. By far the greatest per-

centage of significant learning is derived from life experience rather than formal education, and while a great deal of learning occurs in both domains, more is identified as work related. Next we address the impact that fluctuations in the two arenas have on learning.

Learning in Good Times and Bad

Another major question we had concerned when learning occurs. Is it when things are going well? Is it related to change in one of the domains? Recall that our participants were asked to list their memorable learning experiences along with the year in which these experiences occurred. This enabled us to categorize these learning events according to the position of the work and love vectors at that time. Learning might have occurred, for example, when both work and love were rated good, or work could have been okay and love bad. Altogether there are nine possible combinations of these domain ratings. These are listed in Table 9.3, along with the total number of learning events from our sample that occurred at each of the nine work/love combinations.

Table 9.3. Number of Significant Learning Events.

Work	Love	Male n = 112	Female n = 293	Total Learning Events
Good	Good	185	415	600
Good	OK	54	177	231
Good	Bad	32	164	196
OK	Good	35	96	131
OK	OK	28	84	112
OK	Bad	21	75	96
Bad	Good	13	46	59
Bad	OK	7	28	35
Bad	Bad	25	38	63

The results of this analysis are dramatic and very significant. Approximately ten times more learning occurs when things are going well in both domains than when things are going badly in both, and this is equally true for women and men. Interestingly, when work was rated good and love rated okay or bad, more learning events occurred than when love was rated good and work rated okay or bad. This suggests that work exerts a dominant influence similar to what we saw in the earlier analysis of work- and love-related learnings, where more were located in the work arena.

The theory that perhaps helps us the most in understanding why more learning occurs when things are going well is the theory of margin proposed by McClusky (1970). He suggests that there is a relationship between the demands confronting a person, which he calls *load,* and the resources, or *power,* the person has to deal with them. He calls this relationship *margin,* and he argues that more learning occurs when the load is small and the power large, creating excess margin. When things are going well in both work and love, the demands or load facing a person are presumably smaller than they are when things are going badly; we can also presume that a person's resources to deal with circumstances — their power — is greater in these good times. According to McClusky's theory, then, there is more margin when things are going well and therefore more learning should occur. And in our study it clearly does.

In addition to having them fill out our questionnaire, we also collected data about learning from the nineteen people we interviewed, sixteen of whom were profiled in Chapters Five, Six, and Seven. These interviews confirmed the fact that dramatically more learning occurs when things are going well in both arenas. We also gained some insight into why this is true. Further, the interviews enabled us to see differences in the type of learning that occurs when things are going well or badly. We will examine both of these findings.

Two of the people we interviewed talked about why their learning picks up when things are going well. The first is Norman, the college professor we met in Chapter Six, who discusses his learning especially in reference to how things are going within his family:

> I don't particularly find that when there's a strain
> or things are negative that I learn a whole lot. I

think there's been a theory that kind of goes along the line that how are you going to learn unless things are adverse. And I say, I don't do my best learning when things are adverse. I don't particularly have good days when Cathy and I have had a difference or a conflict, or when my children and I have had some differences of opinion. I don't particularly find that as an opportune time to grow and develop. It's when there is a heavy load that I'm confronted with, in combination with the relationship being really good and no conflict, [that] I grow the most. . . . I want things to be good in the family/love relationship. When those are good, the sky's the limit in terms of what I can do. But when things are in conflict, I am preoccupied with the conflict and feeling bad about the conflict, preoccupied to the point that all the other stuff, while it may be true, it's like it's held off in a way, and not allowed to come in and have its full play.

Norman's description echoes McClusky's theory of margin. For him, conflict adds to his stress or load while reducing his power to deal with it; the loss of margin means he learns less. Ellen, the human resource consultant from Chapter Seven, agrees and relates this idea to her experience in graduate school: "I think conflict is distracting, and I think that when you're growing and learning a lot, you like to focus on that and move something through or follow a lead on something and come to some conclusion. That's something that I would say about my master's that it did for me. I had a period there of eighteen months, and I started with my thoughts in my head and really moved them down the road significantly and fairly quickly, without a lot of distraction or a lot of conflict. And so that's why it was a good time for me. I got lots of positive feedback in the work setting for what I was doing."

We noticed in our interviews that various kinds of learnings took place when the arena in which they were located was rated as good. Among these were professional training, learning to relate to one's adult children, formal education, adjusting to marriage, and getting in touch with one's creativity. The learnings that occurred when the domain was rated as bad were not only fewer in number, they were also less varied. Examination of the characteristics of these bad times helps to explain why this is true.

The conditions that mark the good times — the absence of conflict and the resulting freedom to focus on learning — are dramatically absent in the bad times. But it is more than conflict that makes learning difficult when things are going badly. There is also the presence of pain, something that Katherine, from Chapter Seven, speaks to when she says that in bad times she is not aware of learning, that her mind is on other things: "At the time I realized I was in great pain and all I was looking for was a way out." We can see that pain and conflict appear to be major factors that impede learning when things are going badly in a person's life.

Our interviews give us evidence of more, however. The learning that occurs in hard times often appears to be of a different character from the learning that happens when things are going well. Ellen, reflecting on her divorce, notes that more than a relationship was changed: "The divorce was challenging a value system that I had been given since childhood, so what I was learning is that I didn't have to keep that value system, that I could make my own." Ann, the history and sociology professor with the parallel pattern, suggests the bad times open her to new awareness: "As long as things are going well, there are probably some things I never realized. I have to hit a snag and say, 'Oops, the snag showed me where I don't have it together.' When I hit a snag, generally the reason I hit the snag is because there are some things that I really am not being realistic about, and I hit them and I work through them."

Matt, the minister with the steady/fluctuating pattern, speaks of these types of learnings in terms of transitions: "There were moments when there are issues in your life and something breaks the pattern and you deal with it and that needs to change, and that's sort of what transition means; even if the externals don't change, something changes that releases a transition." The "snags" or the things that "break the pattern" sound like the disorienting dilemmas that Mezirow (1990) argues trigger the process of perspective transformation. Our study suggests that these dilemmas are more likely to be present when things are going badly in a particular arena, at least for those perspective transformations that are more sudden and dramatic.

In our study we found examples of perspective transformation located in both work and love, and appearing with equal frequency in all three patterns. These transformations, whether sudden or gradual, are momentous events in people's lives, and they result in significant changes for them. We have seen some examples of the dramatic transformations already. Remember Matt's experience of being fired as associated pastor of his church, and how he came to understand that life is not always fair. Or Frank's change in perspective after he saw American troops deployed to maintain order in Washington, D.C. Another example of a more sudden perspective transformation is offered by Katherine, though for her the situation was a mixture of bad and good. She discusses the change in herself the year her daughter was born and her mother died:

> I realized my mortality . . . I realized that I was here for a short period of time. The next generation has arrived, the other generation has left, you're the next generation to go. It really was a shock. . . . I felt that if I want [my doctorate] I would have to keep going regardless of what's going to happen here. It just gave me a whole new set of motivation to finish things because I know that I don't have that much time. I use my time much more wisely now. In fact, it has affected how I deal with friends and everything. If someone is bothering me and I can't resolve it after a couple of tries, I think differently about them. I just cut people out of my life, things I've never done before. It changed my values.

Ellen also talks about the impact of death, in her case her father's, and what it has meant for her understanding of herself:

When my dad died, the learning there was . . . I
would say, I grew up. I wasn't a little girl anymore.
Because he was the stable force in my life and had
been all my life. I don't think I really realized that
he is the reason for who I am. Because he's the one
who said to me, "You can be anything you want
to be." I was not going to be a nurse, I was going
to be a doctor. You know, push it. He was the one
who told me I could be anything. . . . But the thing
I learned most from him is that I was in charge,
I was in control, and I was responsible for my own
happiness. It was freeing. It was also scary. . . . I
was no longer daddy's little girl, ever again. I was
truly out of the nest. So I'd say that's what the learning was.

In these cases, the perspective transformation is sudden
and occurs when the domain in which it is located is rated as
bad, or, as in Katherine's case, when it is mixed. But a perspective change can also occur gradually, in which case it is less
likely to be situated only in bad times. One example is given
by another person we interviewed, Monica, a fifty-two-year-
old nurse who has a divergent pattern. She describes her development as a feminist, a process that began when she read Betty
Friedan's *The Feminine Mystique* but that evolved over several
years. She notes: "It kind of changed my outlook on my role
as a woman. It raised my consciousness to let me really look
at some things that I had felt really resentful about, like being
stuck at home with small children while my husband traveled,
and not being able to do the things that I wanted to do. That
and just the attitudes of society towards women. That was a
very eye-opening thing for me." Over time she began to value
herself more and to become more assertive both at home and
at work.

Our analysis of when learning occurs in relationship to
the fluctuations of the work and love arenas reveals several
things. First, the greatest amount of learning occurs when things
are going well in both arenas, a finding that supports McClusky's

(1970) theory of margin. Further, work seems to exert the predominant influence; more learning occurs when it is rated good but love is rated okay or bad than when love is in the good position. Second, the learning that takes place during these good times is also more varied than the learning that happens when things are not going well. And finally, learning that results in a sudden perspective transformation is more likely to occur when things are going badly. We turn now to examine some of the ways that learning links the spheres of work and love.

The Work, Love, and Learning Connection

We noted earlier in this chapter that the events that gave rise to the vectors of work and love in our study were also the sources of learning in a person's life. In this section we will look at some of the major sources of learning in each arena, focusing on both informal or life-experience learning and on formal education.

Work itself is a source of learning. This was made especially clear in two interviews. The first is that of Katherine, who we met in the discussion of the divergent pattern. She emphatically locates her identity in the work domain, even saying at one point that "the work is me personally." But she goes on to link this with education: "The work for me is not just work; work is usually [connected with] returning to school or with something school-related." This is not surprising in her case since what she calls "the professional side" of herself is related to her intellectual abilities: "If I feel like I'm tapping into the intellectual side of myself, then I feel quite fulfilled, quite happy." It is appropriate that she is following an academic career. And remember that earlier in her life, her formal education was directly related to the development of her sense of independence and autonomy. For Katherine, then, the link between work and learning is intrinsic.

Another person we interviewed, Brendon, a forty-three-year-old engineer with a divergent pattern, demonstrates a different connection between work and learning. For him there is a positive correlation between significant learning and job satisfaction, one he discovered when he completed our questionnaire: "I hadn't seen until tonight where work and learning are so inter-related. When one is on an up cycle, the other is too, but when learning starts falling off, work starts falling off or vice versa. In my case, it's like starting out in a new career or new job that I get real hungry to learn all about it and do a lot of digging. Then it's like, once I feel like I have learned or mastered the job or learned all there is to learn about it, then I begin to lose interest in it, and that's when the jobs aspects of life begin to drop off. If the learning process ends, then the interest in the job begins to wane and falls off." Brendon's graph does show cycles of stability and change, and his explanation that these cycles are related to learning — at least in the work arena — is a plausible one.

Don, the college professor who also has a divergent pattern, notes that a learning experience in the work domain can also have an impact on love: "Back in the 1970s, when I went to this first workshop on the freshman movement, it was based on work in the area of human potential. I was just turned on by this. Shortly thereafter my wife and I started to get some marriage counseling. You know, one thing almost prompted the other, so that the professional experience in dealing with personal relationships led me to want to investigate this on a personal level. In that way there was some sort of a carryover."

There were also examples of learning in the love arena that triggered a change in work. Nathan, the nurse-practitioner who had lost his infant son to SIDS, transferred what he had learned from that personal tragedy to his work domain, becoming a SIDS counselor for other parents who suffered that loss. And we saw earlier how Katherine's experience of her mother's death and her daughter's birth motivated her to pursue her doctorate without further delay. All of these stories illustrate the multiple ways learning can function as a link between work and love in adult life.

Two sources of learning were predominant in the love domain. The first was the experience of parenting. Thelma describes it as a radically new experience in her life; learning how to deal with babies "took some of the corners off" her more rigid personality:

I was an only child and I wasn't used to children. I married when I was [older], so handling babies and children was not what I considered exactly a natural thing to happen. I thought, "Here's this baby and what do I do with it?" I found it to be really scary at first having an infant at home. We called it "infant"; we didn't even call it "she." My husband was the same way . . . so we were pretty stiff parents to begin with. . . . My mother said having children takes some of the corners off a little bit. I was probably too rigid, and then I think I kind of went the other way after being home with the kids; I kind of gave up and lost the edge I had.

For Thelma parenting was a new and challenging experience in part because it came later in life. Another participant in our study, Sandra, a thirty-nine-year-old counselor with a parallel pattern, noted how the challenge of parenting was increased because she was young:

I had never had any smaller brothers or sisters, or any child to babysit, so this was totally new. I had to learn how to change diapers, I had to learn about formulas, I had to learn how to wake up and not sleep so sound. . . . I was in my early twenties and I never thought that I would be a mother at that age. Suddenly when my son was born [I realized] "Hey, I have got to do all these things: I am his mother. I can't, you know, say I don't want to do this, I don't want to get up." So then I realized the significance of a mother or parent. I realized and I understood what parents went through, the sacrifices they had to make for their children. . . . I don't think that I probably would have totally appreciated the things my mother had gone through, the sacrifices that she made, if I had not become a parent myself.

Peter, the educational consultant we met in Chapter Five, describes the birth of his son as an opportunity to reconstruct the close relationship he had with his father, a poignant theme since his father had died unexpectedly five years before. But he also talks about a widened sense of responsibility: "You know, I slow down when I drive now. I can drive 80 mph and kill myself but I can't drive 80 mph and let my son get in an accident. I slow down when I go through a subdivision, and I've always cared about children, [but now] I care more about everybody else's children because then you can empathize with what's going on. . . . It's tremendously different for me, the relationship I have with a child after I had my own child."

We have already seen the importance of parenting for Ann, the history and sociology professor, since it has enabled her to understand and forgive her own parents for their emotional abuse of her as a child. She summarizes the heart of that learning as "the internalization of the concept of unconditional love." For all these people, parenting offers a broadened perspective on life, one that is more inclusive and more responsible. Each of them is changed by the experience, and everyone we interviewed describes that change as positive and highly significant in their lives.

If birth was a common learning experience in our study, death was, too. Almost everyone had experienced the death of at least one parent, and many listed this event as one of their most significant learning experiences. Peter talks about his father's death:

> My father was a Baptist minister; I say that to explain that I had some experience with sorrow and pain, loss and death. I had played the piano in fifty or sixty funerals . . . it's not like this was my first exposure. And we had lost family members. . . . The thing was that my father was, in almost every respect, my best friend. I lost a dad but I lost a minister and I lost a best friend. And I didn't realize until that time, which we never do, I'm sure, but I didn't realize how much of me and how much

of my emotions was invested in him. So that was
a tremendous learning experience to just cope with
that, because I had always known that regardless
of the situation, he was always my stable force I
could always fall back on. . . . I had to reevaluate
who I was and where I was going without my
father. . . . It was the major crisis in my life.

We saw a similar theme in Ellen's discussion of her father's
death, especially in the way it changed her understanding of
herself. Like Peter she had to reevaluate who she was once she
realized that she was now "truly out of the nest." The loss of
a parent reshaped both their worlds.

Sandra lost her mother eight years ago. She comments
on how this changed her philosophy of life: "I realized that you
should not take things for granted; you should live each day
as though it is your last day. Because I took for granted my
mother would always be there . . . and there were a lot of things
that I would have said and done with her had I known that she
was going to depart her life at such an early age. . . . So if you
see a person and you want to say, you know, 'How are you doing?' or 'You look nice,' you should say that . . . because I don't
know whether tomorrow I'll be able to say it."

These discussions of the impact of the death of a parent
or other family member, both from our interview data and from
the learning segment of our questionnaire, indicate something
of the magnitude of this event in people's lives. It clearly is a
transformative learning experience, and it has implications for
how people see themselves as well as how they understand life.

In addition to informal learning derived from life experiences in both arenas, there are formal learning experiences
that relate to either work or love. All nineteen people we interviewed had their bachelor's degree, and most also had a master's.
Many discussed the significance of this type of learning, but the
character of that significance varied. Some, like Ed, who went
back to school in order to change careers, valued it for the professional credentialing it provided. Others used it as a way of coping with adversity. Matt enrolled in a doctoral program when

he was fired so that he would have "some reason to quit" his church position. Katherine was better able to cope with her mother's sudden death because she was in school. Nathan admits that Vietnam was a factor in his decision to go on to graduate school. A few people, like Ann, spoke of valuing their formal education for the sake of the learning itself; she described herself as satisfying "interest whims" through her schooling. Finally, several people said it was important for what it taught them about themselves. We have seen how Katherine used her college years to develop personal autonomy. Vivian, who returned to school to get her master's when her children were adults, described that experience as affirming her capability: "When I was in college I made good grades . . . but after twenty-five years can you still do something? So it was really good to go back, and that first report card was something. Then, from then on, it was just 'I can!'" For the most part, these statements of the significance of formal education are more personal than utilitarian.

We have examined the life experiences in both work and love that give rise to learning and have noted how learning in one arena can have an effect on the other. Likewise, formal education has a significant impact on both arenas.

Summary

In this chapter we have examined what we have learned in our study about the connections between work, love, and learning in adult life. We began by seeing how significant learning events were distributed in our sample, and found that there were essentially no differences by gender, pattern, or life stage. There were significantly more learning events located in the work than in the love arena, however.

We then examined the differences in learning in relation to the ratings of the domains. When work and love are both rated good, about ten times more learning occurs than when both domains are rated bad. But we also noticed a difference in the character of the learnings at these times. There is a greater likelihood of a perspective transformation or a restructuring of meaning from those learning events that occur when a domain is rated as bad.

Finally, we saw that life experiences in both arenas are the sources of significant learning. In the work domain we observed the link between learning and identity as well as between learning and job satisfaction. And in the love arena we examined the common learning experiences located in parenting and in dealing with death. We concluded with a discussion of the impact of formal education on both domains. Our findings make clear that learning is intrinsic to the domains of work and love, and unites them at a fundamental level.

CHAPTER TEN

Learning from Experience

There is no question that we are shaped by our experiences; developmental and life-phase theorists all take that as a given. Less clear is how that shaping occurs. Yet, as Ingham suggests, development without learning is inconceivable: "Can you imagine who or what you would be if you did not learn? My guess is that you would be just about the same as when you emerged from the womb. The world would still be the 'buzzing, blooming' confusion experienced at birth. Of course, you would be physically larger—but it is unlikely you would have lived to be your present age. Indeed, it is also unlikely that you or any other member of the species *Homo sapiens* would exist if we had not become capable of learning. When viewed in these terms, it becomes apparent that learning is fundamental to human existence" (1987, p. 148).

Exactly how learning facilitates development is less obvious, in part because the developmental process has not been extensively studied from a learning perspective. The focus of developmental research has been more on outcome than on process, in no small part because the outcomes can be identified and studied whereas the underlying process is less discernible. Yet most developmental theory implies a process that involves more than biological change as the source of development. Influential studies of intellectual development (Perry, 1970), ethical and moral development (Kohlberg, 1973; Gilligan, 1982), and psychosocial development (Erikson, 1980) all suggest sequential changes that enlarge a person's capacity in these areas, an expansion that arises not so much from biological changes within the person as from his or her engagement with experience over time. That engagement with experience is what we would call learning.

Studying how we learn from experience presents complex challenges to researchers. First, the tremendous variety of life-experience learning makes generalizations difficult. Further, each example of such learning is embedded in a particular context, and the role these multiple contexts play in the learning process is difficult to assess. This is one type of learning that cannot be studied by isolating it in a laboratory; here life is the laboratory and it is anything but neat. In addition, these learning experiences are usually accessed in retrospect and are seldom availble for study as they occur. Representations of them are therefore somewhat distorted by time and by personal interpretation.

Our own study shares these limitations. Because our data are retrospective, we were not able to study learning as it occurred. But from the "Work, Love, and Learning in Adulthood" questionnaires and the interviews we were able to gain some insight into that process. Certainly our findings on the learning that occurs in good times and bad tell us some important things about perspective transformation and how it relates to development. In addition, we have data on the significance our participants gave their major learning experiences, enabling us to see the meaning of these experiences for them. These data give us a window into the role that this learning plays in the development of their capacities to work and to love. In this chapter we will discuss those findings.

We will begin by examining some of the developmental literature that relates to learning, particularly those studies that address the changes in the ways we structure meaning in our lives. Then we will discuss our findings about what makes learning significant in adulthood and will examine how this advances our understanding of the connection between adult development and learning.

Development and the Structuring of Meaning

How learning occurs from life experience has received little attention in the adult developmental literature. We must look instead on the borders of the educational literature, at those points where it intersects with psychology. The person who stands most prominently at the intersection between psychology and learning is Carl Rogers. As we discussed in Chapter Three, his contribution was to connect the process of learning to the structure of the self. He understood the self as being impelled toward growth by the principle of the actualizing tendency, "the inherent tendency of the organism to develop all its capacities in ways which serve to maintain or enhance the organism. . . . It involves development towards the differentiation of organs and of functions, expansions in terms of growth, expansion of effectiveness. . . . It is development toward autonomy and away from heteronomy or control by external forces" (1959, p. 196). This directional growth is effected through learning.

Research into the changes in how meaning is structured gives us even more insight into the process of life-experience learning. These changes in meaning-making can be construed in two ways, both of which allow us to have a greater capacity for dealing with evolving life experiences: as expansion of the ways in which we think about and interpret our experience, and as transformation of the meaning system itself. There is an obvious connection between expansion and transformation; in a practical sense they form a continuum, with greater and greater expansion of our thought leading to a transformation of our meaning systems. However, it is useful to focus on the cognitive changes that underlie expansion in order to understand how this gives rise to the transformation of meaning perspectives.

One theory that has significantly advanced our understanding of how our thought expands as we engage experience is that of Perry (1970, 1981). Studying Harvard students over the course of their undergraduate years, he noticed that they developed increasingly complex interpretations of their educational experience. This gave rise to a map or scheme of cognitive and ethical development that has several stages. At first students think in dualistic terms, believing that knowledge is absolute and that things are either right or wrong. The next stage is multiplicity; at this point they believe everyone has a right to his or her own opinion and all views have equal merit. This is followed by relativism; here various points of view are subject to evaluation and knowledge is seen as contextual. Finally students are able to establish commitments within a relativistic world and, in so doing, to forge a personal identity. Throughout the schema Perry makes it clear that how we think about the world shapes how we act in it. Cognitive and ethical development, therefore, are linked.

Building on Perry's work but focusing on women in both formal and informal learning situations, Belenky, Clinchy, Goldberger, and Tarule (1986) outline five positions that describe how women know. These are (1) silence, where women are passive and defined by others; (2) received knowledge, in which knowledge comes from others and not themselves; (3) subjective knowledge, where knowing is located within the self; (4) procedural knowledge, in which objective methods are used to know something; and (5) constructed knowledge, an integrated position that recognizes both subjective and objective ways of knowing and sees all knowledge as contextual. As in Perry's schema, we see an expansion here in the ways in which experience is thought about and rendered meaningful.

Several researchers develop the idea that learning leads to a transformation of the meaning system itself. Gould understands development as a process of transformation from childhood consciousness to adult consciousness, a movement that involves the risky task of "reformulating our self-definition" by reworking "the irrationalities of childhood" (1978, p. 25). Childhood consciousness is built on a series of assumptions that instill a feeling of safety; in adulthood, however, these assumptions are dysfunctional and limit growth. Gould summarizes these childhood beliefs about ourselves and our world as four major false assumptions:

1. I'll always belong to my parents and believe in their world.
2. Doing it their way, with willpower and perseverance, will bring results. But when I become too frustrated, confused or tired or am

simply unable to cope, they will step in and
show me the right way.
3. Life is simple and controllable. There are no
significant coexisting contradictory forces within me.
4. There is no evil or death in the world. The
sinister has been destroyed [p.40].

These assumptions do not function at a conscious level
in adulthood; instead, they serve as unconscious protective
devices against unresolved childhood fear and anger. They can
only be transformed by first being exposed, probed, and replaced
by adult beliefs that are more congruent with lived reality. Gould
notes that this transformation process involves a type of internal dialogue that is more than intellectual, a struggle between
deep forces within the person. When the transformation is successful, it results in "a new level of passion for life, accompanied by a greater sense of internal freedom and power" (1980,
p. 223). He concludes that transformation, understood in this
way, is "the central concept of adult development" (p. 223).

Whereas Gould sees human growth as involving transformations of meaning, Kegan goes a step further and argues
that the concept of person is more verb than noun, and that
we must understand "human being as an activity" (1982, p. 8).
That activity is one of rendering experience coherent or meaningful, and it is central to the psychological concept of the ego
or the self. Meaning-making, Kegan argues, is what human beings do; and that activity is the way the self is given form. He
proposes a model for understanding the progressive changes in
the self as the individual matures that traces the development
of the activity of meaning-making, a model he calls *constructive-
developmental*. It is constructive in that it attends to the creation
of meaning, a continuous process that is basic to human existence; to be human is to render experience meaningful. And
it is developmental in that our capacity to engage in this human activity evolves across the life span. Kegan, then, suggests
that "the evolution of the activity of meaning [can be under-
stood] as the fundamental motion in personality" (1982, p. 15).

Daloz (1986) makes a similar argument about the developmental impact of formal education on adults. He contends that the goal of education is the development of the whole person and that development is facilitated by the caring relationship between the teacher and the student. The teacher assumes the role of mentor, providing guidance and support as the student negotiates this growth process — a process that involves "taking apart and putting together the structures that give our lives meaning" (p. 236). Using both current developmental theory and ancient myth, Daloz suggests that growth follows a three-stage pattern of separation/initiation/return. The self separates or grows beyond the earlier conceptualization of itself and of the world. The initiation into the new state requires finding different ways of structuring meaning, of perceiving the self and the world. This can mean a radical transformation. The return is the synthesis, the integration of the whole at a higher level of understanding, and a reengagement with the world in a new way. Daloz assumes that formal education has the potential to function in this transformative way, and he argues that educators have a moral responsibility to facilitate this process.

What Gould, Kegan, and Daloz describe is essentially a process of transformational learning in which engagement with life experience results in the restructuring of personal meaning systems. As we saw in Chapter Three, the learning theory that offers the best explanation of this process is outlined by Mezirow (1981, 1990) in his description of perspective transformation. Occurring either suddenly or gradually, this process is triggered by certain life experiences that challenge an individual's current meaning system and result in a change or restructuring of that system. When those life experiences are normative, with the events expected to occur at generally predictable times in the life course, then this kind of learning is most recognizable as developmental in character. But the nonnormative or unexpected events also foster development.

We have already seen a number of examples of perspective transformation in our interview data to illustrate this. Ellen spoke about her divorce challenging the value system she grew up with and inviting her to forge a set of values that were more truly her own. Then later she talked about the way her father's death somehow completed her passage into adulthood. Matt's experience of being fired altered how he saw the world; after that he knew that life is not always fair. And for Sandra it was the experience of parenting that changed not only how she acted but also how she understood herself. These and other examples make it clear that transformational learning experiences advance the developmental process by significantly enlarging a person's meaning system, leading to the superior meaning perspective that Mezirow describes as "more inclusive, discriminating, permeable, and integrative . . . [enabling adults] to better understand the meaning of their experience" (1990, p. 14).

We have reviewed some of the major research that explores the connection between adult development and learning as the restructuring of meaning, both in terms of expansion of our thought and transformation of our meaning systems. Perry tracks the changes in thought and behavior that result from the experience of formal education; Belenky and her colleagues argue for similar stages in women's ways of knowing. Gould's psychological studies construe growth as transformations in meaning, while Kegan argues that there is a developmental progression in our very capacity to make meaning in adulthood. Daloz addresses more broadly the transformational character of adult education. Finally, we returned to Mezirow's theory of perspective transformation and saw how it helps explain how these transformations take place. We turn now to our own findings regarding the significance of learning and examine how this expands our understanding of the learning/development connection.

What Makes Learning Significant?

When we asked the participants in our study to identify memorable learning experiences, they reported events that included both the predictable (marriage, birth, first job) and the unpredictable (car accident, winning an award), and that encompassed learnings that came from life events as well as those from formal education. This reaffirmed our belief that all of life holds the potential for learning. It also made us examine more closely the intrinsic connection between experience, learning, and development, that is, how our capacity to work and to love is expanded through our engagement with life experience. We will examine that connection first, then discuss our findings related to the significance of learning.

Experience and Learning. Dewey (1938) argued that not all experiences educate; understanding why this is true would give us a place to begin our analysis of those experiences that educate particularly well. The work of Mezirow (1981, 1990) and Jarvis (1987a, 1987b) gives us a way of conceptualizing this.

If all experience is mediated through a personal meaning system as Mezirow suggests, then we can construct a continuum of experience for each learner. This is illustrated in Figure 10.1. Experiences would range from those that are to-

Figure 10.1. Continuum of Learning Experiences.

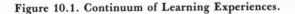
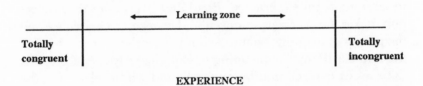

tally congruent with the current meaning system to those that are totally incongruent. Both extremes account for experiences that do not educate, but for different reasons. When an experience is too congruent, it fails to get the learner's attention because nothing new is happening; this accounts for Jarvis's category of nonlearning. When an experience is too incongruent, it can, as Mezirow suggests, present too much a threat to the current meaning system and be rejected out of hand. In this situation, too, learning fails to occur. Where learning does occur is somewhere between the extremes on the continuum, in what we are calling the *learning zone* for that person. Here the experience is different enough from prior experience to get the learner's attention, but not so different as to threaten his or her established identity and worldview. The more an experience approaches the incongruent end of the continuum, however, the more likely it will precipitate transformational learning and the restructuring of the learner's meaning perspective.

Conceptualizing the connection between experience and learning in this way influenced how we defined learning itself. Multiple definitions of learning were available to us. Some theorists focus on changes in behavior, others emphasize cognitive change, and still others, like Mezirow, focus on the restructuring of meaning systems. We understand learning to involve *attending to* and *reflecting on* an experience that results in some *present* or *future change* in a person's behavior, attitudes, knowledge, beliefs, or skills.

An experience must do more than gain an individual's attention; for learning to occur, the person must reflect on that experience. Educators agree about the importance of reflection in the learning process. Usher (1985) argues that it is the key to learning from experience. Boyd and Fales note that reflection makes the necessary connections between an experience and the person's meaning system, defining it as "the process of creating and clarifying the meaning of experience (present or past) in terms of self (self in relation to self and self in relation to the world). The outcome of the process is a changed conceptual perspective" (1983, p. 101).

Learning is also linked to change, but that change need not be immediate. The process is probably more often incremental, with change resulting only as particular learning experiences accumulate. The perspective transformations that are gradual rather than dramatic certainly would fall into this category of more incremental learning.

Using these understandings of the concepts of experience and of learning, we turn now to examine our findings about the significance of learning.

Toward an Understanding of Significance. When we asked participants in our study to identify "formal, informal, or personal learning experiences that were especially meaningful, significant, or intense," we also asked them to explain the nature of their significance. We gave several examples from our data in Chapter Nine; here are several more.

Learning Experience	*Significance*
first job	academic skills alone are not sufficient to effect change
family illness	learned how to accept and handle tragedy
going to college	I can function away from Mom!
divorce	recognized my inner coping strengths
death of mother	death is a reality in life; there is no utopian existence

Our analysis of significance dealt with the data in the second column. Two assumptions guided our work here. First, we assumed that the judgment of what is significant is personal and subjective. And second, because of this subjective evaluation, we assumed that the significance of the same event would vary from person to person. Given this necessary variability, our goal was to determine if there was a common inner structure among the statements of significance. Because the learning experiences identified were selected for their importance to the learner, we believe that these experiences figured prominently in the learner's development. Thus, analysis of the underlying structure of their significance would provide some insight into the connection between learning and the developmental process.

Through analysis of the learning data from the "Work, Love, and Learning in Adulthood" questionnaire as well as the data gathered in our interviews, we were able to discern that inner structure of significance. We found that the significance of a learning experience has two components. First, it is an experience that personally affects the learner either by resulting in *expansion* of skills and abilities, sense of self, or life perspective, or by precipitating a *transformation* that involves the whole person. And second, it is an experience that is subjectively valued by the learner. The first component is the personal impact that a significant learning experience has on the learner. It must change the learner in some way. Expansion is meant to capture the notion of growth and enhancement that is fundamental to the concept of development. The three areas of expansion — skills and abilities, sense of self, and life perspective — should be seen as dimensions of significance, the arenas in which significance is located. Some learnings will have more than one dimension to their significance. Transformation occurs when the expansion is not limited to one dimension but encompasses the whole person. The second component is the subjective valuation the person gives the learning experience. This places a personal stamp on the experience and amounts to a naming of its importance in the person's life. This component acknowledges the fact that some learning experiences result in expansion of some dimension of the person but not in a way that is personally valued. An example might be a factory worker who learns how to perform a particular task on the job but who assigns no personal value to having that skill and therefore does not consider it significant.

As we noted, expansion has three dimensions: skills and abilities, sense of self, and life perspective. Many people valued a learning experience because it enlarged their skills and abilities in a particular area. One man, referring to an experience of job training, said its significance was "learning survival skills; having confidence to be able to do whatever is needed in my area." A woman listed a job she had as significant because "it taught me to work with others." One of the younger women in our study listed the experience of being out on her own as valuable for teaching her "how to manage money." Another man also listed being on his own as an important experience, but it was significant for him because of "learning how to fend for myself; surviving." One woman, writing about the experience of intimacy, said its importance was in learning "how to maintain some independence and still be in a relationship." In each of these cases, the person experiences an increased ability to deal with certain situations; his or her capacity to function is enlarged in some way that is deemed valuable. The experiences are far ranging and occur in both the work and love arenas, but what unites them is this expansion of personal capability.

The dimension we are calling sense of self relates to the impact of learning on the person's identity. The sense of self is expanded in two ways: either through development of greater independence and autonomy, or through the establishment of an increased sense of relatedness or connection. Obviously adults seek to balance both of these movements across the life span, with each at times predominating in development. What we have in our data are marker events that point to those times when there is a redressing of this balance.

The movement toward independence was often noted in relation to separation from the family of origin or within the context of a committed relationship. One woman, reflecting on the experience of intimacy, wrote, "I can keep my sense of self in a healthy love relationship," while another realized that "I could make my own choices and could break free if my decisions didn't feel right anymore." Many noted that the breakup of a relationship made them more independent. Other sources for increased independence were work experiences and formal education. One woman spoke of college as important because "it taught me to be independent and responsible; it was my first step towards being an adult"; another woman said that college helped her recognize that "I am in control of my life." Many listed work experiences as increasing their sense of autonomy; comments like "my first job helped me accept responsibility for my actions" were common.

An expanded sense of connectedness was most frequently expressed in terms of relationships. One young man wrote: "With sex comes responsibility; I'm on my way to becoming an adult." Many spoke of the experience of marriage and family as significant because, as one man expressed it, "I'm no longer responsible for only myself, I'm responsible for other people." Parenting was a particularly powerful experience in this regard; it was described poignantly by one woman as the experience of being "totally needed and totally accepted." But tragic events could also generate this sense of connection; one woman, the victim of rape and battering earlier in her life, spoke of how it increased her empathy and understanding of other women in similar situations. We also had examples of religious experiences that fostered a sense of unity. That sense of connection, then, could be felt toward those immediately present as well as toward a larger, possibly even unseen, community.

The final dimension of expansion involves changes in life perspective. We noticed that this could take two forms. It could be a broad philosophical understanding about life in general, or it could be more specific and localized. One woman, as an example of the first kind of enlarged perspective, learned from a particularly difficult family crisis that "things happen as they should and *will* work out." Another comment that frequently accompanied experiences of suffering and death was that "life is fragile and precious." A more localized example of a broadened perspective was given by a man who said that "married life is very complicated" as he reflected on his divorce. Or a woman said about a work experience that "anything is possible with a group who believes it is possible." In all these instances, the person's perspective on the world changed as a result of the learning experience.

But a learning experience can have more than one dimension of significance, as our interviews made clear. Katherine, whom we met in the chapter on the divergent pattern, provided an excellent example of this when she talked about the significance of her formal education. Recall that she had begun college in the nursing program because that was what her father wanted. It did not take long for her to realize that she wanted something else, however, and she changed majors. It was at that point, she said, that "I realized I had control of my life." Her learning here fostered the development of a more independent self. She also came to know herself better and to understand that her intellectual abilities were central to her self-definition: "A lot of my self-concept is really tied up in what I would call the professional side of myself [and that is] academically related [and] of an intellectual nature." Her education also gave her the skills necessary to pursue a career in speech communications. So we see in her discussion of one learning experience several dimensions of significance, all of which expanded her in different ways.

The effect of a learning experience can result in more than expansion, however; it can also lead to transformation of the whole person. The concepts of expansion and transformation must be understood not as discrete categories but rather as positions on a continuum. The experience of expansion can be self-contained and specific, involving one dimension of the person's life and not resulting in change in other areas, or it can be an increment within a gradual transformation that involves the whole person. This reflects both the dramatic and the more gradual types of perspective transformation that Mezirow (1990) describes.

In Chapter Nine we presented several examples of perspective transformation from our interview data. Some people experienced a more dramatic perspective transformation: Matt was fired from his ministerial position; Frank left the defense industry after seeing American troops deployed in Washington, D.C.; Katherine's daughter was born within weeks of her mother's death; Ellen was divorced the same year her father died; and Sandra became a mother earlier than she expected. Others, like Ann responding to the experience of parenting and Monica talking about her development as a feminist, described a more gradual transformation process. With all these examples, however, we can see the intrinsic connections between expansion and transformation. In all cases they experienced change in aspects of themselves that expanded their ability to understand and deal with the world. This echoes Mezirow's description of perspective transformation as resulting in "more inclusive, discriminating, permeable, and integrative perspectives" (1990, p. 14). What Mezirow describes here is the dynamic that underlies the process of maturation, that expansion of an adult's capacity to effectively engage his or her life experience. This expansion is driven by learning and culminates in the development of wisdom.

In our data all the significant learning experiences identified were essentially growth enhancing. The learning was not always pleasant or easy, as we saw in Matt's case, for example, when he learned that "life isn't always fair," but the result is a positive one in that the learner is able to deal more effectively with reality. We believe, however, that it is also possible for a significant learning experience to constrict a person, leading to a perspective that is more rigid and less integrative of new experience. This would explain the development of the fanatic or, less dramatically, of someone who has withdrawn from others and become bitter and lonely. Change is not solely expansive and linear, but learning is as central in these situations as it is in the more positive cases we saw.

To summarize what we have learned about the significance of learning, we can see several connections. These are represented in Figure 10.2. All experience, both life experience and formal education, has the potential for learning. No learning occurs when an experience is either too congruent or too incongruent with prior experience, thereby falling outside the learning zone. For learning to occur, the experience must be attended to and reflected on. Further, a learning can be significant or nonsignificant. Significance means that a learning experience is subjectively valued and has a personal impact on

Figure 10.2. Learning from Life Experience.

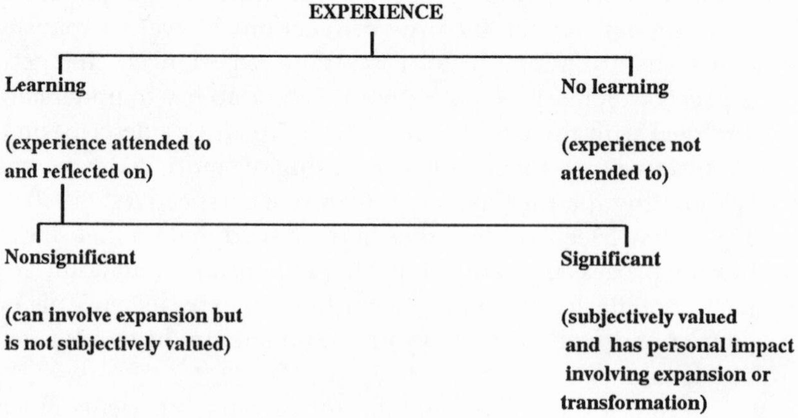

EXPERIENCE

Learning   No learning

(experience attended to   (experience not
and reflected on)   attended to)

Nonsignificant   Significant

(can involve expansion but   (subjectively valued
is not subjectively valued)   and has personal impact
                                                      involving expansion or
                                                      transformation)

the learner involving expansion or transformation. It is this expansive or transformative character of significant learning that reveals the intrinsic connection between learning and adult development.

Summary

In this chapter we have discussed the connection between learning and adult development. We reviewed some of the developmental literature that points to this connection, particularly those studies relating to the structuring of meaning in adult life as a way of explaining how the capacity to work and to love is expanded as adults mature. We examined several theories related to the expansion of our capacity to think about and interpret our experience, particularly the work of Perry on cognitive and ethical development. And we addressed the actual transformation of meaning systems in the work of Gould, Kegan, and Daloz. Mezirow, with his theory of perspective transformation, offers the best explanation of how learning accounts for these transformations.

Finally we described our own findings about the structure of significance underlying major learning experiences. We found that significance has two components. First, a learning experience is significant when it personally affects the learner by resulting in expansion of his or her skills and abilities, sense of self, or life perspective, or by resulting in a transformation that involves the whole person. And second, the learning experience must be subjectively valued by the learner. Together these two components describe the developmental character of significant learning.

CHAPTER ELEVEN

Understanding
Work, Love, and Learning

This chapter affords us an opportunity to step back from our study and assess its implications for both theory and practice. That is, what have we learned about work, love, and learning in adult life? What contributions do we make to the literature on adult development and learning? What might be the benefits of having individuals assess their own patterns of work, love, and learning? Finally, how might practitioners in human services and education make use of these findings? Thus this chapter is divided into two major sections. In the first we discuss what we consider to be the major contributions of our study to theory in adult development and learning. The second part of the chapter focuses on how individuals and practitioners might make use of these insights in their daily activities.

Work, Love, and Learning: What Have We Learned?

In some ways it is difficult for us to highlight just a few findings, given the richness of the data provided by both the questionnaires and the interviews. Respondents shared with us their life experiences, some painful, some joyous; this helped us to better understand what Freud meant when he said maturity was the capacity to work and to love. We were also able to better understand how learning functions in developing this capacity.

Discovery of Three Patterns. Clearly, a major contribution of this study is the discovery of three distinct patterns of work-and-love interaction. There is a parallel pattern in which both arenas move in tandem. Changes in one are reflected by changes in the other. The steady/fluctuating pattern is characterized by one arena remaining stable throughout, while the other fluctuates freely. In the divergent pattern, there is change in both arenas, but the changes appear to be independent of and sometimes in apparent opposition to one another. We were surprised by the stability of these patterns, at least over the twenty-year period of the graph, and speculated that these modes of interaction might be reflecting personality types.

It was also interesting to discover that only a few people with the parallel pattern tended to fuse the two domains, that is, to view them as one and the same. Most people in all three patterns saw their work arena as separate from the love arena. This separation perhaps reflects our culture's tendency to define work in bureaucratic, industrialized terms, keeping it separate conceptually and physically from the love dimensions of our lives. Further, we should note that we reinforced this dichotomy by the very way we structured the study: We specified two separate domains and asked our participants to think about their lives in those terms. That only a few people resisted this dichotomy gives evidence of the powerful influence culture has on the way we think about our experience.

Identification of the Stabilizing Factor. In looking more closely at the interaction between work and love, we discovered differences by pattern in three areas: domain emphasis, the stabilizing factor, and modes of interaction. We feel that the discovery of the stabilizing factor is particularly important because of its connection to the notion of balance and well-being. The stabilizing factor is what allows adults to have a sense of organization and control in their lives. For those with parallel patterns, the tandem movement of the arenas—the rhythm of the pattern itself—created the sense of stability. In the steady/fluctuating pattern, stability was located in the internal benefit derived from the steady domain. Finally, in the divergent pattern, work, and the control our respondents felt by emphasizing work, provided a sense of stability in an otherwise chaotic life.

Whatever the source of stability, it seemed to allow respondents to cope with both domains in their lives. This need to deal with *both* work and love is of course inherent in Freud's description of a healthy, mature adult. Much of the literature speaks to the need to balance, at least tentatively, work and love, and that such balance is related to development (Rohrlich, 1980; Smelser, 1980a; Kegan, 1982). Numerous studies have also found a fairly strong connection between attending to both domains and psychological well-being (Vaillant, 1977; Baruch, Barnett, and Rivers, 1983; Lancereau, 1987; Dimidjian, 1982; Hinand, 1984). Our data suggest that the stabilizing factor in each of the patterns allows one to achieve some balance, harmony, or integration of the two domains, and this balance is related to well-being. The sketch from the book *Johnny Cottontail* that is included later in the chapter touchingly summarizes this connection between work, love, and well-being.

Failure to Uncover Gender Differences. Another important finding in our study was the lack of gender differences in the distribution of the patterns, or in the naming of a dominant domain within the patterns. That is, we found no evidence whatsoever that women emphasize love more than work, or that men focus on work at the expense of love. Most of the empirical research reviewed in Chapter Two also supports this conclusion. This lack of gender differences may be due to the nature of our sample. It may also be that associating women with love and men with work is outdated stereotyping. Using a more diverse sample, it would be interesting to see if such associations are either socioeconomic or cohort specific.

Recognition of the Role of Learning in Development. What we learned about the intrinsic connection among work, love, and learning strikes us as another important contribution. It is our contention that maturity is an ever-evolving state having no predesignated endpoint. If maturity is, as Freud stated, the capacity to work and to love, then we see this capacity as continually growing and enlarging and a result of a person's interaction with, and learning from, life experiences. We discovered how this works. First, all life experiences (and we include formal education as one of life's experiences) hold the potential for learning. Some we do not attend to either because they are congruent with previous experience and go unnoticed, or, at the other extreme, they are too antithetical to our beliefs and values to be accommodated at all. The ones we do attend to can lead to a change in our perspective. Learning is in the attending to and the reflecting on the experience. The learning becomes significant when it personally affects us and is subjectively valued. Sometimes the result is a more developed perspective, ability, or skill, and sometimes the result is a transformation. In any case, learning seems to be the key to becoming more mature.

With regard to learning, we also discovered that the work and love events of people's lives functioned in two ways—as a stimulus for other learning, and as a source of learning in and of themselves. For example, a divorce might motivate someone to learn new career skills. Or a geographical move might result in learning about a different culture. This finding echoes Aslanian and Brickell's study (1980), which distinguishes between events that triggered learning and the transition period that followed. Triggers and transitions can occur in different areas of life. We also found that people learn about themselves and about life in general as a result of directly grappling with a particular life event. Becoming a parent and coping with the death of a loved one were found to be particularly powerful learning experiences. Finally, our explorations of work, love, and learning led to one surprising finding with regard to the timing of learning in adult life. It might be recalled that approximately ten times more learning occurred when things were going well in both the work and love arenas. Apparently people need the energy and resources available in good times to engage in significant learning.

Thus we consider the discovery of three patterns, the stabilizing factor, the lack of gender bias, and the role of learning in development to be the major findings of this study. We would like to elaborate on how the conceptual framework and the design of our study led to these findings, in the anticipation that future research will be conducted in this area that would extend our knowledge about work, love, and learning even further.

Using Life Events to Study Development

As discussed in Chapter Four and in Resource A, we used a qualitative design to gain insight into the interaction of work, love, and learning in adult life. We treated the "Work, Love, and Learning in Adulthood" questionnaire — with its journal-like listing and subjective rating of life events, the graphs of these events, and the respondents' comments — as a source of qualitative data, from which we inductively derived three distinct patterns of interaction. Although there are precedents for using graphs to study adult development, our design is the first that we know of that allows for the visualization of the interaction between work and love, and the location of learning in relation to this interaction. This design could be used as a prototype in future studies of work and love.

Underlying all of our findings is the life event framework that we used to structure the study. Life events in the work and love arenas anchored the study, defined the patterns of work and love, and were listed as sources of significant learning. We would like to explore further how this framework facilitated our investigation.

As mentioned in Chapter Four, the study of adult development is the study of change over time. Investigators attempt to map the commonalities of human experience, at least within a particular social context, while at the same time preserving the uniqueness of individuals. A life event framework allows for both in that every adult has a personal history made of life events that is different from every other adult's history. Yet each society has a set of normative life events that results in "most people follow[ing] a relatively orderly progression through their life" (Kimmel, 1990, p. 83). In our study, respondents listed both normative and nonnormative life events as part of their personal life course.

Normative life events are those events that are assumed to occur at particular times in people's lives. Each society determines when it is appropriate for events to occur; such expectations can change over time, but at any point in time there are clear expectations of when certain events should take place. Neugarten explains:

There exists a socially prescribed timetable for the ordering of major life events: a time in the life-span when men and women are expected to marry, a time to raise children, a time to retire. This normative pattern is adhered to more or less consistently, by most persons within a given social group. . . . For any social group it can easily be demonstrated that norms and actual occurrences are closely related. Age norms and age expectations operate as a system of social controls, as prods and brakes upon behavior, in some instances hastening an event, in others, delaying it. Men and women are aware not only of the social clocks that operate in various areas of their lives but also of their own timing; and they readily describe themselves as "early," "late," or "on time" with regard to the major life events [1976, p. 16].

Certainly the on-time occurrence of expected, normative life events is what leads to some commonality of experience in the life cycle. Hundreds of life events listed by men and women in our study were normative and on time. One thirty-nine-year-old teacher, for example, fell in love at nineteen, got married at twenty-two, started teaching elementary school the same year, had children at ages twenty-four, twenty-six, and thirty-two, dropped out of work and stayed home after the birth of the second child, and went back to work when the youngest turned five. A forty-five-year-old male respondent was married at age twenty-four, had two children within the next three years, and had a parent die by the time he was forty-four. For the work arena he noted obtaining several degrees and periodic increases in responsibilities at work. For many of the men and women in our sample, the predictable, normative events of marriage, birth of children, illness or death of parents, graduations and job moves occurred at the expected times in their graphs. Kimmel comments on how normative work and love events structure our lives: "Not only do we tend to share implicit timetables about family events (marriage, parenthood, grandparenthood, widowhood in that order) and occupational events (first job, serious job, promotion, last chance to change jobs, reaching the peak, retirement), but we even have a timetable for death (the oldest die first). . . . We, as members of society who share these norms, tend to organize our lives in relation to these timetables, whether they fit us precisely or not" (1990, p. 83).

The timing of these normative life events is central to the stability of adult life. Timing is an artifact of the social context at a particular point in time. As society changes, there are changes in the timing of life events and the rhythm of the life course. Several such shifts were reflected in our study. Commonly listed were divorce and remarriage (sometimes several times for the same person), delayed parenthood, multiple job or career changes, dropping in and out of formal education, and so on.

There is another type of life event that militates against the life cycle being totally predictable. That is the nonnormative or idiosyncratic life event, which is defined as an event that is unanticipated and unplanned—one that most people do not expect to experience. Winning a lottery, being fired, the death of a child, a major illness, and so on are examples of nonnormative or unanticipated life events. Numerous examples of this type of event are scattered throughout our sample: bankruptcy, job loss, the death of a child, the death of a sister caused by a drunk driver, caring for a sibling's children, rape, religious conversion, being selected to teach in an honors program, winning a prize for artwork. Some people seem to have more than their share of unanticipated events. One fifty-five-year-old woman in our sample reported her house being burned down and having to live in a motel for several months. Seven months later her barn was destroyed. Four years later she won a trip to Europe. Finally there is the nonevent—one that a person expects to occur but that does not, such as not getting married, or not being promoted as anticipated.

Normative events lend regularity and predictability to the life course, while nonnormative events would seem to disrupt the rhythm of our everyday lives. Our respondents listed both types of events (although there were significantly more normative events), and yet we were able to detect three distinct, stable patterns of work/love interaction. This finding suggests that the patterns reflect personality types or perhaps styles of relating to or adapting to life events. Smelser, for example, suspects that working and loving might be "different names for a very similar process of human adaptation" (1980a, p. 5). Thus, with their characteristic modes of interaction, the three patterns might represent three adaptational styles.

In our study, significant learning occurred in response to work- or love-related life events (see Chapters Nine and Ten). The intrinsic connection between work, love, and learning in adult life arises from life events — marriage, births of children, family moves, jobs taken and lost, promotions, travel. The same events that define a person's work-and-love pattern become the sources of significant learning. Educators speak of the lifelong learner, pointing to studies that document the extensive participation in formal and informal learning. However, we have seen that learning is lifelong in a far deeper sense: Life itself is the locus of learning.

Certainly there is some commonality to this learning and the development that results from it. The normative events of adult life — experiences like becoming financially responsible for oneself, committing to an intimate relationship, developing professional capabilities, assuming responsiblity for the care of others, dealing with the deaths of loved ones — these shape us as adults in our culture and we learn from them, becoming more mature, more seasoned, and hopefully wiser.

Yet there are also life events that are nonnormative, that cannot be predicted, that startle and surprise us out of the normal flow of our lives. Sometimes these are wonderful experiences that are the stuff of dreams: an award for the work that for years was unnoticed, being reunited in later life with a childhood sweetheart, being offered an opportunity to travel. Others are tragic: the inexplicable death of an infant, losing a job because of a corporate takeover, or being emotionally abused as a child. These events shape us too, but not always in ways that can be predicted. We become gentler and more loving, or bitter and angry. And our life course itself can be radically redirected.

It is not the events in and of themselves, but the *learning* that we derive from these events — both the ones we can predict and the ones that come as a total surprise — that shapes our lives. It is the person himself or herself who determines the meaning of these life experiences, and thus the individuality of the life course is preserved. We have also found that there is some commonality in the process of maturing. We engage in, attend to, reflect on life events, which leads to a change, large or small, in how we react to subsequent experiences. The process is ongoing and lifelong.

In summary, the life event framework provided a workable means of exploring the connections between work, love, and learning in adult life. First, we uncovered three distinct patterns of interaction. Second, we identified a stabilizing factor in each pattern that we feel is related to notions of balance and well-being. Third, we found no gender differences in any of our results. Fourth, we found learning to be the key to understanding how maturity evolves from interaction with life events.

Implications for Practice:
The World of Work and Love Revisited

In a sense, any research study has three phases: It begins in the world we live in, asking questions and gathering data about that world; then it moves beyond everyday life in the process of analysis, getting the large picture of what is going on in that world; and finally it returns to the everyday world to situate what it has learned in that context and to ask what difference the new understandings make to real life. This final section is our effort to make that return trip.

Work and love are the major arenas of adult life. They form the basis of our identity and they organize how we relate to the world. And they get a lot of our attention. Consider Freud's dictum about the capacity to love and to work being the basis of maturity. We will not find this idea developed or even mentioned anywhere in his extensive writings; it was, in fact, something he is reported to have said to someone, perhaps in response to a question and therefore more spontaneous than planned — the exact context remains unclear. That this one pithy statement should have been remembered at all shows that it captures what we know to be intuitively true. It is remembered, we believe, because it gives expression to our lived experience.

We have a lot of knowledge about the arenas of work and love, and that knowledge derives from our experience. We know how important it is to have both dimensions in our lives, and we are taught from an early age to attend to both. These cultural values are reflected clearly in the institutionalized forms of each domain — the bureaucratically defined areas of work in job and career, and socially defined expressions of love in marriage and the family — but they also find expression in literature and the arts. Consider one example, the children's book *Johnny Cottontail*. In Figure 11.1 we see the rabbit sitting alone and disconsolate at his table, all because he has no work to do and no one to love. This is not just a lesson for children; it represents beliefs within our culture about what constitutes a satisfying life. In it we see that the very idea of adulthood is composed of both working and loving.

People also feel that both areas of life should be satisfying. It is not enough that we have work, we want that work to be meaningful. Likewise in love we value quality relationships. Sometimes that concern assumes comic proportions, as it does in the "Cathy" cartoon in Figure 11.2, but the cartoon is funny precisely because it captures our personal experience. Being accurate is an issue because our satisfaction in work and love varies, and we wish it could be more uniformly high.

Finally, we want to find a healthy balance between work and love in our lives, yet both our experience and the extensive literature on this issue indicate the difficulty in achieving this. How do we effectively integrate both domains on a day-to-day basis? Are there ways to balance the two and thereby increase our sense of well-being? The fact that these questions of balance continue to confront us is proof enough that the answers still elude us.

These are the major questions that present themselves when we consider the two arenas of adult life. Our study began in response to them and, as we have seen, it has offered some theoretical and conceptual answers that we believe are significant. But the real-world question still remains: what difference does our study and its findings make in the world we live in? We

Figure 11.1. A Scene from *Johnny Cottontail.*

He had no one to love.
He had no work to do.
He was not happy.

Source: Friskey, M. *Johnny Cottontail.* Philadelphia: McKay, 1946. Courtesy of the Kerlan Collection, University of Minnesota Libraries. Reprinted with permission.

will address that question from two perspectives. First, we will assess the value to individuals of using the "Work, Love, and Learning in Adulthood" questionnaire as a way of reflecting on these dimensions of their lives. And second, we will explore how educators and human service practitioners can use our questionnaire and our findings in their work with adults.

Figure 11.2. Cathy's Assessment of Work and Love in Adulthood.

Individual Reflection on Work, Love, and Learning. We already have experience with individual use of the "Work, Love, and Learning in Adulthood" questionnaire in our study itself, since it was the means by which we collected our data. In order to assess the impact that completing the instrument had on people, we added a "Comments" section on the last page where we asked participants to "share any reflections you have related to the experience of completing this activity, or comments of any kind." Over a third of our participants responded with extensive comments. These can be categorized according to particular gains in self-knowledge and comments on the benefits of the reflection process itself.

Numerous comments had to do with insights gained about oneself. In some there is a sense of awe at having negotiated through the maze of life events, planned and unplanned. "I've gone through a lot," summed up one thirty-four-year-old. "I've come a long way!" emphasized another. Yet another wrote, "I am amazed at the inner strength it took to survive the emotional roller coaster of my life and I feel proud of myself for those triumphs." Others were more detailed about what they saw: "This activity gave me a chance to formalize my adult experiences and how they have shaped my life. Growing up, I had many dreams and goals. I realized at age twenty-eight that I had accomplished many of my childhood goals, and I became very unhappy due to lack of direction. Since then I have developed new goals for my life and my work, leading to increased happiness." A fifty-eight-year-old arts administrator discovered the following about her life: "As I look back over the 'peaks and valleys' I wonder that I kept my sanity some of those times. . . . What gave me an escape hatch was the personal satisfaction derived from creative pursuits on the side—affording me fresh 'second winds' even in the midst of stale air. Teaching Sunday School, learning new things, and losing myself in producing art were literally lifesavers." One of our youngest respondents, a twenty-three-year-old medical technician, discovered this about life: "I realized that until this year, I experienced major events as extremes—either good or bad. Since graduation from my undergraduate institution, and subsequent entrance into 'the real world,' I've learned to realize that there *is* middle ground; not everything needs to be one extreme or the other. I didn't see that until I drew the graph!"

Self-knowledge also grew from examining one's work and love patterns. One woman discovered that "'bad' assessments usually are when I am so obligated to the needs of others there is no time left for me!" Another found out that even though she had been on an "intense emotional roller coaster," her achievements had not suffered. "I am surprised," she wrote, "because my emotions colored my feelings about my achievements. Until

I made this graph I would've described my achievements as so-so." A forty-six-year-old man found out that as he has gotten older his "perspectives are more consistent. I realize I don't need the things I once thought I did and I enjoy the ones I have more." Finally, one respondent said of the activity, "It sums up eight years of therapy."

The reflection process that was involved in filling out the "Work, Love, and Learning in Adulthood" questionnaire generated its own set of comments. One of our young adults wrote, "It *really* made me think to actually write this down and consider it. Ought to do this every ten years or so!" Another thanked us for the opportunity "to reflect on my 'ups and downs' and on what I consider important to have learned. I can see that I hold as most valuable those learnings about myself, about human beings, about how we generate and limit our lives." Another suggested that "similar exercises would be helpful to anyone seeking counseling to see the causes and effects of their current or past ups and downs, especially if they are not usually introspective." A couple of people commented on the process being uncomfortable and unsettling, but yet "most worthwhile."

It appears that reflecting on the arenas of work and love in the way we have suggested enables individuals to gain some distance on their lives and to attain a more holistic perspective. In doing so they see relationships not only between the domains but among various factors in their lives that have shaped them. They learn more about themselves and their strengths and weaknesses, as well as about the factors that promote well-being and those that impede it. In short, this reflection itself becomes a learning experience with the potential to enhance personal growth.

Implications for Practitioners. Ours is an age of specialists, and this is as apparent in the human service field as it is elsewhere. It is the norm rather than the exception to have professionals who focus on one aspect of adult life; we have marriage counselors, family therapists, community activists, career counselors, spiritual directors, adult educators, human resource personnel, and other professionals who are equipped to assist adults with particular areas of their lives. Those who have a more holistic approach, who deal with all aspects of adult experiences in an integrated fashion, are the exception. Yet it is precisely such an integrated approach that offers the greatest potential for growth.

We believe that the greatest benefit our study offers to human service practitioners — to educators, counselors, social workers, and others concerned with the personal growth and development of adults — is such a holistic approach. By facilitating reflection on both work and love, defined in the broadest possible way to include a vast range of adult experience, individuals are being asked to attend to all aspects of their lives at one time. Only then can they begin to see the connections between the different aspects of their lives and to note patterns of behavior that link or separate the two arenas. Such a panoramic view affords an important opportunity for significant personal growth.

The "Work, Love, and Learning in Adulthood" questionnaire and our findings can be used in several ways. For counselors the questionnaire provides a useful evaluation and assessment tool. Having clients reflect on their lives in this way early in the treatment process will facilitate the identification of major issues in both domains, as well as reveal the overall style or orientation of clients to their life experience. The period of time reviewed can be extended to encompass all adult years. The questionnaire also presents a way of reviewing the life course that is immediate and can be easily discussed with the counselor. It thus provides an excellent initial exercise within the therapeutic process.

Beyond its uses in assessment, the questionnaire and our findings present opportunities for the development of insight in work with adults individually and in groups. Certainly identification of their pattern of work and love interaction would help enable adults to see their overall style of dealing with their life experience. An increased understanding of the stabilizing factor in their lives would be particularly interesting and useful. Knowledge of this would mean that individuals could maximize this aspect of their lives, increasing their overall sense of well-being. Within a group context the questionnaire could be used to demonstrate the varying styles adults adopt to deal with the major arenas of their lives. Acknowledging legitimate differences fosters acceptance of styles other than one's own. This could be particularly useful in marriage counseling, where differing styles could be sources of conflict.

The questionnaire can be used to look forward as well as backward, however, and this itself is a significant feature. Because we found that each pattern was largely maintained across the twenty-year period, it seems reasonable to project forward and to anticipate those normative events that lie ahead. Understanding of one's pattern could be used to facilitate adaptation or adjustment to later predictable life events such as retirement, empty nest, or widowhood. For example, a person whose pattern is steady/fluctuating with love as the steady domain may have more difficulty coping with empty nest or widowhood than a person whose steady domain (thus, stabilizing factor) has been work. Conversely, a person with a divergent pattern in which work is emphasized may have less difficulty with empty nest and widowhood but more difficulty with retirement.

Likewise, once people's particular style of work/love interaction is clear it would be possible to think about how they would deal with crises or other unpredictable events in the future. Thus adults would be encouraged to be more proactive in engaging their life experiences. This can also be done by groups of people in community settings who face shared problems that fall into one or both arenas. Together they could learn alternative ways of dealing with those issues, becoming proactive in their engagement with their environment.

For educators in various settings, the "Work, Love, and Learning in Adulthood" questionnaire and the findings of our study could foster the same kind of insight and personal growth that it does in therapeutic settings. Additionally, it could serve as a vehicle for experiential learning about adult development in general and, more specifically, about the development of the capacity to work and to love. The educator could effectively illustrate the major theories of adult development with use of the questionnaire by the students, or work inductively by beginning with the students' life experience and build toward theory. The importance of life events in shaping development would be particularly well illustrated by this method.

For courses in adult learning, use of the questionnaire helps explicate the important role that learning plays in the developmental process. Because the bulk of that learning derives from life experience, students will have an opportunity to study firsthand a mode of learning that has received limited attention in the literature. This will expand their awareness of the scope of learning in adult life.

Finally, we believe that our findings will influence the way educators think about the learning that goes on in their classrooms. Rather than focusing primarily on the instrumental dimension of that learning, they will be able to see the personal impact that learning has on their students. This should help them become attuned to the transformative potential of formal education experience and help them see themselves as facilitators in the developmental process of their students.

When we make the return trip, then, from our findings back to the world in which we as adults live, we see multiple ways in which what we have learned in this study can be used. The questionnaire offers individuals a way to reflect on their lives in a holistic way, providing insight into themselves and their way of engaging experience and leading to enhanced personal growth. And for practitioners it provides a means of facilitating that reflection to augment their work with adults in various settings.

Summary

In this chapter we have highlighted the major findings of our study and attempted to show how practitioners can apply them to their daily activities. Generated by Freud's notion of maturity as being the capacity to work and to love, our study explored both the interaction of these central forces in adult life and the intrinsic link between learning and the development of this capacity. Using a life event framework, we discovered three distinct patterns of interaction, which we called parallel, steady/

fluctuating, and divergent. Each pattern has its own special characteristics, one of which — the stabilizing factor — we identified as a major contribution to the adult development literature. This is because this factor seems to be linked to balance, integration, and sense of well-being. Surprisingly, we found no gender differences with regard to any of our findings, suggesting that work and love are valued equally by both men and women. Finally, as a result of our study we are better able to understand the link between learning and development, or the evolution of maturity. Significant learning from life events results in an expansion or a transformation, enlarging a person's capacity to work and to love.

In this chapter, we also suggested how these findings could be put to use by individuals and practitioners in education, human services, and community groups. Drawing from comments from the participants in our study, we noted that using the "Work, Love, and Learning in Adulthood" questionnaire led to insights about oneself, and about the reflection process itself. It is clear that such an exercise, whether done alone, in groups, or with a trained professional, could be in and of itself a learning experience leading to growth and development. We thus come full circle to a better understanding of Freud's pithy but profound statement that maturity is the capacity to work and to love.

Notes on Methodology

This study began as most research does, with the researchers being curious about or puzzled by a phenomenon for which there is little information or satisfactory answers. In particular, we were interested in understanding the interaction among work, love, and learning in adult life. A review of the literature in these areas produced few studies on the interaction of work and love, and even less on the place of learning in developing the capacity to work and to love, which is how Freud defined maturity. With no well-developed theory or research base to guide this study, and no well-tested instruments (questionnaires) with which to assess this interaction, we chose an exploratory, qualitative research design as the only feasible means of addressing our questions.

The Design of the Study

Research in adult development focuses on delineating how adults change as they age, determining the sources of change, and predicting patterns of change or development. As discussed in Chapter Four, there are numerous frameworks that can be used for studying development. The centrality of working and loving in adult life combined with a life-event framework formed the basis of this study. Cross-sectional, longitudinal, and sequential research designs are used when specific variables are investigated such as intelligence, self-concept, or coping mechanisms and there is enough theory to generate hypotheses. There are hundreds of studies on various dimensions of adult development using these quantitative designs (Rybash, Roodin, and Santrock, 1991). Qualitative designs are used when less is known about an aspect of development, when many rather than a few variables are suspected of being important, when the context of people's lives may be interrelated with the phenomenon of interest, and when discovery and understanding rather than verification are sought. Interviews, documents, and observations are the major sources of data in qualitative studies (Lincoln and Guba, 1985; Patton, 1980; Bogdan and Biklen, 1982; Merriam, 1988). In addition to data collection, sample selection and data analysis (including issues of validity and reliability) are treated somewhat differently in qualitative research than they are in traditional experimental or survey designs. Some have written about combining the two approaches in the same study (Miles and Huberman, 1984; Smith and Louis, 1982).

Our study design is primarily *qualitative,* although we do collect data from over 400 adults. Our purpose was to uncover, if they existed, discrete patterns of interaction of work and love in people's lives, and to understand the place of learning within those patterns of interaction.

Sampling

Our sample can be described as a *purposeful* and a *convenient* sample, both of which are common in qualitative research (Patton, 1980). In purposeful sampling, the investigator selects respondents, cases, or situations on purpose, because it is from them that he or she can learn the most about the phenomenon under investigation. This nonprobability sampling makes sense as long as the researcher "expects mainly to use his [or her] data not to answer questions like 'how much' and 'how often' but to solve *qualitative* problems, such as discovering what occurs, the implications of what occurs, and the relationships linking occurrences" (Honigmann, 1982, p. 84). The nineteen men and women that we interviewed for this study were selected because they had a particular pattern of work/love interaction and because they were articulate and introspective enough to provide us with insights into their pattern and their learning. The sample from whom we collected the "Work, Love, and Learning in Adulthood" questionnaires was both convenient and purposeful. Original workshop participants who came from across North America volunteered to distribute the forms with their classes. Since nearly all of our participants were engaged in formal or informal learning (including cooperative extension, church, and community groups), we felt that they would be a good sample in that they would probably be able to reflect on and delineate the connection between learning and their work and love experiences.

Since a nonrandom sampling technique was used, we are unable to generalize the findings in a statistical sense to a larger population of adults. However, in qualitative research the goal is to discover new insights into a previously ill-defined or unknown phenomenon, rather than determine causation or describe the distribution of a known phenomenon. Thus rather than *statistical generalization* (also known as *external validity*), what we have in our research is what Stake (1978) calls *naturalistic generalization*. Naturalistic generalization draws on tacit knowledge, intuition, and personal experience. According to Stake, this process of naturalistic generalization is arrived at "by recognizing similarities of objects and issues in and out of context and by sensing the natural covariations of happenings" (1978, p. 6). Generalization, then, is the search for patterns to explain experience, the "sensing" of "natural covariations of happenings." This is precisely what occurred in our investigation of work/love interaction, in which we uncovered three distinct patterns. We might also think of our findings in terms of reader or user generalizability. This involves letting the reader or the user determine the applicability of the study's findings to his or her own particular situation.

Data Sources and Data Analysis

Traditional sources of data for the study of adult development are biographies (Levinson and others, 1978), journals (Progoff, 1983), clinical practices (Erikson, 1963; Gould, 1978), surveys, and interviews (Levinson and others, 1978; Sheehy, 1976; Vaillant, 1977). Our two sources of data were interviews and the "Work, Love, and Learning in Adulthood" questionnaires. The development of this questionnaire as well as precedents for graphic representations of developmental processes are discussed in detail in Chapter Four. What we would like to point out is that for the major portion of our analysis we treated the information provided by the questionnaires as qualitative data. We asked people to identify major work and love events, and to rate the years of those events as good, bad, or okay. These events were personally and subjectively evaluated. There were no "right" answers, nor were we testing any hypotheses. These data, then, were more like diary or journal entries than objective survey data. The same is true for the learning section, in which we asked people to identify significant learning experiences, when they occurred, and what made them significant. What we sought was respondents' subjective interpretation of the interplay of work, love, and learning in their lives.

Our findings of course hinge on this subjective listing and evaluation of work, love, and learning events. Although we broadly defined work as "noteworthy work experiences, paid or volunteer; formal education," and love as "interpersonal relationships, family events; social life; leisure activities," the interpretations of these definitions was left up to individual respondents. We also realize that these definitions, as well as the dualism inherent in dividing work and love into two separate domains, reflect culturally bound, Western paradigms and values.

There are other limitations to our journal-type instrument. Because it spans a twenty-year period (1969–1989), we were unable to capture what might have been major events in early adulthood for the older adults in our sample. A fifty-five-year-old respondent, for example, would have listed events beginning at age thirty-five. There are two mitigating factors with regard to this issue, however. First, the average age of our respondents is 37.6, and two-thirds of our sample are between 20 and 40 years old, meaning that a twenty-year period covered the majority of our respondents. Second, our analysis of the stability of the patterns (see Chapter Eight) revealed that the pattern of work/love interaction does not change over time. It would be interesting to see if the patterns remain stable if people were able to graph an additional five, ten, or even twenty years.

An additional limitation has to do with the good, bad, and okay ratings of the years. Our instructions asked people to rate each year "as you remember experiencing it at the time." It is difficult to know how accurate these assessments are. While a few people had trouble assigning a rating to those years in which something good and something bad had happened, most of our respondents did not have a problem, perhaps because many of the life events listed had had a major impact and were easy to recall. Furthermore, an occasional inaccurate rating or a year left blank would not have changed the basic structure of any one person's graph.

We considered the information given in both the life-events and the learning sections of the questionnaire to be qualitative data. We analyzed these data and the interview data using the *constant comparative analysis technique of grounded theory*, a qualitative research methodology developed by Glaser and Strauss (1967). The method is largely inductive; one instance, event, or statement is compared with the next in an attempt to find some sort of order, pattern, or theme in the data. Tentative categories, themes, or hypotheses are then tested against the data in a constant movement between discovery and verification, inductive and deductive analysis. In our study the graphs were analyzed inductively, that is, one was compared with another and these were compared with a third, and so on. Three major patterns or categories emerged. Likewise, the statements about the significance of learning on the second page of the questionnaire were categorized into types of significance. Finally, we analyzed the interview data inductively, which allowed us to discover and confirm identifying characteristics of each pattern of interaction.

Our analysis did contain a quantitative component in that we had enough graphs (405 in the final sample) to be able to assess the distribution of the patterns, once we had derived them, according to gender and life stage. We also had enough quantitative data on the number and type of significant learning events to determine their distribution by pattern, gender, and position on the graphs. While this was interesting material, we consider these findings to be secondary to the major findings of the study that emerged from the analysis of the qualitative data. Through that paradigm and the sample selection and data analysis that accompanied it, we were able to discover three patterns of work/love interaction, and could better understand the connection between learning and development.

Validity and Reliability

Judging the worth or value of a research study depends on its validity and reliability. That is, can we believe and trust the findings of a study? Regardless of the type of study, validity and reliability concerns permeate all parts of a research study from conceptualization to interpretation of findings. For survey and experimental studies there are well-developed guidelines for ensuring for validity and reliability. Qualitative research also has ways of handling these concerns, many of which we incorporated into this study.

We have already discussed *external validity* or the extent to which our findings can be generalized to a larger population. Of even more concern is *internal validity,* the extent to which we are observing and perhaps measuring what we think we are measuring. That is, how well do one's findings actually match with reality? How trustworthy are the data? We employed two strategies for ensuring internal validity, *triangulation* and *member checks.* One form of triangulation is the use of multiple methods of data collection. We used interviews and the "Work, Love, and Learning in Adulthood" questionnaires. Data from each of these sources converged with regard to pattern identification. Second, our interviewees were selected based on their pattern type, and we asked them to elaborate on their work/love interaction. This strategy functioned like a member check, in which one takes findings and interpretations back to the people from whom they were derived, asking them if the results (in this case our identification of the pattern types) are plausible. Later interviews were also used to "check" on the characteristics of the patterns that had emerged from earlier interviews.

The notion of reliability in quantitative research depends on repeatability; that is, if the study is repeated the same results should occur. Qualitative research, however, seeks to describe and explain a phenomenon from the perspective of those most closely involved. The researcher interprets these perspectives or understandings and reports them as findings. Because multiple interpretations of the same data are possible, it is not possible to achieve reliability in the traditional sense. Thus, Lincoln and Guba (1985, p. 288) suggest we replace traditional notions of reliability with the concepts of "dependability" or "consistency." That is, "rather than demanding that outsiders get the same results, one wishes outsiders to concur that, given the data collected, the results make sense — they are consistent and dependable" (Merriam, 1988, p. 172). Again, triangulation is one technique for ensuring reliability. In our study we have visual representations of the patterns in the graphs, and we have interview data that concur with the graph data. Furthermore, we made use of investigator triangulation in determining the patterns. As explained in Chapter Four, four doctoral students independently categorized samples of graphs, and all identified the same three patterns.

Once the three pattern types were inductively identified, we set about categorizing all of the graphs. Three investigators did this, working independently of each other. Table A.1 demonstrates the reliability of this categorizing process. As the table shows, there was total agreement among the three raters for 275 or 67.1 percent of the graphs, versus what would be expected by chance (46 or 11.5 percent). There was no agreement on only 5 graphs and these were deleted from the analysis.

In summary, ultimately the reader must decide how trustworthy our findings are. We have attempted to clearly present the conceptual framework and procedures we used to conduct this study, and to support our findings with data from both the interviews and the questionnaires. A final "check" on the validity of our findings would be for each reader to determine his

Table A.1. Interrater Reliability Figures.

Agreement	Expected Through Chance		Observed	
	n	%	n	%
Total agreement	46	11.1	275	67.1
Two out of three agree	273	66.7	130	31.7
No agreement	91	22.2	5	1.2

or her own pattern of work/love interaction, to reflect on significant learning in relation to this pattern, and then to compare these results to those in our study.

Determining Your Own Pattern

To determine your own pattern of work and love inter-action, first on a piece of paper construct a chart with two major columns, one labeled *WORK* and the other labeled *LOVE*. In the left-hand margin list the years chonologically; in the middle, between the two columns, leave space for two ratings. (See Exhibit B.1; for a copy of the entire questionnaire to use as a reference see Exhibit 4.1 in Chapter Four.)

Exhibit B.1. The Chart.

	WORK	rating		LOVE
1971				
1972				
1973				
1974				
1975				
(continue)				

To complete the chart, first try to recall the significant events that occurred in your life for each year in each domain beginning with the year of the earliest event (or the year in which you turned 18). The work domain includes noteworthy work experiences, paid or volunteer, and formal education. The love domain includes interpersonal relationships, family events, social life, and leisure activities. You may not recall major events for every year, but complete as much of the chart as you can.

236

Next, consider each year's events by domain and decide whether your experience of work or love that year was good, okay, or bad; then indicate that rating on the chart. Your judgment here should be how you remember experiencing those events at that time, not how you subsequently evaluate them. For example, one woman listed a divorce in the love column for 1972. It was a painful experience at the time, so she rated it as bad, even though the ultimate consequences of this event were beneficial to her. The goal here is to capture the quality of the experience at the time it occurred.

Once you have completed the chart, the next step is to graph the work and love ratings. On a separate piece of paper, draw two lines perpendicular to each other. On the horizontal axis, list the years chronologically; on the vertical axis, place the ratings, good, okay, and bad, in that order. (See Figure B.1.)

Figure B.1. The Graph.

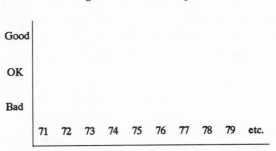

Now plot the ratings for each domain by year. It is helpful to do one domain first, completing a vector for that domain, then the other. It is also helpful to use different marks for each domain; on our own questionnaire people used x's for work and o's for love. When a year has no rating, maintain the rating of the previous year. The result will be two vectors representing your experience of work and love over the last twenty years. (See Figure B.2.)

The final step is to determine which pattern of work/love interaction you follow. For guidelines here, consult the beginnings

Figure B.2. A Sample Graph.

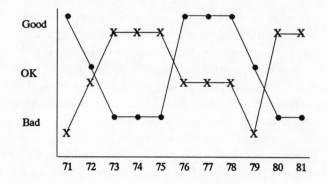

of Chapters Five, Six, and Seven, where specifications of each
pattern are outlined. However, broadly speaking, if the overall
movement of the vectors is in tandem, the pattern is parallel;
if one vector is unchanging while the other changes freely, it
is steady/fluctuating; and if the vectors appear to move independently of one another (as is true in Figure B.2), then the pattern is divergent.

References

Allman, P. "The Nature and Process of Adult Development." In M. Tight (ed.), *Adult Learning and Education.* London: Croom Helm, 1983.

Aries, E., and Olver, R. "Sex Differences in the Development of a Separate Sense of Self During Infancy: Directions for Future Research." *Psychology of Women Quarterly,* 1985, *9,* 515–532.

Aslanian, C. B., and Brickell, H. M. *Americans in Transition: Life Changes as Reasons for Adult Learning.* New York: College Entrance Examination Board, 1980.

Atchley, R. C. "A Continuity Theory of Normal Aging." *The Gerontologist,* 1989, *29* (2), 183–190.

Back, K. W. "Mathematics and the Poetry of Human Life and Points In-Between." In K. W. Back (ed.), *Life Course: Integrative Theories and Exemplary Populations.* American Association for the Advancement of Science Selected Symposium 41. Boulder, Colo.: Westview Press, 1980.

Back, K. W., and Bourque, L. B. "Life Graphs: Aging and Cohort Effect." *Journal of Gerontology,* 1970, *25* (3), 249–255.

Bakan, D. *The Duality of Human Existence: An Essay on Psychology and Religion.* Chicago: Rand McNally, 1966.

Baruch, G., Barnett, R., and Rivers, C. *Lifeprints: New Patterns of Love and Work for Today's Women.* New York: McGraw-Hill, 1983.

Basseches, M. *Dialectical Thinking and Adult Development.* Norwood, N.J.: Ablex, 1984.

Belenky, M. F., Clinchy, B. M., Goldberger, N. R., and Tarule, J. M. *Women's Ways of Knowing: The Development of Self,
Voice, and Mind.* New York: Basic Books, 1986.

Block, J. "Some Enduring and Consequential Structures of Personality." In A. I. Rabin and others (eds.), *Further Explorations in Personality.* New York: Wiley-Interscience, 1981.

Blumenthal, P. J. "Male Physicians in Young Adulthood: An
Assessment of Goals and Satisfactions in Their Work and
Family Lives." Unpublished doctoral dissertation, Univer-
sity of Texas Health Science Center at Dallas, 1981.

Blumstein, P., and Schwartz, P., *American Couples: Money, Work
and Sex.* New York: Morrow, 1983.

Bogdan, R. C., and Biklen, S. K. *Qualitative Research for Educators: An Introduction to Theory and Methods.* Newton, Mass.: Allyn
& Bacon, 1982.

Borman, K. M., and Frankel, J. "Gender Inequities in Child-
hood Social Life and Adult Work Life." In K. M. Borman,
D. Quarm, and S. Gideonse (eds.). *Women in the Workplace:
Effects on Families.* Norwood, N.J.: Ablex, 1984.

Boshier, R., and Collins, J. B. "The Houle Typology After
Twenty-Two Years: A Large-Scale Empirical Test." *Adult
Education Quarterly,* 1985, *35* (3), 113–130.

Boyd, E. M., and Fales, A. W. "Reflective Learning: Key to
Learning from Experience." *Journal of Humanistic Psychology,*
1983, *23* (2), 99–117.

Boyd, R. D., and Myers, J. G. "Transformative Education."
International Journal of Lifelong Education, 1988, *7* (4), 261–284.

Bracken, D. W., and Gier, J. A. "Work/Family Issues in U.S.
Companies: Your Personal Life Is Some of Our Business!"
The Exchange. Atlanta, Ga.: American Society for Training
and Development, Jan. 1990.

Bridges, W. *Transitions.* Reading, Mass.: Addison-Wesley, 1980.

Carnevale, A. B. "The Learning Enterprise." *Training and Development Journal,* 1986, *40* (1), 18–26.

Carnevale, A. B. "The Learning Enterprise." *Training and Development Journal,* 1989, *43* (2), 26–33.

Chodorow, N. *The Reproduction of Mothering.* Berkeley: University of California Press, 1978.

Costa, P. T., Jr. and McCrae, R. R. "Still Stable After All These Years: Personality as a Key to Some Issues in Adulthood and Old Age." In P. B. Baltes and O. G. Brim, Jr. (eds.), *Life Span Development and Behavior.* Vol. 3. New York: Academic Press, 1980.

Costa, P. T., Jr., and McCrae, R. R. "Personality in Adulthood: A Six-Year Longitudinal Study of Self-Reports and Spouse Ratings on the NEO Personality Inventory." *Journal of Personality and Social Psychology,* 1988, *54,* 853–863.

Cross, K. P. *Adults as Learners: Increasing Participation and Facilitating Learning.* San Francisco: Jossey-Bass, 1981.

Daloz, L. A. *Effective Teaching and Mentoring: Realizing the Transformational Power of Adult Learning Experiences.* San Francisco: Jossey-Bass, 1986.

Daniels, P., and Weingarten, K. *Sooner or Later: The Timing of Parenthood.* New York: Norton, 1982.

"Dear Abby." *Atlanta Journal and Constitution.* Apr. 9, 1990, p. C-2.

Demuth, N. *Musical Forms and Textures: A Reference Guide.* (2nd ed.) London: Barrie and Rockcliff, 1964.

Denzin, N. K. *The Research Act: An Introduction to Sociological Methods.* Chicago: Aldine, 1970.

Dewey, J. *Experience and Education.* London: Collier-Macmillan, 1938.

Dewey, J. *Democracy and Education.* New York: Macmillan, 1961. (Originally published 1916.)

Dimidjian, V. J. "A Biographical Study of the Psychosocial Developmental Issues in the Lives of Six Female Psychotherapists in Their Thirties." *Women and Therapy,* 1982, *1,* 27–44.

Donne, J. *Complete Poetry and Selected Prose.* Edited by J. Hayward. London: Nonesuch Press, 1930.

Erikson, E. H. *Childhood and Society.* (2nd ed.) New York: Norton, 1963. (Originally published 1950.)

Erikson, E. H. *Identity: Youth and Crisis.* New York: Norton, 1968.

Erikson, E. H. *Identity and the Life Cycle.* New York: Norton, 1980.

Erlich, H. S., and Blatt, S. J. "Narcissism and Object Love: The Metapsychology of Experience." *Psychoanalytic Study of the Child,* 1985, *40,* 57–79.

Evans, R. *Dialogue with Erik Erikson.* New York: Harper & Row, 1967.

Farone, P. A. "The Adult Developmental Patterns of Career-Committed Women Who Make a Transition to an Integrated Lifestyle." Unpublished doctoral dissertation, University of Pittsburgh, 1981.

Fine, R. "The Protestant Ethic and the Analytic Ideal." *Political Psychology,* 1983, *4* (2), 245–264.

Fiske, M., and Chiriboga, D. A. *Change and Continuity in Adult Life.* San Francisco: Jossey-Bass, 1990.

Flavell, J. H. "Cognitive Changes in Adulthood." In L. R. Goulet and P. B. Baltes (eds.), *Life-Span Developmental Psychology: Research and Theory.* New York: Academic Press, 1970.

Ford Foundation. *Work and Family Responsibilities: Achieving a Balance.* New York: Ford Foundation, 1989.

Freud, S. *Civilization and Its Discontents.* Edited and translated by J. Strachey. New York: Norton, 1961.

Gaylin, W. "Love and the Limits of Individualism." In W. Gaylin and E. Person (eds.), *Passionate Attachments.* New York: Free Press, 1988.

Gerson, K. *Hard Choices: How Women Decide About Work, Career, and Motherhood.* Berkeley: University of California Press, 1985.

Gilligan, C. *In a Different Voice.* Cambridge, Mass.: Harvard University Press, 1982.

Glaser, B. G., and Strauss, A. L. *The Discovery of Grounded Theory.* Chicago: Aldine, 1967.

Gordon, J. "Training's 1986 Salary Survey." *Training,* 1986, *23* (11), 35–51.

Gould, R. L. *Transformations: Growth and Change in Adult Life.* New York: Simon & Schuster, 1978.

Gould, R. L. "Transformations During Early and Middle Adult Years." In N. J. Smelser and E. H. Erikson (eds.), *Themes of Work and Love in Adulthood.* Cambridge, Mass.: Harvard University Press, 1980.

Hale, N. "Freud's Reflections on Work and Love." In N. J. Smelser and E. H. Erikson (eds.), *Themes of Work and Love in Adulthood.* Cambridge, Mass.: Harvard University Press, 1980.

Hardin, P. "Generativity in Middle Adulthood." Unpublished

doctoral dissertation, Department of Leadership and Educational Policy Studies, Northern Illinois University, 1985.

Havighurst, R. *Human Development and Education.* New York: McKay, 1972.

Hendrix, L., and Johnson, G. D. "Instrumental and Expressive Socialization: A False Dichotomy." *Sex Roles,* 1985, *13* (11/12), 581–595.

Hinand, G. "Psychological Well-Being at Midlife: A Study of a College Class of 1959." Unpublished doctoral dissertation, School of Education, Boston University, 1984.

Hodgson, J., and Fischer, J. "Pathways of Identity Development in College Women." *Sex Roles,* 1981, *7,* 681–690.

Honigmann, J. J. "Sampling in Ethnographic Fieldwork." In R. G. Burgess (ed.), *Field Research: A Sourcebook and Field Manual.* London: Allen & Unwin, 1982.

Houle, C. O. *The Inquiring Mind: A Study of the Adult Who Continues to Learn.* Madison: University of Wisconsin Press, 1961.

Ingham, R. J. "Context and Learning." In Lifelong Learning Research Conference Proceedings, no. 8. College Park: Department of Agriculture and Extension Education, University of Maryland, 1987.

Jarvis, P. *Adult Learning in the Social Context.* London: Croom Helm, 1987a.

Jarvis, P. "Meaningful and Meaningless Experience: Toward an Analysis of Learning from Life." *Adult Education Quarterly,* 1987b, *37* (3), 164–172.

Josselson, R. *Finding Herself: Pathways to Identity Development in Women.* San Francisco: Jossey-Bass, 1987.

Kacerguis, M. A., and Adams, G. R. "Erikson Stage Resolution: The Relationship Between Identity and Intimacy." *Journal of Youth and Adolescence,* 1980, *9,* 117–126.

Kanter, R. M. "Jobs and Families: Impact of Working Roles on Family Life." In P. Voydanoff (ed.), *Work and Family: Changing Roles of Men and Women.* Palo Alto, Calif.: Mayfield, 1984.

Kegan, R. *The Evolving Self: Problem and Process in Human Development.* Cambridge, Mass.: Harvard University Press, 1982.

Kidd, J. R. *How Adults Learn.* (2nd ed.) New York: Cambridge Books, 1973.

Kimmel, D. C. *Adulthood and Aging.* (3rd ed.) New York: Wiley, 1990.

Knowles, M. S. *The Modern Practice of Adult Education: From Pedagogy to Andragogy.* (2nd ed.) New York: Cambridge Books, 1980.

Knox, A. B. *Adult Development and Learning: A Handbook on Individual Growth and Competence in the Adult Years.* San Francisco: Jossey-Bass, 1977.

Kohlberg, L. "Continuities in Childhood and Adult Moral Development Revisited." In P. Baltes and W. Schaie, *Life Span Development Psychology.* New York: Academic Press, 1973.

Kohn, M. L., and Schooler, C. "Job Conditions and Personality: A Longitudinal Assessment of Their Reciprocal Effects." *American Journal of Sociology,* 1982, *87,* 1257–1286.

Kolb, D. A. *Learning Style Inventory Technical Manual.* Boston: McBer, 1976.

Kolb, D. A. *Experiential Learning: Experience as the Source of Learning and Development.* Englewood Cliffs, N.J.: Prentice-Hall, 1984.

Lancereau, F. R. "Reported Experiences of Work and Love of Young Married Professional Women." Unpublished doctoral dissertation, New York University, 1987.

Levinson, D., and others. *The Seasons of a Man's Life.* New York: Knopf, 1978.

Lidz, T. *The Person, His and Her Development Throughout the Life Cycle.* New York: Basic Books, 1976.

Lifton, R. J. *The Nazi Doctors.* New York: Basic Books, 1986.

Lincoln, Y. S., and Guba, E. G. *Naturalistic Inquiry.* Newbury Park, Calif.: Sage, 1985.

Loevinger, J. *Ego Development: Conceptions and Theories.* San Francisco: Jossey-Bass, 1976.

Loewenstein, S. F. "The Passion and Challenge of Teaching." *Harvard Educational Review,* 1980, *50* (1), 1–12.

Looney, J. G., and Lewis, J. M. "Competent Adolescents from Different Socioeconomic and Ethnic Contexts." *Adolescent Psychiatry,* 1983, *11,* 64–74.

Lowe, J. *The Education of Adults: A World Perspective.* New York: OISE Press, 1975.

Lukas, E. "Love and Work in Frankl's View of Human Nature." *International Forum for Logotherapy,* 1983, *8* (2), 102–109.

Lynch, A. Q., and Chickering, A. W. "Comprehensive Counseling and Support Programs for Adult Learners: Challenge to Higher Education." In N. K. Schlossberg, A. Q. Lynch, and A. W. Chickering, *Improving Higher Education Environments for Adults: Responsive Programs and Services from Entry to Departure.* San Francisco: Jossey-Bass, 1989.

McClusky, H. Y. "An Approach to a Differential Psychology of the Adult Potential." In S. M. Grabowski (ed.), *Adult Learning and Instruction.* Syracuse, N.Y.: ERIC Clearinghouse on Adult Education, 1970.

McCrae, R. R., and Costa, P. T., Jr. *Personality in Adulthood.* New York: Guilford, 1990.

Marcia, J. E. "Identity in Adolescence." In J. Adelson (ed.), *Handbook of Adolescent Psychology.* New York: Wiley, 1980.

Massey, R. F. "Erik Erikson: Neo-Adlerian." *Individual Psychology Journal of Adlerian Theory, Research and Practice,* 1986, *42* (1), 65–91.

Merriam, S. B. *Case Study Research in Education: A Qualitative Approach.* San Francisco: Jossey-Bass, 1988.

Merriam, S. B., and Caffarella, R. M. *Learning in Adulthood: A Comprehensive Guide.* San Francisco: Jossey-Bass, 1991.

Mezirow, J. "A Critical Theory of Adult Learning and Education." *Adult Education,* 1981, *32* (1), 3–24.

Mezirow, J., and Associates. *Fostering Critical Reflection in Adulthood: A Guide to Transformative and Emancipatory Learning.* San Francisco: Jossey-Bass, 1990.

Mickelson, R. A. "Why Does Jane Read and Write So Well? The Anomaly of Women's Achievement." *Sociology of Education,* 1989, *62,* 47–63.

Miles, M. B., and Huberman, A. M. *Qualitative Data Analysis: A Sourcebook of New Methods.* Newbury Park, Calif.: Sage, 1984.

Morgan, E. "Toward a Reformulation of the Eriksonian Model of Female Identity Development." *Adolescence,* 1982, *17,* 199–211.

Mortimer, J. T., Lorence, J., and Kumka, D. S. *Work, Family, and Personality: Transition to Adulthood.* Norwood, N.J.: Ablex, 1986.

Mortimer, K. M., and Sorensen, G. "Men, Women, Work, and Family." In K. M. Borman, D. Quarm, and S. Gideonse (eds.), *Women in the Workplace: Effects on Families.* Norwood, N.J.: Ablex, 1984.

Murstein, B. I. "A Taxonomy of Love." In Sternberg, R. J., and Barnes, M. L. (eds.), *The Psychology of Love.* New Haven, Conn.: Yale University Press, 1988.

Neugarten, B. L. "Adaptation and the Life Cycle." *Counseling Psychologist,* 1976, *6,* 16–20.

Nicola, J. S., and Hawkes, G. R. "Marital Satisfaction of Dual-Career Couples: Does Sharing Increase Happiness?" *Journal of Social Behavior and Personality,* 1985, *1,* 47–60.

Nieva, V. F., and Gutek, B. A. *Women and Work: A Psychological Perspective.* New York: Praeger, 1981.

Parsons, T. *The Social System.* New York: Free Press, 1964.

Patton, M. Q. *Qualitative Evaluation Methods.* Newbury Park, Calif.: Sage, 1980.

Penland, P. "Self-Initiated Learning." *Adult Education,* 1979, *29* (3), 170–179.

Perosa, S. L., and Perosa, L. M. "The Mid-Career Crisis in Relation to Super's Career and Erikson's Adult Development Theory." *International Journal of Aging and Human Development,* 1984–85, *20* (1), 53–68.

Perry, W. *Forms of Intellectual and Ethical Development in the College Years.: A Scheme.* New York: Holt, Rinehart & Winston, 1970.

Perry, W. "Cognitive and Ethical Growth: The Making of Meaning." In A. W. Chickering (ed.), *The Modern American College: Responding to the New Realities of Diverse Students and a Changing Society.* San Francisco: Jossey-Bass, 1981.

Piotrkowski, C. S. *Work and the Family System: A Naturalistic Study of Working-Class and Lower-Middle Class Families.* New York: Free Press, 1978.

Progoff, I. *Life-Study.* New York: Dialogue House Library, 1983.

Raskin, P. M. "The Relationship Between Identity and Intimacy in Early Adulthood." *Journal of Genetic Psychology,* 1986, *147,* 167–181.

Roberts, P., and Newton, P. M. "Levinsonian Studies of Women's Adult Development." *Psychology and Aging,* 1987, *2* (2), 154–163.

Rogers, C. R. *Client-Centered Therapy: Its Current Practice, Implications, and Theory.* Boston: Houghton Mifflin, 1951.

Rogers, C. R. "A Theory of Therapy, Personality, and Interpersonal Relationships as Developed in the Client-Centered Framework." In S. Koch (ed.), *Psychology: A Study of a Science.* Vol. 3: *Formulations of the Person and the Social Context.* New York: McGraw-Hill, 1959.

Rohrlich, J. B. *Work and Love: The Crucial Balance.* New York: Summit Books, 1980.

Roznafszky, J. "The Relationship of Level of Ego Development to Q-Sort Personality Ratings." *Journal of Personality and Social Psychology,* 1981, *41,* 99–120.

Rubin, L. *Women of a Certain Age: The Midlife Search for Self.* New York: Harper & Row, 1979.

Rubin, Z. "Does Personality Really Change After 20?" *Psychology Today,* 1981, *15* (5), 18–20, 23, 25, 27.

Rybash, J. W., Roodin, P. A., and Santrock, J. W. *Adult Development and Aging.* (2nd ed.) Dubuque, Iowa: Wm. C. Brown, 1991.

Sangiuliano, I. *In Her Time.* New York: Morrow, 1978.

Schlossberg, N. *Counseling Adults in Transition.* New York: Springer, 1984.

Schlossberg, N. K., Lynch, A. Q., and Chickering, A. W. *Improving Higher Education Environments for Adults: Responsive Programs and Services from Entry To Departure.* San Francisco: Jossey-Bass, 1989.

Sears, R. "Sources of Life Satisfaction of the Terman Gifted Men." *American Psychologist,* 1977, *32* (2), 119–128.

Shaw, J. S., Francois, F., Filler, H., and Sciarillo, U. "The Thoughts of Persons in an Urban Environment." *Journal of Social Psychology,* 1981, *115,* 293–294.

Sheehy, G. *Passages: Predictable Crises of Adult Life.* New York: Dutton, 1976.

Smelser, N. J. "Issues in the Study of Work and Love in Adulthood." In N. J. Smelser and E. H. Erikson (eds.), *Themes of Work and Love in Adulthood.* Cambridge, Mass.: Harvard University Press, 1980a.

Smelser, N. J. "Vicissitudes of Work and Love in Anglo-American Society." In N. J. Smelser and E. H. Erikson (eds.), *Themes of Work and Love in Adulthood.* Cambridge, Mass.: Harvard University Press, 1980b.

Smelser, N. J., and Erikson, E. H. (eds.). *Themes of Work and Love in Adulthood.* Cambridge, Mass.: Harvard University Press, 1980.

Smith, A. G., and Louis, K. S. (eds.). "Multimethod Policy Research: Issues and Applications." *American Behavioral Scientist,* 1982, *26* (1) (entire issue).

Sorensen, G., and Mortimer, J. T. "Implications of the Dual Roles of Adult Women for Their Health." In J. T. Mortimer and K. M. Borman (eds.), *Work Experience and Psychological Development Through the Life Span.* American Association for the Advancement of Science Selected Symposia Series, no. 107. Boulder, Colo.: Westview Press, 1988.

Spade, J. Z. "Bringing Home the Bacon: A Sex-Integrated Approach to the Impact of Work on the Family." In B. J. Risman and P. Schwartz (eds.), *Gender in Intimate Relationships: A Microstructural Approach.* Belmont, Calif.: Wadsworth, 1989.

Stake, R. E. "The Case Study Method in Social Inquiry." *Educational Researcher,* 1978, *7*, 5–8.

Sugarman, L. *Life-Span Development: Concepts, Theories and Interventions.* New York: Methuen, 1986.

Tough, A. *The Adult's Learning Projects.* Toronto: Ontario Institute for Studies in Education, 1971.

Tough, A. "Major Learning Efforts: Recent Research and Future Directions." *Adult Education,* 1978, *28* (4), 250–263.

U.S. Department of Education, Office of Educational Research and Improvement, Center for Education Statistics. *Digest of Education Statistics – 1987.* Washington, D.C.: U.S. Government Printing Office, 1987.

U.S. Department of Labor, Women's Bureau. *Facts on Women Workers.* Fact Sheet No. 88-1. Washington, D.C.: U.S. Government Printing Office, Jan. 1988.

Usher, R. "Adult Students and Their Experience: Developing a Resource for Learning." *Studies in the Education of Adults,* 1985, *18*, 24–34.

Vaillant, G. E. *Adaptation to Life.* Boston: Little, Brown, 1977.

Weiss, R. S. *Staying the Course: The Emotional and Social Lives of Men Who Do Well at Work.* New York: Free Press, 1990.

White, M. S. "Ego Development in Adult Women." *Journal of Personality,* 1985, *53,* 561–573.

Willemsen, E. W. "Terman's Gifted Women: Work and the Way They See Their Lives." In K. W. Back (ed.), *Life Course: Integrative Theories and Exemplary Populations.* American Association for the Advancement of Science Selected Symposium No. 41, Boulder, Colo.: Westview Press, 1980.

Index

251

Educational consultant. *See* Peter
Educators, implications for, 225–226
Elementary school teacher. *See*
  Thelma
Ellen: compared, 68, 169; and de-
  velopment, 199–200, 207; diver-
  gent pattern for, 140–146, 151,
  154, 155, 156, 157; and learning,
  183, 184, 185–186, 191
Engineer. *See* Brendon
Erikson, E. H., 4, 5, 8, 11–12, 14,
  15, 54, 106, 194, 230
Erlich, H. S., 8, 164
Evans, R., 5
Expansion, and development,
  196–197, 204–207
Experience, and learning, 201–202.
  See also Life events

F

Fales, A. W., 202
Farone, P. A., 25, 26, 64, 166, 167
Filler, H., 16
Fine, R., 3, 9
Fischer, J., 12
Fiske, M., 45
Flavell, J. H., 46
Ford Foundation, 20
Francois, F., 16
Frank: compared, 2–3, 68; and de-
  velopment, 207; divergent pattern
  for, 151–154, 156; and learning,
  185
Frankel, J., 19
Frankl, V., 5
Freud, S., 1, 3–4, 5, 8, 9, 14–15,
  23, 56, 176, 210, 212, 218, 226,
  227, 228
Friedan, B., 186
Friskey, M., 220n

G

Gaylin, W., 3, 4
Gender differences: and concepts of
  work and love, 4, 8, 10; and development, 196–197; in identity
  and intimacy, 23, 34; lack of,
  212; and learning to work and
  love, 12–14; in patterns,

159–160; research on, 18, 31–35;
  in steady/fluctuating pattern,
  126–127; in thought contents, 16.
  See also Men; Women
Generalization model, of interaction,
  168–169. *See also* Spillover effect
Generativity, in work and love, 5
Gerson, K., 21–22
Gier, J. A., 32
Gifted children, longitudinal study
  of, 25, 30
Gilligan, C., 11, 12–13, 23, 35,
  106, 160, 194
Glaser, B. G., 69, 232
Goldberger, N. R., 197
Gordon, J., 40
Gould, R. L., 54, 197–198, 199,
  200, 209, 230
Guba, E. G., 229, 234
Guidewite, C. 221n
Gutek, B. A., 20–21, 32, 33, 168

H

Hale, N., 3–4
Hardin, P., 17
Harvard University: graduates of,
  28–29, 35; student development
  at, 196–197
Havighurst, R., 44–45
Hawkes, G. R., 6, 33
Hendrix, L., 10
Hill, M. M., 37–38
Hinand, G., 17, 34–35, 160, 212
Hodgson, J., 12
Homemaker. *See* Nadine
Honigmann, J. J., 229
Houle. C. O., 41–42
Huberman, A. M., 65, 229
Human resource consultant. *See*
  Ellen
Human service practitioners, impli-
  cations for, 224–225

I

Identity: gender differences in, 23,
  34; and learning to work and
  love, 11–14; in steady/fluctuating
  pattern, 106–107
Independence, expansion of, 205